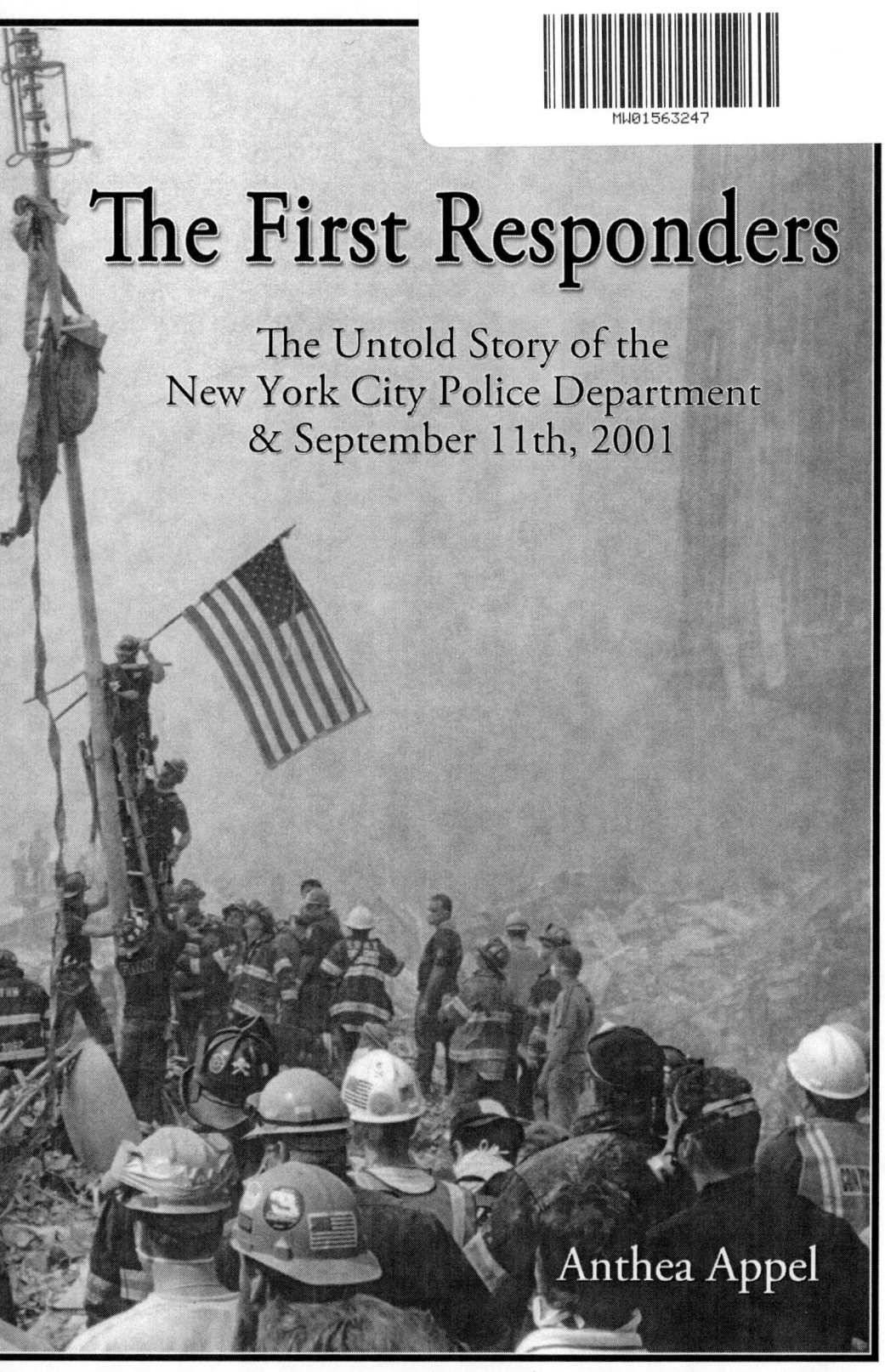

The First Responders

The Untold Story of the
New York City Police Department
& September 11th, 2001

Anthea Appel

INNERCIRCLE PUBLISHING

The First Responders
The Untold Story of the New York City Police Department
& September 11th, 2001
Copyright © 2009 Anthea Appel

ISBN: 1-882918-25-8

Edition 1

Page Design by: Chad Lilly
Cover Design by: Anthea Appel & Chad Lilly
Cover Creation by: Chad Lilly
Cover Photo: Anthony Garvey

*Special Thanks to David Margules
for his inspiring photos
www.fromdusttilldawn.com*

www.antheaappel.com

All Rights reserved. No part of this book may be reproduced in any form or by electronic or mechanical means, including information storage and retrieval systems, without permission in writing from the publisher, except by a reviewer who may quote a brief passage in a review.

Are You Aware?
www.innercirclepublishing.com

This book is dedicated to the twenty-three New York City police officers who lost their lives in the terrorist attack on September 11th, 2001:

Sgt. John G. Coughlin
Sgt. Michael S. Curtin
Sgt. Rodney C. Gillis
Sgt. Timothy A. Roy
Det. Claude D. Richards
Det. Joseph V. Vigiano
P.O. John D'Allara
P.O. Vincent Danz
P.O. Jerome M. Dominguez
P.O. Stephen P. Driscoll
P.O. Mark J. Ellis
P.O. Robert Fazio
P.O. Ronald P. Kloepfer
P.O. Thomas M. Langone
P.O. James P. Leahy
P.O. Brian G. McDonnell
P.O. John W. Perry
P.O. Glen K. Pettit
P.O. Moira A. Smith
P.O. Ramon Suarez
P.O. Paul Talty
P.O. Santos Valentin Jr.
P.O. Walter E. Weaver

... and in loving memory of my brother, Mark.

- *Acknowledgments* -

"My thanks to all the police officers and civilians
who told me their stories. Without them,
this book could not be possible."

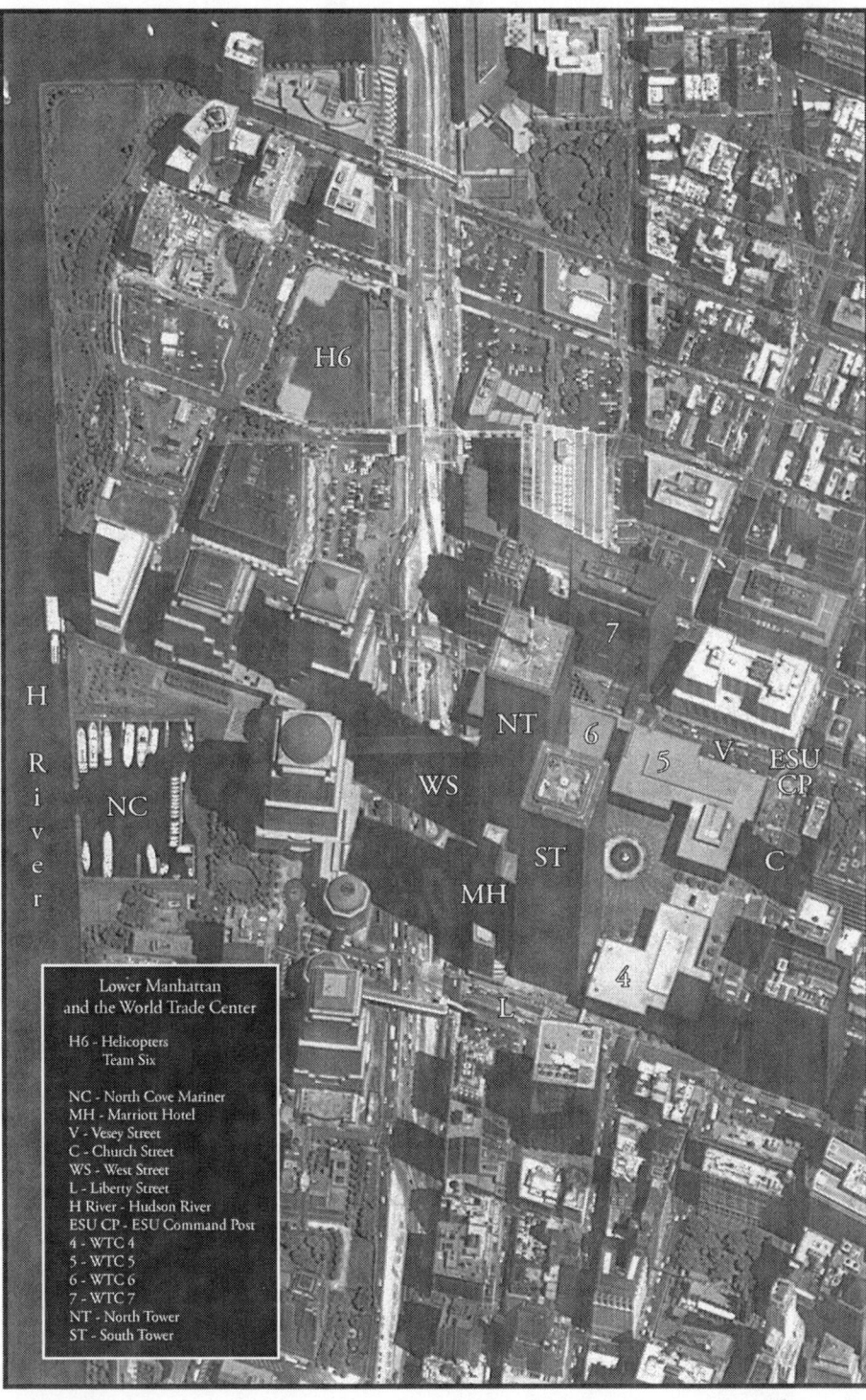

- Contents -

Introduction 9

1. 8:46 AM: The Attack Begins 15
2. 9:03 AM: Team One On The Plaza 27
3. 9:03 AM: The Response 37
4. 9:03 AM: Eight-Truck 65
5. 9:25 AM: Team Three Inside The North Tower 70
6. Team One Inside The North Tower 76
7. 9:45 AM: Team Five On The Plaza 83
8. Team Six: Waiting For The Helicopters 87
9. 9:59 AM: Team Five On The Plaza 95
10. 9:59 AM: Team Three Inside The North Tower 104
11. 9:59 AM: Team One Inside The North Tower 107
12. 9:59 AM: Down On The Streets 112
13. Team Three: Inside The North Tower "We Can't Get Out!" 122
14. Team One: Strange Encounter In The North Tower 125
15. 10:29 AM: Team Five On The Plaza 134
16. 10:29 AM: Team Three Escapes The North Tower 142
17. 10:29 AM: Team One Escapes The North Tower 147
18. Team Five: Sanctuary 153
19. Team Three: Trapped! 161
20. After The Collapse 171
21. The Survivors 178
22. Hoaxes & Bomb Scares 209
23. Buried Alive 217
24. The Rescue Of John McLoughlin 238

25	The Flag Raising At Ground Zero 253
26	Search & Rescue 265
27	The Black Boxes 281
28	The Missing 283
29	The Toxic Dust 299
30	'Chernobyl On The Hudson' 308
31	Remembering The Guys 314
32	Christmas At Ground Zero 321
33	The Closing Ceremony 323
34	Repose 326
	Glossary 328
	Afterword 333

The First Responders

- Introduction -

This book is the story of September 11th, 2001, and the terrorist attack of the World Trade Center as experienced by the New York City Police Department. On that day twenty-three police officers lost their lives, fourteen of whom, were assigned to the Emergency Service Unit.

I retired from the NYPD in the spring of 2002, about six months after 9/11. When I look back over my twenty years on the force, there are two "moments" in my career that stand out in my mind where I felt the most proud. The first was the day I graduated from the police academy and, as a brand new cop in my stiff, black leather and crisp blue uniform, I walked my foot post up and down Sutphin Boulevard in Jamaica, Queens. I thought this was the best job in the world. The second proudest day came at the end of my career, and that was September 11th. For me, the courage and sacrifice of these officers was what I knew this job was all about.

It's said that 9/11 may be the best-documented event in all of history, and there certainly have been enough books written about it. No doubt, every September 11th for years to come Barnes & Noble will pull out a "9/11 table" with books on the subject stacked in little neat piles. But on the anniversaries that have gone by so far, I couldn't help noticing most of these books were written either by journalists or firemen—virtually nothing from, for, or about the NYPD (there is, however, one picture book).

Precious little has been written about what the Police Department did on 9/11, and that little has been largely critical. We were blamed both by the media and the Fire Department for the break down in communication that allegedly occurred during the attack

The 9/11 Commission Report did nothing to set the record straight. The families of the victims killed on that horrific day wanted an explanation from our government as to why 9/11 happened. They wanted to know how our intelligence agencies—the FBI and the CIA—had failed the American people. The victim's families pressed for an investigation, and a ten-man panel was assembled to oversee the commission. Eighteen months later, in the summer of 2004, their final report was presented to the public.

The 567-page *Report* (at the affordable price of ten dollars) sold faster than a new Tom Clancy novel, and in less than a week, it was in its second printing. And, why not? It had all the earmarks of a best seller: suspense, intrigue, politics, mystery, and espionage. If you turn to chapter nine, you'll find a two-page description of NYPD's response to the attack. Actually, it was not a bad job of summarizing the actions of the NYPD on September 11th, but there was something really missing: *there was no direct testimony from the "first responders," the police officers who were on duty at the time of the first attack and who rushed to the scene to deal with the chaos as it began to unfold.* And it wasn't only the *Report* itself from where direct testimony was missing. The police had never been asked to give their perspective on the story. It strikes me as amazing that nobody had ever talked to the cops themselves about their experience. A few of the guys did do interviews for the foreign press, but nobody in this country has ever asked these first responders, and I mean the guys actually inside the Towers, "Hey, what happened? What did you see? What did you do? What was it like?" Not even the brass in the Department had been interested in talking to these guys.

I've written this book to make up for this gap in the public record concerning what happened on the morning of September 11th, 2001. I wanted to know what they saw, how they felt, and what they did. I wanted to give these police officers a face and a name. I thought the best place to begin was to talk to the first responders. But I had to decide which officers I was going to speak to. Since I was a patrol officer myself, I thought it would be easiest to interview other patrol officers, but that was only until I learned approximately 2,000 police personnel responded to a "Level-Four Mobilization" once the attacks were reported. So I decided to concentrate on the Emergency Service Unit (ESU). They had a smaller, initial response to the scene, they were better organized, and they kept an account of the whereabouts of their men. The Emergency Service Unit comprises our Rescue/SWAT teams. I tracked down as many ESU first responders as I could find (some of the officers are still on active duty but many of the men mentioned in this book have retired). Over a cup of coffee, we talked for an hour or two, or sometimes three, and I heard their stories.

At first, I wasn't sure how these officers would react to my probing them, or if they'd want to talk at all: I know how cops can clam up, but this wasn't the case about 9/11. If anything, they were surprised anyone would want to hear their stories. They thought anyone who wasn't personally affected by 9/11 wouldn't care about it anymore, but they were happy to tell their tales.

Cops are such good storytellers this book practically wrote itself. It's put together almost verbatim from our interviews. In a way, this book is a collective memoir told by these officers, for this is how they remembered that day, how they experienced it. For the most part, the stories are told one by one, officer by officer, but there are a few instances where two officers, standing in the same place at the same time, looking in the same direction saw things slightly differently. In these instances, I have sometimes combined both points of view. Usually this involves only slight discrepancies in the time frame of an event. But a lot of guys will tell you on that day, time didn't seem to exist.

All three-hundred-plus members of the Emergency Service Unit are based throughout the five boroughs: Queens, Brooklyn, Bronx, Staten Island, and Manhattan. But they aren't restricted by precinct boundaries. If something was happening in Queens, the Bronx ESU would be there in a flash. They know each other as brothers. Each face is familiar to all. They train together, they climb bridges together, they "rappel" off buildings together. They watch each other's back in the dark and unfamiliar hallways and stairwells of the most dangerous and unpredictable parts of the City. On any ordinary day, one minute they can be lowering themselves down ropes and pulleys to pluck a jumper off the 59th Street Bridge, and the next minute be in Brooklyn in full battle gear, ready to bust through a barricaded door in a tense, three-hour long, armed stand-off in a hostage situation.

The one thing that separates ESU members from the precinct cops is a strong sense of discipline. That isn't to say a patrol officer doesn't have discipline, far from it; after all, the police department is a para-military organization where rank is respected and orders are followed. But it's a little different in ESU, because of the type of work the officers do and the kind of weapons they carry. Things as gun control and teamwork are constantly drilled into their heads. An ESU cop always knows what his partner will do and he always knows the next move another team member will make.

The dialogue in this account is approximate—it's based on what the officers could recall from memory. It was impossible to double-check radio transmissions inside the Towers because ESU cops communicated with each other on the "Tactical-g" (Tac-g) frequency, and Tac-g doesn't operate on a "repeater." That meant no transmissions were recorded. Hence, the dialogue comes from actual conversations as reported to me by the surviving officers. In many instances, two or more officers participated in or heard the same conversations and were able to collaborate in reconstructing what was said.

Throughout the events on 9/11, most of the action involving different Teams of officers was happening at the same time; but, rather than describe each phase of an event, jumping from one team to another, I've allowed things to unfold fully with one team and then back track to another team at a different location, then going back again to the original team as another event developed.

There were six ESU "Teams" of first responders, plus the men at the Command Post (CP). These Teams were organized on the spot as officers arrived at the CP and were unrelated to the ESU unit the officer was regularly assigned. Below, I have listed the members of each Team by name and the rank they held on September 11th, the "Truck" number (ESU Command), and the borough they served. At the head of each Team I give the Tower—North or South—where they responded. In Team One you'll notice there is one member that isn't an ESU cop. His name is Tim Morley. He hooked up with ESU but he never appeared on their roster.

Command Post: (Church and Vesey)
PO Kenny Winkler, ESU 1, Manhattan South

The First Responders

PO Billy Lutz, ESU 1, Manhattan South
Lt Stephen Reardon, ESU 6, Brooklyn

Team One: (North Tower)
Lt Venton "Vic" Hollifield, ESU 3, Bronx
Sgt Dominick Amendolare, ESU 1, Manhattan South
PO Cliff Allen, ESU 1, Manhattan South
PO Roger Mack, ESU 1, Manhattan South
PO Dave Norman, ESU 1, Manhattan South
Det Timothy Morley, OCCB, Brooklyn North Narcotics

Team Two: (South Tower)
Sgt Rodney Gillis, ESU 8, Brooklyn
PO Ronnie Kloepfer, ESU 7, Brooklyn
PO Santos Valentin, ESU 7, Brooklyn
PO Jerome Dominguez, ESU 3, Bronx
PO Walter Weaver, ESU 3, Bronx

Team Three: (North Tower)
Sgt Mike Curtin, ESU 2, Manhattan North
PO John D'Allara, ESU 2, Manhattan North
Det Joseph Vigiano, ESU 2, Manhattan North
PO Vincent Danz, ESU 7, Brooklyn
PO William Beaury, ESU 7, Brooklyn
PO Mark DeMarco, ESU 1, Manhattan South
PO Stephen Blihar, ESU 10, Queens North

Team Four: (South Tower)
Sgt John Coughlin, ESU 4, Bronx
PO Stephen Driscoll, ESU 4, Bronx
PO Brian McDonnell, ESU 1, Manhattan South
PO Thomas Langone, ESU 10, Queens North
PO Paul Talty, ESU 10, Queens North
PO Joseph McCormack, ESU 4, Bronx

Team Five: (South Tower)
Lt John Murphy, Floyd Bennett Field, Brooklyn
PO David Brink, ESU 3, Bronx
PO Mike Garcia, ESU 3, Bronx
PO Richard Hartigan, ESU 4, Bronx
PO Steve Lanoce, ESU 4, Bronx
PO Evan Schwerner, ESU 4, Bronx
PO Robert Steinman, ESU 4, Bronx

Team Six: (Air Rescue Team)
Sgt Paul Hargrove, ESU 10, Queens North
PO Peter Appice, ESU 10, Queens North
PO Steven Stefanakos, ESU 10, Queens North
PO Richard Winwood, ESU 10, Queens North
PO Franco Berarducci, ESU 4, Bronx

The First Responders

8:46 AM: The Attack Begins

On September 11th, 2001, at 8:46 in the morning, Lieutenant Venton "Vic" Hollifield was walking down Rector Street, a quiet, two-block section of Lower Manhattan, in the financial district, and only a stone's throw from the World Trade Center. Hollifield was an Emergency Service cop from the South Bronx, and the reason he was down there was because he had a 9 o'clock appointment at the Corporation Council, a Departmental hearing board at 30 Rector Street, between Greenwich and West.

He squeezed his unmarked police car into a parking space on a side street. He walked leisurely. There was plenty of time—fourteen minutes, to be exact—to get to where he was going, but suddenly the sound of a low flying plane grabbed his attention. The engine was loud and seemed to be coming from somewhere it didn't belong. He looked up between the tall office buildings and caught sight of the two skyscrapers of the World Trade Center at the exact moment a commercial jetliner crashed into the North Tower. He saw the impact: a giant ball of orange flames and black smoke.

He grabbed his radio off his gun belt and transmitted a message over SOD (Special Operations Division) police radio channel hooked up to every SOD unit in the five boroughs: Emergency Service, Aviation, K-9, and Harbor. He said, "Emergency Service portable with an emergency transmission!"

A transmission as that demands attention. A cop's radio is an important tool—sometimes it is more important than his gun. If he needs help, all he has to do is shout into his radio the cross-streets of his location—that's all, nothing more—and every cop listening will know he's in trouble and they'll know where he's in trouble. They don't ask questions, they just step on the gas and go!

As soon as the dispatcher acknowledged the lieutenant, he said: *Be advised a plane has crashed into the World Trade Center!*

The next thing Hollifield did was to make his way to the Trade Center. Drive or go on foot? The narrow Lower Manhattan streets didn't provide much room for all the traffic that was trying either to get closer or away, or pull over and watch the smoke and flames—so, he ran. He fixed his eyes on the fire and let it lead him to the site. As he was running, he heard an Emergency Service Unit (ESU)—One-Truck—putting themselves over the air that they were responding. When he arrived at the Trade Center he tried to think of the best location to mobilize the units. He knew he only had a few moments before the Emergency Service trucks would be rolling in, so he had to think fast.

In ESU, the Commands are called "Trucks" and are designated by a number from One to Ten. The ten Trucks are divided up between the five boroughs: One-Truck and Two-Truck are in Manhattan; Three-Truck and Four-Truck are in the Bronx. There is only one ESU command in Staten Island: Five-Truck. Brooklyn has three commands: Six-Truck, Seven-Truck, and Eight-Truck. Nine-Truck is in South Queens and Ten-Truck in North Queens. Each Command works out of separate workstations attached to the rear of a given precinct. For example, One-Truck in Manhattan South is next door to the 13th Precinct on 21st Street; Eight-Truck is in the rear of the 9-0 Precinct in Brooklyn; Ten-Truck in Flushing, Queens is attached to the back of the 1-09 Precinct, and so on.

Four blocks bordered the World Trade Center: the eight lanes of West Street, four running north and four south, parallel to the dock area and beneath the Westside Highway along the east bank of the Hudson River. Then there was Liberty Street to the south, a brief walk from the Battery; and Church Street, a step away from Saint Paul's Church, on the east. To the north was Vesey Street.

At first, Hollifield radioed to mobilize at West and Vesey, but as he got closer to the intersection he saw it was a bad idea. It was too close to the North Tower. There were large chunks of debris raining down into the street from where the plane had struck the building. He walked west until he found a spot still close but far enough away to be safe. He stopped at the corner of Church and Vesey Street, and then he rerouted the Emergency Service Units to that spot.

The first Emergency Service Unit to arrive at the World Trade Center was One-Truck, headquartered at 21st Street and Second Avenue, near Gramacy Park. It was the closest command to Lower Manhattan's financial district. One-Truck's quarters sat next door to the 13th Precinct and directly behind them was the Police Academy, with its front entrance facing 20th Street. It was an upscale neighborhood of 19th century brownstones, restaurants, shops, and punk-clad fashion-forward students congregating in front the Fashion Institute of Technology. On 21st Street was a gridlock of police cars: the precinct's RMPs (radio mobile patrol), marked and unmarked, two-wheeled or three-wheeled scooters, ESU's three or four Radio Emergency Patrol vehicles (REPs), and in the garage, the "Big Truck"

The Big Truck is what they call the two-ton utility Mack. It's about the size of a garbage truck and carries every conceivable piece of rescue and tactical equipment from blowtorches to machine-guns to jumping bags. In order to drive the Big Truck, an ESU police officer has to be qualified as the "chauffeur." It's his job to know what equipment is stored in the trucks and where. On jobs, the chauffeur distributes the equipment to the men so they can go in and do the work. He remains with the Big Truck at all times and safeguards the heavy weapons, such as, rifles, shotguns, and machine guns that are kept in the bins.

ESU also has a second type of rescue vehicle called the REP, or Radio Emergency Patrol, as mentioned above. It's a smaller Ford truck with an attached utility cabin that sits on a four-wheel ambulance chassis. It's loaded with everyday emergency tools, such as, the "Jaws of Life", saws, bolt-cutters, etc., and are ready to handle everyday emergency jobs such as "pinned" jobs (vehicle accidents with trapped passengers inside) or evidence search at a crime scene. The REPs are identified as "Adam" or "Boy" cars. The Adam-car is the first response vehicle and the Boy-car is back up. If the job is too big for the both of them—such as, an armed hostage situation or a jumper on the 9th floor of an apartment building—then they call in the Big Truck.

On Tuesday morning there were five cops from the "Third Squad" working in One-Truck: Sergeant Dominick Amendolare, police officers Cliff Allen, Dave Norman, Roger Mack, and Brian McDonnell. The squads in ESU are small, one sergeant and four to six men. There are three squads within a platoon, each designated with a number, and working opposite hours. On September 11th, the Third Squad's tour started at 7:00 AM, and overlapped the midnight tour that would be coming in at 8:35 AM. Usually, in the morning, while drinking their coffee, they'd have some kind of in-service training. It could be a training tape or reviewing a new tool or maybe one of the guys went to a new class in rescue techniques and he'd bring back some information.

This morning, Allen and Norman had brought in a windshield-removing tool that glaziers use to take out large plate glass in high-rise buildings. In Manhattan, One-Truck responded to a lot of scaffold rescues. A scaffold would go awry, and a window washer or a construction worker would be dangling in midair up the side of a building. The windshield-removing tool was designed to surround the glass and cut the glue out. Then two large suction cups would stick to it and remove the glass and the stranded worker would be pulled in through the window.

The tool was on the kitchen table. Norman opened the instruction manual and mulled over the first page, and then he began to read it out loud. He'd read one sentence, stop, let the information sink in, and then read the next sentence, stop again, and so on.

The quarters at One-Truck were cramped, with only three rooms: the office and radio-room in the front, lockers and bathrooms in the middle, and a kitchen with a large table and a TV in the back. The TV was on 24/7, usually tuned to a news program such as NY1. The rooms were all connected with no doors. Mark DeMarco, a cop from the Second Squad, was getting dressed in the locker room. His tour was scheduled to start at 3:15 PM, but this was the day of the mayoral primaries and he had come in early to work overtime at the election polls.

DeMarco was a seasoned veteran. He had twenty-eight years on the job and twenty-two of those years were in ESU. Anytime a cop goes passed his twentieth year, the younger guys with less time will look at him as if he's crazy and say, "*Wha'd'ya still doin' here?*" And guys as DeMarco would always answer, "Because I'm still havin' fun." But now

The First Responders

he was fifty years old and had nearly three decades of service. The fun was gone and he'd decided to retire. He was grabbing any overtime the guys trickled down to him so he could fatten his pension: half-pay from a job that didn't pay that well to begin with.

DeMarco could hear the guys talking in the other room, but he wasn't really paying attention. He was sitting on a bench, bent over his knees and tying his shoelaces. From that angle he could see the boots of the midnight tour coming in the locker room. It was their end of tour and they were changing to go home.

Suddenly, at 8:46 AM, every single radio in the three room quarters—from the one lying on the kitchen table to the radios lined up in their slots in the re-charger—started blaring Hollifield's emergency transmission. Amendolare, Allen, Norman, and Mack dropped what they were doing and ran down the stairs, through the garage, out to the street, and down to the trucks parked on 21st Street.

McDonnell didn't leave with them straight away. He was the odd man and didn't have a partner and he was waiting for a "fly guy" to come down to One-Truck to work with him in the Boy-car (to "fly" or "flying" are terms used to describe somebody that's sent out of his command to either fill in for manpower at another command or to work a detail). But the fly guy never showed up. Usually, the odd man would jump in the back of the Big Truck and ride to the job that way. But McDonnell's REP was loaded and he couldn't abandon his equipment. He didn't know what to do. Should he wait for his partner, or leave? He gave the thought thirty seconds and then decided to ride his truck solo down to the Trade Center.

As the Third Squad rushed out of quarters they passed one of the midnight cops, Kenny Winkler, on the stairs. He asked what all the excitement was about and they told him a plane had crashed into one of the Twin Towers. Immediately, Winkler turned around and ran back to the locker room. He yelled to the guys rushing out the door to wait for him because he was going to go with them and help out. Winkler grabbed his uniform out of his locker and raced back down the stairs to catch up with the men boarding the trucks.

Norman and Mack were Adam-One and they were already racing

their REP down 21st Street. They made a sharp right turn at the corner of Second Avenue, hit the siren to open the traffic, stepped on the gas and, in a ghostly white blur with flashing red lights, plowed through Manhattan's rush hour traffic to the Trade Center.

The Big Truck sat idling in the garage. The corrugated metal garage doors were rolled open as was usual on a warm and sunny day. Allen was behind the wheel of the Big Truck and Sergeant Amendolare sat shotgun waiting for Winkler to jump on board. The back of the truck was tall enough for a man to stand. The equipment stored inside was secured to the ceiling, floor, and walls, or stashed in metal bins so it wouldn't toss around on high-speed responses or hair-pin turns, but a man riding in the back would have to sit between the bins and hold on tight. There was one cushioned seat cut into the side with a leather handle strap to wrap the wrist around and a metal bar to grab onto. Finally, Winkler leaped in and the rear doors slammed shut. Allen stepped on the gas and they were off.

On the ride down, Norman noticed the radio was calm, and that made him think it must have only been a light aircraft had crashed into the Tower—tragic, but not catastrophic.

It was only a few weeks before some daredevil had tried to fly around the Statue of Liberty in a parachute-light aircraft (a light-weight aircraft with a powered parachute capable of lowering the whole plane to the ground in the event of an emergency). The aircraft hit the statue and the parachute wrapped around Lady Liberty's arm that holds the torch. The man tried to self-rescue by climbing up the arm using his rope extenders. A police scuba team just happened to be on a launch in the New York Bay. They climbed up the arm and nabbed the stunt pilot in mid-escape. The police pulled the man and the parachute in and escorted him down the stairs.

When the Adam-One car was a few blocks away from the Trade Center on West Broadway, they could see the extent of the damage. Norman was driving and he leaned forward over the steering wheel and looked up through the windshield at the burning North Tower. He saw a huge hole on the north face side of the building somewhere around the 94th floor. Orange flames and black smoke were pouring out as an erupting volcano and he turned to Mack and said, "This is no light aircraft."

He still didn't know it was a commercial airliner that had crashed. The initial transmission on the radio only said "a plane"; it hadn't said what kind of a plane. Then Norman added, "That's a big hole. This is bad."

The Big Truck was driving south on Broadway. When they reached Vesey Street, they swung a right. On West Broadway, Adam-One swung a left at Vesey. Simultaneously, the two trucks converged towards Church Street as two locomotives on a head-on collision. They kept one eye on the crowd of pedestrians in the street and then darted out of the way while the other eye zeroed in on Hollifield as he stepped off the curb and flagged them down.

The two ESU trucks came to a screeching halt. Norman and Mack jumped out of their REP, and Allen and Amendolare exited from the front seat of the Big Truck. Then the back doors of the Big Truck opened and out jumped Winkler. He was still in his civilian clothes: a pair of knee length jean shorts, sneakers, and a dark blue T-shirt with One-Truck's insignia in white letters written on the back. Even though he had grabbed his uniform out of his locker before he jumped in the back of the truck, he never changed his clothes, because half way down to the Trade Center he suddenly realized he didn't bring his uniform pants.

Winkler asked Allen to switch places. Allen was the chauffeur and he was going to stay with the Big Truck while Winkler and the other guys went to the North Tower. But since Winkler was also a chauffeur and was out of uniform, Allen agreed to go to the Tower and Winkler would stay with the Big Truck.

Now that the assignments were settled, it was time to gear up. There was no time to waste! It was: Jump out of the truck! Grab the equipment and go! They knew the drill. There was a brief discussion about what equipment to carry. They all agreed they'd put on their blue safety helmets, Larakus belts for rappelling, and Scott-packs, a self-contained breathing apparatus with an air tank and a heat-resistant plastic mask. They'd also carry a medical bag equipped with a respirator, extra O-2 bottles, assistant masks, burn kit, resuscitator, KED extrication, splints, stretchers, and bandages. Plus, they'd carry a bag of entry tools: Hurst tools, halogen tools, bolt cutters, pry bar, bow saw, sledge hammer, come-along tool, hack saw, and an ax. When all of this equipment was put together it weighed about eighty pounds. And once they were suited up, they'd throw an added 200-300 feet of rope on their backs.

They also discussed what they were going to do inside the Tower. They knew there would be a lot of injured people, so they decided their mission would be to go somewhere in the middle of the building—around the 30th or 40th floor—and set up a triage. It was below the fire line and a safe distance to treat the wounded.

The next important thing was communications. They switched their radios to the tactical frequency, Tac-g for short. Tac-g is what Emergency Service uses to stay in contact with one another. They do it on every job so that the only voice they hear on the radio is another ESU guy. It has a range of about ten blocks. Tac-g has no repeater, and that means the transmissions don't get recorded. Outside scanners can't pick up the frequency, and that keeps the prying ears of the press away.

Amendolare and his three cops designated themselves as Team One. They were first on the scene. None of the other ESU trucks had arrived yet, but they were on their way. Their radio transmissions could be heard over the air telling Central they were responding to the Trade Center, or double-checking the location of the mobilization point at Church and Vesey. There wasn't any other emergency personnel present, yet, except for one fire rig pulling up to Church Street and getting their own guys out and ready, and a few precinct cops scrambling up and down the streets.

As Team One was about to take the first step towards the Tower, Hollifield announced he was going in with the team. He took the lead position, but he forgot one important thing: he wasn't wearing any safety equipment. The men made a small ruckus and protested nobody could join the team without protective gear. Roger Mack took Hollifield back to the truck and made sure the lieutenant put on a helmet and a Scott-pack.

Their Big Truck only carried two Scott-packs, and that meant they didn't have extra equipment to throw around. Mack knew there was one left, but when he looked inside to get it he saw it was gone. A Bomb Squad cop named Joe Nolan had just arrived from the 6th Precinct, on West 10th Street. He had gone inside the truck and helped himself to the last Scott-pack. Winkler chased after him, asked for it back, and then gave it to Hollifield.

Hollifield had only been in ESU for two years. Before that he had been in the South Bronx-borough-wide-anti-crime detail of the Street Crime Unit. He was forty-five years old and over six feet tall with a salt and pepper receding hairline and a mustache. He was gruff on the outside, and a squared away guy on the inside. Hollifield was street wise and tough, all the qualities you need to work the bad streets of the South Bronx. Going from there to ESU might have been a culture shock, but being the boss meant being the boss. The guys he was with were experienced Emergency cops. Each one of them had at least ten years in the unit. They knew what they had to do so well they could do it in their sleep. They were trained in rope rescues and they were certified Emergency Medical Technicians (EMT). Plus, they all had some kind of extra-curricular skill that would come in handy. Cliff Allen was a physician's assistant, and for anything doing with fire, they could look to Dave Norman, who had been a Nassau County volunteer fireman for twenty years.

The Twin Towers sat on an elevated plaza, five stories above the street. In order to get up to the plaza, Team One had to take either the escalators or the stairs, half way down Vesey Street at West Broadway. As they were walking in that direction they saw Brian McDonnell and Mark DeMarco finally arriving at the command post. They had a late start, but the team wasn't going to wait for them.

Allen was surprised to see McDonnell. The last time he had seen him was back at quarters and it looked as though he was staying behind. But some time after 9/11, Allen said when he watched the video footage of September 11th on the TV news, there was a REP tailgating his truck. He couldn't see the driver, or the identification number on the side panel, but he believed it was McDonnell.

When McDonnell pulled up to Church and Vesey, he parked his REP further east on Vesey Street, a half a block away near Broadway. In the few short minutes it took him to grab his gear and run up to the command post, Amendolare and the others were gone.

While Winkler was standing at the command post, a lot of injured civilians and precinct cops were walking up to him. He had heard over the radio somebody wanted to set up a triage in Building Seven, directly across from the Trade Center on Vesey. Winkler didn't think that was a safe distance. He transmitted back he was moving the triage to City Hall Park on the other side of Broadway and at the end of Vesey. Then he grabbed McDonnell and told him to direct the walking wounded to the park.

DeMarco arrived shortly after McDonnell. He was late because he was in the middle of changing his clothes when everybody ran out the door. He was wearing his dress uniform with his silver shield—appropriate garb for sitting at the polls all day. He had to change into his ESU work clothes: dark blue cargo pants and a dark blue shirt with his stitched in name and shield number. After he changed, he ran down to the street and grabbed the last REP, drove south on Second Avenue, cut cross-town for a few blocks, and then drove south again. He remembers he was driving so furiously that he has no idea what streets he took. In a flash he was on West Broadway that took him right up to Vesey Street, directly across from the Trade Center.

DeMarco parked his REP on West Broadway and ran across Vesey to catch up with his command. In his excitement he ran passed a body lying in the middle of the street. Winkler jumped out into the intersection and shouted to DeMarco, "There's a guy layin' over there! He's hurt bad!"

DeMarco skidded to a stop, turned around, and saw a man sprawled out on the ground. It looked as though he had been hit by a piece of aircraft. There were chunks of wreckage around him—fuselage and piping. He was lying on his stomach, but all the clothes on his back had been ripped off and his skin looked scraped and raw as though he had been dragged down the street. DeMarco crouched down and examined the man's injuries. Suddenly, McDonnell came running up behind him and said, "What're we gonna do?"

"We gotta get this guy outta here," DeMarco exclaimed.

There were objects crashing all around them. Angry-looking pieces of glass and airplane fragments were whizzing passed their heads, and it was obvious the longer they stood out in the open, the greater their chance of getting nailed by one of them.

DeMarco ran to his REP and grabbed a scoop stretcher. He brought it back to the man on the ground and then he and McDonnell placed him on the stretcher. Suddenly, two paramedics appeared, as if they had popped out of the ground. They reached over the two cops' head, snatched the stretcher and, running as hell, disappeared around the corner of a building. It happened so fast it took DeMarco, still crouched in a pose as if looking at the injured man, a second or two to realize the man was actually gone.

Now that the injured civilian was taken care of, DeMarco turned his attention to gearing up and getting with his unit. He ran back to his truck for his Scott-pack. As he hoisted the straps over his shoulders, McDonnell ran over to him again, anxious and excited, and said, "What do we do now?"

McDonnell was a fairly new guy in ESU. DeMarco only know him from passing by between shifts, but every time he had seen him he always had a serious expression on his face. DeMarco would tell him to lighten up, and McDonnell was just beginning to take that advice and relax and smile a little more.

"Brian, we're gonna be here a long time." DeMarco said. "We gotta take things as they come. We first gotta get ourselves organized. Don't worry, we'll get a game plan together."

DeMarco saw more ESU trucks pulling up and parking across the street. He could see other cops getting their gear on and gathering in a group. Maybe those guys had a plan. But even if they didn't, if a bunch of cops stand around long enough, eventually some boss will walk over and give them something to do.

"Go to the corner and I'll be right over," said DeMarco. He felt McDonnell might feel a little more secure with other guys around him.

After McDonnell walked away, DeMarco leaned inside his truck and tried to pry away a tool stuck between the seats, but something made him stop what he was doing, as if someone tapped him on the shoulder to pay attention. Through the windshield of the truck everything came into focus. Hundreds of people were standing motionless in the street with upturned startled faces. They were watching the Tower burn as if it was a tenement fire.

Suddenly, an explosion. A giant fireball shot out of the South Tower, somewhere around the 73rd floor. A thick wave of heat poured over him. A shower of glittering, silver confetti fell from the sky. DeMarco felt a weird sense of awe. He couldn't take his eyes off what he was seeing. For one split second he felt as though he was watching a movie. *This couldn't be real; it has to be special effects!*

The people in the street began to scream. Then in unison, as a herd of spooked zebras, they turned on their heels and ran north on Church Street. DeMarco looked up and saw falling from the sky at rocket speed a deluge of debris heading straight at him. He didn't run; instead, he belly-flopped across the seat of his R.E.P. Objects were pounding the ground and whacking his truck with a God-awful, pummeling clatter. The door was open and his feet were dangling outside. He felt vulnerable. He thought *this was a bad idea. I should have run when everybody else ran.* He squeezed his eyes shut and waited for something to crash through the windshield.

Suddenly, silence! The pounding had stopped! Was the coast clear? He backed off the seat and slid out of the truck and onto his feet. DeMarco looked up and down the block and saw every car parked on the street had been demolished by the falling debris.

A sick, sinking feeling went through his guts. Now, DeMarco knew—everyone knew. Every cop, every fire fighter, every New Yorker knew—they all knew: this was not an accident. This was a terrorist attack.

The First Responders

9:03 AM: Team One On The Plaza

The officers of Team One, Lieutenant Hollifield, Sergeant Amendolare, Cliff Allen, Roger Mack and Dave Norman, were on the plaza when the South Tower was struck. They had walked down the alleyway between Buildings Five and Six that led towards the center of the plaza and were holding their position underneath the overhang of Building Five.

Building Five was known as the Chase Building and Building Six was the Customs House. These two buildings appeared almost identical with their top-heavy, ell-shaped exteriors. The upper floors looked as a square cap screwed off a box with the middle exposed in a kind of a gap that came out into a platform. They were only eight stories high and were dwarfed by the Towers. Their dull, metallic black contrasted with the shiny silver skyscrapers. The only bit of color was from the neatly manicured shrubs in large cement planters placed against Building Five.

Right in front of where Team One had placed themselves was an outdoor café with round metal tables and chairs where you could sit and relax with a cup of coffee and look out across the five-acre plaza. Dozens of blue plastic chairs were lined up in tidy rows, and behind that, more chairs piled up in blue columns. Whoever laid out the seating arrangement hadn't finished the job. During the afternoon there was to be a concert. Somebody was going to sing and play music. But now there was just empty chairs facing an empty stage.

Across the plaza, Team One saw hundreds of people running, going nowhere, looking for a way to escape. The frightened people were dashing randomly into the open and then running back against a building every time something fell from the North Tower. American Airlines Flight 11 had crashed into the north facade of the building around the 95th and 96th floor. The plane dipped just before impact and that caused the wingspan to slice through seven floors from the 93rd and up to the 100th. Large sections of stainless steel wrapped around the high beams were falling from the huge hole. If anybody had been hit by one of these sections it would've torn their head off.

The cops wanted to get the people to run the other way—away from the Tower where the debris was falling. They thought the best way to divert them was to use the blue chairs and block the alleyway between the two buildings. If they could herd the first few people in that direction, the crowd, though confused and terrified, would follow the leader. They grabbed the chairs and lined them across the plaza while yelling and pointing for the people to run to their right.

Just then, the second plane, United Flight 175, struck the South Tower. A thick, hot wind swept over the team and the crowd and new chunks of debris began to rain down upon them. The team immediately pulled back under the concrete awning just in time to miss a huge, flaming tire crash into the plaza. It landed directly in front of them, with its landing gear still attached, the twisted metal sticking up in the air as a dead chicken lying on its back, embedded in a crater and emanating a stench of burning rubber.

Everyone thought it was a secondary explosion from the plane in the North Tower, but what had blown up? Then suddenly a man jumped up from behind the burning wreckage and ran towards them screaming hysterically a plane had hit the second Tower. He was a police lieutenant dressed in a disheveled business suit; his gold shield hung out of his breast pocket, and he had on his head a vintage riot helmet that probably hadn't seen the light of day since the 1970s. He was running back and forth, waving his arms, the helmet bopping around as a huge pumpkin.

Dave Norman grabbed the lieutenant, held him still, and said, "What plane? What do you mean a plane hit? What kind of a plane?"

The lieutenant looked at the cop as though he had two heads and screamed, "What fuckin' difference does it make what kind of a fuckin' plane it is?"

"Calm down," said Norman. He wasn't in the mood for a sarcastic answer. From where he was standing, it was hard to see what was going on thirteen-hundred feet above his head, and all he saw was a big ball of fire shooting out from the other side of the South Tower.

The lieutenant cried, "It was a big fuckin' plane!" Then he broke loose from the Norman's grip and disappeared behind one of the buildings.

The First Responders

They heard Winkler and others on the radio confirming what they had begun to guess. Voices were stepping over each other and words as "terrorist" and "attack" were blasting over and over again.

At first, they had one building on fire and now there were two. Team One looked up at the North Tower and they looked up at the South Tower. They saw the debris of building parts and plane parts crashing all around them and in the plaza, and then they looked at each other and said, "Which tower do you want to go to?"

It was an important question. They'd have to run through an obstacle course of wreckage while, at the same time, dodging a deluge of metal and glass falling from the sky. After a brief discussion, they decided to stay on course and continue to the North Tower. It was the closest to them, and therefore, was probably the path of the least resistance.

Suddenly, a plainclothes detective in a suit and tie named Tim Morley ran up to the team. Just minutes before, he had been a few blocks away at 26 Federal Plaza attending a joint FBI-NYPD Departmental training course in interrogation techniques. When the first Tower was struck, the instructor, Agent Fermin, came into the classroom and announced the North Tower was on fire and the class was canceled. "Call your command, go home, do whatever you want," he said. That was it, no further explanation.

The classroom had emptied out and most of the guys either rushed to the phones or just stood around in the hallway, wondering what they were supposed to do, but Morley wanted to see what was going on. He ran to the street and, when he saw the air was full of black ash, he followed it down Broadway. As he ran, he placed one hand over the gun in his waistband. He didn't want anyone to see it and get scared, and he didn't want it juggling against his side. His other hand was holding a dark blue canvas bag that contained his study material for the upcoming sergeant exam in December.

When he got to the Trade Center, he took the stairs up Building Seven and walked across the Plexiglas overpass to the plaza. He saw a Port Authority guard, and he asked, "Where's NYPD?"

"On the plaza," said the guard.

The only cop he saw on the plaza was another detective, also, in a suit and tie—probably from the same classroom—crouching down and taking cover behind a wall. Morley joined him, and they started calling out for survivors. There was a heap of clothing lying out in the center of the plaza. Morley could see an arm sticking out and the glitter of a ring. He wanted to run over and "save" that person, but the other detective stopped him and said, "Don't risk your life for the dead". Morley looked again. The arm was all that was left of whoever it was lying there.

The bright, morning sunlight reflected off the pavement. Morley saw the globe glowing with white fire. Then a huge shadow momentarily darkened the plaza. It was the second plane flying into the South Tower.

The impact rocked the foundation as an earthquake. Hard and soft debris rained down. Some of it was pieces of metal and glass and some of it was body parts. Morley was worried about his eyes getting cut by the shearing glass, so he quickly turned his back and stuck his face in the tight corner of a wall. He couldn't see what was going on around him, but he felt it and heard the noise.

He heard a whirling sound—*whooh-whooh-whooh*—as the blades of a helicopter spiraling through the air, but it was the broken wing of the airplane spinning to the ground. It bounced a couple of times on impact and then came to a stop nearby, somewhere behind him.

Morley waited until the noise subsided and then, when he felt it was safe, he pulled himself out of the corner and saw the dark blue uniforms of five ESU officers walking into the plaza. It was Team One and they were hugging the building line, coming towards him. Morley thought, "This is it? Only five guys? They're gonna need my help." They were burdened with huge duffle bags of equipment. Morley felt sorry for them. He wanted to help the way he might if he saw somebody's grandma carrying heavy bags of groceries. Morley put his house keys and cellphone in his pants pocket, took off his jacket and folded it around his canvas bag and went inside Building Five. He tucked his jacket and the bag in a corner against the lobby wall and then came back outside, and walked over to Team One. The men had put their equipment bags on the ground and were taking a two-second breather before making their next move to the North Tower. Morley bent down and grabbed one bag of tools and another bag containing a thousand feet of rope and hooked on to the rear of the team.

Lieutenant Hollifield looked back to see who was tagging along and did a double take. He knew Morley from his Street Crime days, but they hadn't seen each other in five years. Hollifield had worked the midnight shift in the Taxi Squad and Morley patrolled on the "four-to-twelves." Even in those days, however, they only knew each other as a familiar face, somebody they passed in the hallway.

Hollifield said, "Wha'd'yer think you're doin'?"

"I'm goin' with you," said Morley.

"No you're not"

"Yes, I am."

Their argument went back and forth.

"You're not ESU. You don't have a Scott-pack," said the lieutenant.

"Well, if it gets too smoky I'll turn around."

"And you don't have a helmet."

"You want a helmet?" said Morley, challenging. "I'll give you a helmet."

Morley put down the bags and picked up one of the café tables and held it above his head as an umbrella and said, "Here's my helmet."

Hollifield tried not to laugh. But with that comeback how could he resist? Morley got his quick induction into ESU and now it was time to get to the North Tower.

To do this, they'd have to run out in the open. The closest entrance to the Tower was blocked by plane debris. They'd have to run cross the plaza and enter from the north side of the Tower. They plotted a quick route in their mind—there weren't that many options. They'd first run to the Customs House, that sat opposite the North Tower. The building had an overhang they could crouch under, and there was a gap of about thirty feet before the Tower's entrance. They held their breath, kept their heads down, and ran as hell across the plaza towards the Customs House.

It's weird the things that get noticed in the middle of a catastrophe. On the plaza, easy listening "elevator music" was playing over the outside speakers. And as Morley was running across the plaza, he was watching a small crowd on the mezzanine of the South Tower waving through the tall glass windows. There he saw a pretty, blonde-haired woman step forward from the crowd and put her face up against the window. He quickly caught sight of her. She was waving and jumping up and down, and he thought she looked as if she was cheering them on "Go! NYPD! Go!"

The men darted under the protective concrete awning of the Customs House. They stood close to the building, and when it was safe, they made a quick dash across the small space of plaza that separated the Customs House and the North Tower. They entered the mezzanine, a balcony that encircled the building's atrium. A Plexiglas parapet with a waist-high metal railing secured the edge of the balcony. The atrium was a large open space extending five stories from the main lobby, one level down from the mezzanine. All around it were tall windows, draped with colorful banners that filtered the sunlight.

Team One stepped up to the railing and took a quick mental snapshot of the layout of the interior. For the evacuation it was important to remember where all the exits were and that the elevators and the stairs were in the back, and two of the three main staircases ended on this level. They could see office workers pouring down the stairs and around the balcony to get to the escalators that would take them to the main lobby and then to the underground shopping mall that led to the street.

They looked around for other uniform rescue workers. They leaned over the railing and saw, below in the lobby, a clutch of firemen rushing back and forth in a busy frenzy. It was the Fire Department's Command Post.

Team One ran to the escalators and walked down the moving steps. At the bottom, they met Battalion Fire Chief, Joseph Pfeifer. He looked overwhelmed, and every time another fire chief walked in, the plans seemed to change and change again. Above the noise and the constant interruptions—one person or another trying to get the chief's attention—Pfeifer told Sergeant Amendolare and Lieutenant Hollifield he was awaiting additional units. The sergeant told the fire chief he'd be taking his team somewhere between the 30th and 40th floor to set up a triage. Pfeifer acknowledged this, but advised them the elevators didn't work.

Chief Pfeifer was from Engine Seven Ladder One, at 100 Duane Street and near the Financial District in Lower Manhattan. He was an unassuming man in his mid-forties, short and thin, with a dark mustache. At 8:45 AM—one minute before the attack—Pfeifer and his fire company were out on a routine "odor of gas" condition at Church and Lispenard Streets. They were fifteen blocks from the Trade Center and had a clear view of the Twin Towers, south on Church Street. The firemen had with them a French filmmaker named Jules Naudet. He had been bunking at the firehouse and tagging along on jobs for the past two months, trying to put together a film about the day and the life of a probationary fireman. Naudet was frustrated with his project because nothing exciting was happening at the firehouse and he couldn't get any provocative firemen-in-action photographs. The "odor of gas" job turned out to be unfounded.

As Pfeifer and his men were packing up to leave, they heard the loud zooming engine of a low flying plane. The firemen looked up to see where the sound was coming from. Naudet's camera was rolling. He tilted his camera and panned across the top of the buildings until he caught sight of a large commercial airliner crashing into the North Tower. The camera's microphone recorded a boom and the astonished expletives of the firemen. The images blurred and jiggled. He zoomed in for a closer look: big orange flames and black smoke.

Pfeifer jumped into action. He climbed aboard his fire department vehicle, a red SUV Chevy Blazer, and his men boarded their fire rig and raced west across Lispenard Street. Naudet sat in the backseat of the SUV. He filmed the ride and recorded the radio transmissions: "Battalion One to Manhattan," said Pfeifer, over a phone attached underneath the dashboard. "We have a number of floors on fire. It looked like the plane was aiming towards the Building. Transmit a third alarm. We'll have the staging area at Vesey and West Street."

Six blocks later, they swung a left turn on West Street and drove to the Trade Center. Pfeifer was the first Fire Department supervisor to arrive on the scene and he immediately set up the Command Center on the street-level lobby of the North Tower. Naudet asked Pfeifer if he could stay with him and the chief said, "Yes," but warned him to "Stick close to me." Naudet mounted his camera on his shoulder and followed the firemen inside the Tower and recorded the action every inch of the way.

The large lobby windows facing out to West Street by now were empty frames of shattered glass. They had been blown out from the impact of the crash as it sent a blast of fire shooting down the elevator shafts as a thunderbolt down a chimney. The blast burst out through the elevator doors and across the lobby floor. Office workers casually going about their business were either burnt by the blowtorch of fire or thrown out of the building by the concussion of the explosion.

The empty windows were serving as doors, and the firemen were walking in and out. A Port Authority sergeant dashed by, and there was the crashing sound of more windows being broken as newly arrived firemen stormed the command post.

As more firemen scrambled forward, the ESU police team were elbowed out of the way. They found themselves being rolled over by a wave of leather helmets. Fire Commissioner Thomas VanEssen was there, and every time he tried to make a suggestion to his men, he was pushed back, until he found himself standing in the peanut gallery with the cops.

Amendolare stretched himself over the bobbing heads of the frenzied crowd and shouted to Chief Pfeifer. He asked him if there was anything they could do. A newly arrived fire chief interrupted, and with a quick dismissal, said, "We don't need you guys. It's a fire."

On that note, the sergeant realized there wasn't any more they could do or say. The fire chiefs had their hands full and weren't interested in the police. The team turned around and headed for Staircase B.

Staircase B was one of three major staircases. It ran through the center of the building from the lobby straight up to the 105th floor. The other two major stairwells were A and C and they were positioned on the outer perimeter of the building, on the southeast and southwest corners of the North Tower. These two staircases also started at the top floor but ended on the mezzanine, right above the lobby. Besides the three main stairwells, there were shorter stairwells that zigzagged from one floor to the next. The shorter ones were used as a kind of a convenient connection between individual floors. This was probably useful for companies that had offices on several of them.

As the cops were walking up, the civilians were walking down. The staircases were narrow—about the width of two people standing shoulder to shoulder. Team One was hauling bulky tools on their backs and some of the civilians were carrying injured co-workers down the stairs. This made passing each other a little clumsy. At one point, a woman covered with third-degree burns passed them on the staircase. She had blackened skin and a glazed look in her eyes. She couldn't feel the pain where her nerves had been burnt away, and she looked peaceful, as though she didn't know the severity of her burns.

There was a strange silence on the stairs. The team was quiet and the civilians were quiet. Sometimes the people would catch Morley's eye. This made him feel self-conscious. He knew he looked out of place dressed in a white shirt and tie with no jacket, his off-duty .38 caliber handgun in his waistband, and carrying two large, heavy duffel bags of equipment banging against his shins. While at the same time, he tagged behind five ESU cops in dark blue uniforms, air tanks, safety helmets, and their bodies crisscrossed with the buckles and straps of the rescue harness. As the people passed him on the staircase he'd see in their faces a look he had seen before, not as a cop, but of all things—as a bartender. Years ago he used to work in a bar in Bayside, Queens. He remembered how a customer would come in after a long day at work and just flop down on a stool in front of him. They'd give him a look as though they were searching for an answer that everything was going to be all right. Today, in the staircase, Morley didn't have an answer, but he thought perhaps he could distract them so they wouldn't be afraid. He started making small talk with the people. As a friendly game show host, he'd say, "Hey, how're ya doin'? What floor were you on? Introduce yourself to the person in front of you and to the person behind you. You're almost there. Two more flights to go."

Amendalore and Hollifield and the rest of the team looked back at Morley and wondered who the hell he was talking to. Then they realized what he was doing and they liked that idea and everybody started joining in.

The First Responders

9:03 AM: The Response

The South Tower was hit at 9:03 AM. In those desperate seventeen minutes between the first attack and the second, the Emergency Service Unit trucks from the outer boroughs were starting to show up at the command post.

It was a mad race from Brooklyn, the Bronx, Queens, and Staten Island. The traffic was insane. Over the radio, the police were demanding (and getting) clear passage into Manhattan: open lanes through the Mid-Town and Battery Tunnels, and across the Brooklyn Bridge. They had to have one straight line with nobody in the way. There would be no slowing down, no hitting the brakes. It would be eighty-mph automatic pilot and a one way ticket to hell.

To be on an ESU truck in a situation as that sends a rush through your body as nothing else in the world. The heightened state of danger quickens your vision. Your ears shut down. You don't hear the radio and you don't hear the guy talking next to you. What you do hear sounds as far-off, monotonous echoes, except perhaps for the exhilarating scream of the siren. But you do need your eyes. It's important to not become separated from your partner, the other cops on your team, or your sergeant. Staying with your command (together with fear turned into exhilaration and the power of the police department) is what holds you together while the mad race to the rescue is pumping your blood.

Kenny Winkler was waiting for the trucks at the command post. His position as chauffeur escalated into something called the "safety net." This meant he'd be the liaison between the cops and the bosses. It would be his responsibility to put together the teams and to know where everybody was. He kept two radios on at the same time. One was tuned to SOD (Special Operations Division) so he could hear what was going on in the City. The other was tuned to Tac-g so he could stay in contact with the teams in the Towers.

Winkler had twenty years on the job, and sixteen of those years were in Emergency. He was a no-nonsense and take-charge kind of a guy, about forty years old, calm and confident, and had a rugged but youthful face that was a cross between rocker Bon Jovi and the Marlboro man. He was trained in HazMat (Hazardous Material), in the handling of biological, chemical, and radiation material; he was a tactical scuba instructor, a sure shot marksman, and a member of the sniper team. In 1995, he had been with the New York FEMA task force that responded to the Oklahoma City terrorist bombing of the Alfred P. Murrah Federal Building. His supervisors trusted him to call the shots in the midst of chaos and praised him as an ace "E-Man."

The first thing Winkler wanted to do was to put the teams in the staircases, set up a logistic area (a temporary headquarters), and start stripping the trucks of equipment as they pulled in. The teams would be balanced with experienced supervisors and police officers mingled in with the younger and less experienced guys. Winkler wanted to keep the teams small. He had learned in Oklahoma City that you can't expect to accomplish much with a team of thirty guys, but he also knew you couldn't send in a team of two and expect to accomplish anything either. Five, six, or seven officers plus a boss are good working numbers. If they have to carry someone out, they can do it. If they have to set up a hauling system or do CPR, they can do it. Each team would take the same equipment. They'd carry entry tools to knock down doors and ropes to lower somebody or do a self-rescue. They'd all have breathing apparatus, harnesses, medical gear, and their blue, construction worker's safety helmets.

Before Winkler could put teams together, he needed the bosses—and here they came, arriving one after another, not more than a few seconds apart: Sergeants Mike Curtin, Rodney Gillis, John Coughlin, Paul Hargrove, and Lieutenant John Murphy. Once he had them, he needed his cops—and, parked around the command post as a wagon train under siege, were twenty-nine Emergency Service police officers from the Third Squad, or, as they like to call themselves, the "Third Herd." The Third Squad is always working when the shit hits the fan. They were the same bunch of guys who responded when the terrorists attacked the Trade Center in '93. They were old pros at this, and they were back.

Winkler looked around to see what cops were in front of him and either called them over or sent the sergeant to fetch them. There was no time to wait for a guy that hadn't arrived yet, or to deal with cops who wanted to switch teams. It was, "Get your gear, get on this team, and go." Everything was going to be systematic; everything was going to run smoothly.

Sergeant Mike Curtin was from Two-Truck in Harlem. He walked up to Winkler already dressed in tactical gear. He was wearing a ballistic helmet and cradling an MP-5 semi-automatic machine-gun in a sling. Even though Curtin decided to suit up in combat gear, he had the rest of his men stay in rescue mode. He had his driver, police officer John D'Allara, with him; and across the street were Detective Joe Vigiano and his partner, Officer Vinny Danz, who had just "flown" in from Three-Truck in the Bronx. They parked their REP on the west curb of Church Street, fifteen feet north of Vesey.

Winkler and Curtin had a brief discussion about what equipment to take. D'Allara, who was an expert technician with a love for elaborate contraptions, wanted to bring some heavy-duty equipment, including an airbag. Airbags, filled by a hydraulic pump, are used to lift up heavy objects, but they weigh about forty pounds. Not a good idea. Winkler said, "John, you can't bring this stuff up with you. You'll never make it. If you get to a point where you need extra equipment, I'll have somebody bring it up to you." Saying this gave Winkler the idea to set up teams on standby for the specific task of running equipment up the Towers for men who needed equipment.

BROOKLYN

Sergeant Rodney Gillis arrived solo at Church and Vesey. He worked in Eight-Truck, in the 9-0 Precinct, Williamsburg, Brooklyn. He had finished a midnight tour and was hanging around quarters killing time before leaving for his second job. He was down in the garage with Curtis Garvey, an officer from the Third Squad, who had come in for a day tour, and they began doing inventory together on the equipment stored in the trucks. Gillis would read off the serial numbers of the ballistic vests and the ballistic shields and Garvey would write it down.

When the news of the first plane crash into Tower One came over the radio, Gillis and Garvey dropped everything and ran to their trucks. Garvey was assigned that morning to work in the Big Truck, and his partner Pete Linarello, was already sitting behind the wheel and ready to go. Garvey was about to jump in the back and leave the front seat open for Gillis, but he saw the sergeant getting into one of the smaller trucks, REP 5527. Garvey asked him to come with him, but Gillis said, "No." He wanted to bring his own vehicle.

"What do you want me to do?" asked Garvey. His soft Jamaican accent became thicker, as it usually did whenever he got excited. He thought maybe the sergeant wanted him to drive down with him.

"You go with your partner," said Gillis. "I'll meet you in Manhattan."

At that moment, Frank DeMasi and his partner, Jim Nessenthaler were pulling up outside the Eight-Truck's quarters. They were the "fly" car from South Queens and had been sent to Brooklyn to fill in for manpower. They saw the Big Truck pulling away, and they saw Gillis standing on the apron of the garage.

"Hey, Jimmy! Frank! Let's go!" yelled Gillis. "I have a car here. I'm shootin' over the Bridge."

"We're your Adam-car today," said Nessenthaler. "So, we're goin' to switch REPs." The vehicle they drove in from Queens was on its last legs. It was good enough to get from point A to B, but not for eight hours of patrol.

"Rodney, what kind of a load do you have on that car?" said DeMasi.

"It's unloaded," said Gillis. That meant he had no rescue equipment.

The Adam-car was unloaded, too. The fly car is usually never sent to another command with gear, and they knew they couldn't bring an empty truck down to the Trade Center.

"We're goin' to need equipment," said DeMasi."You go ahead. We'll meet you in Manhattan."

Gillis grabbed a set of car keys off a hook that belonged to one of Eight-Truck's spare REPs and tossed them to Nessenthaler. This way, the fly guys could switch trucks. Then the sergeant jumped into his REP and took off. By the time Nessenthaler and DeMasi threw Scott-packs, oxygen tanks, sand bags, ropes, and first aid kits into the bins of their truck, Gillis was already across the Brooklyn Bridge and making his way through Lower Manhattan.

Adam-Eight tried to catch up with Gillis. As they raced over the Brooklyn Bridge, there, across the East River, they could see the North Tower—burning. The hole where the plane went in was so huge you could look right through the building and see the sky on the other side. It didn't look real. More as something you might see in a Wily Coyote cartoon.

Once off the Bridge, they swung around City Hall Park and drove south down Broadway (City Hall is a few blocks from the Trade Center Plaza). It was bumper cars all the way through a massive gridlock, including crowds of dazed pedestrians blocking the streets. As they approached the Towers, the biggest problem was finding a place to park. The first safe spot close to the scene would be as good as any, so DeMasi looked around and pulled the truck over at Cedar and Broadway and parked it there. DeMasi stepped out of his vehicle, took his radio out of his holster, switched to Tac-g, and tried to raise Sergeant Gillis.

"Sergeant Gillis are you on the air? Rodney, you on the air? Sergeant Gillis are you on Tac-g?" said DeMasi.

Three times he called him and three times Gillis didn't answer. Actually, the only reason he was trying to contact the sergeant was because they had agreed to meet up in Manhattan. When Gillis didn't answer, DeMasi assumed he was already in the Tower walking up a staircase and his radio had hit a blind spot, caused by the building's steel structure interfering with transmission. What DeMasi didn't know was that Gillis had no radio.

THE BRONX

At 8:46 AM, Sergeant John Coughlin was in quarters at Four-Truck in the Riverdale section of the Bronx near Yankee Stadium. Today he was assigned as U-4, the Manhattan North supervisor. His job would be to monitor all ESU radio-runs in the Bronx and Upper Manhattan. Also working in Four-Truck were seven police officers: Steve Lanoce, Richard Hartigan, Evan Schwerner, Bobby Steinman, Stephen Driscoll, Franco Berarducci, and Joseph McCormack. Driscoll and Berarducci were out with the Big Truck to Central Repair in Woodside, Queens, to get some minor maintenance work done, and McCormack was on his way out the door to "fly" down to One-Truck to partner with Brian McDonnell. The others were going through their morning routine of loading the equipment on the trucks. One minute later, Hollifield was screaming over the radio that a plane hit the World Trade Center. Everybody's ears perked up, but nobody moved. They turned up the volume and listened for more information. In their mind they pictured a small plane or a helicopter crashing into the building. They figured there would be some causalities and damage, but not enough to demand their response. But that was until they heard a transmission that said bodies were falling out of the building. Now they jumped into their trucks and headed to Lower Manhattan.

In the Soundview section of the South Bronx, Three-Truck had the same reaction. David Brink, Mike Gracia, Eddie Lutz, and Jim Malley were also down in the garage loading equipment on the trucks, and their two other guys, Jerome Dominguez and Walter Weaver, who were assigned to Two-Truck for the day, had already left quarters and were making their way to Harlem. When they heard Hollifield's transmission, Brink and Garcia, who were in the Adam-car, said they'd go down to the Trade Center and check it out. Lutz and Malley would stay behind at quarters so the South Bronx wouldn't be completely stripped of manpower.

Adam-Three was coming from the 4-3 Precinct on Fteley Avenue, a few blocks off the Bruckner, an elevated expressway that ran north and south through the South Bronx. Brink was driving and Garcia was handling the radio. It was an aggravating ride down. Transmissions on the radio were overlapping each other, and Garcia, a new guy in the unit, was concerned he couldn't get on the radio. He turned to his partner and said, "Don't you think we oughta let someone know we're goin'?"

The First Responders

"No, don't worry about it," said Brink. "They'll know that we're goin'."

For the rest of the trip, Brink and Garcia didn't say another word. The siren was wailing and they strained to hear everything coming over the radio. Some of what they heard, such as, unnecessary transmissions, was annoying. First they had to listen to the chiefs getting their tickets punched with the irritating, "Hey, Jack, where are you?" answered by the inane "I'm over here." Or, another chief was asking, "You wanna call a level three or a level four?' After a minute or two of head scratching back and forth over the radio, a decision was finally made to activate a Level Four Mobilization.

After the 1993 terrorist attack on the Trade Center, the then-Chief of the Department, Joseph Anemone, realized the police department needed to set up some kind of a system to get the first responders to the scene of a major incident as efficiently and as quickly as possible. Anemone created the Mobilization Response Procedure. There are four levels of mobilization, with number four being the most serious. Each level determines the number of police that will respond to the scene. Level One mobilizes one sergeant and eight cops, all to come from the precinct where the incident occurs. Level Two mobilizes one sergeant and eight cops from several different precincts, but from within the borough where the need arises. Levels Three and Four can only be ordered by a rank above captain. These levels involve one sergeant and one lieutenant and eight cops from every precinct in the five boroughs and sent to an incident any where in the City.

On September 11th, approximately 2,000 police officers responded to the World Trade Center. Although the Emergency Service Unit determined its own command post, the precinct personnel were directed down by radio to muster at Wall and Pike Street. The Task Force Units were sent to West and Vesey, and the Highway Units to West and Chambers Street.

Central was repeating questions as a broken record. The dispatcher kept asking ESU if they were "eighty-four" (present on the scene).

Central asked, "Has ESU been notified that there's a plane in the building?"

Somebody shouted over the air. "They know!" Then, two seconds later, Central would ask the same question again: "Has ESU been notified that there's a plane in the building?"

What came over the radio next was a sonata of exasperated voices that took pop shots at the dispatcher: "Everybody knows! Stop asking! Shut up! Don't put it over the air no more!"

Then a female voice came over the SOD airways and it sounded as though she was stuck in traffic and was trying to give directions to another car. But instead of speaking into the PA system, she picked up the radio mike and for the next ten minutes all they heard was, "Turn right! Turn right! Get outta the way! Turn right! Turn right!"

Brink was ready to pull his hair out. *Doesn't that stupid bitch know she's on the radio?* Communications got more fouled up. The cellphone in the truck didn't work. He tried to call his girlfriend but couldn't get through. He cursed the phone and threw it on the floor.

Simultaneously, Trucks Three and Four arrived at the World Trade Center— approximately two minutes after the second plane hit the South Tower. A moment later, Sergeant Coughlin pulled up with McCormack at the wheel. They parked next to each other at the corner of West and Vesey Street. The Bronx cops were on the northwest side of the Trade Center and three blocks west from the Mobilization Point. They'd have preferred to have driven to where Winkler and the rest of the ESU trucks were gathered, but Vesey was impassable—littered with plane and building parts.

In the race down from the Bronx, Hartigan had a minor vehicle accident and broke the passenger's side window. He was in the Adam-Four car with his partner, Steve Lanoce, when they got snagged in traffic somewhere south of 56th Street on the Westside Highway. There was a Highway cop standing in the middle of the intersection directing traffic. He tried to clear a path for the emergency vehicles responding to the Trade Center, but there were so many cars piled on top of one another traffic froze, as a snapshot. Hartigan was frustrated and he looked around for another route. To his right he saw two things:

the sight-seeing tour boat, the Circle Line, docked at the pier in the Hudson River, and the black-tarred bicycle/pedestrian path between the highway and the water. There were no people on the path. Hartigan pulled out of traffic and jumped the curb and went flying down the bike path. Then the Highway cop walked into the bike path and stepped in front of the truck. Hartigan slammed on the brakes. The brakes locked and the truck skidded sideways into a stop sign, hit the side view mirror attached to an extension bar, and rammed it into the passenger's side window. The glass shattered and Lanoce was covered in little bits.

"I'm sorry! I'm sorry!" said Hartigan, excitedly. "Are you okay?"

"Richie, don't fuckin' worry about it," said Lanoce, as he picked a piece of glass out of his eye. "Just get us down there in one piece."

Hartigan got the truck back on track and continued down the Westside Highway. When he arrived at West and Vesey, he saw Coughlin and said, jokingly, "Hey, Sarge. Sorry about the window."

The sergeant just shrugged it off with his good-natured laugh and said, "Don't worry about it, lad. We gotta lot more problems today."

That was Coughlin's way. He never sweated the small stuff. He was a big bear of a man, a former Marine, but you'd never find him in a bad mood. He was always laughing, and he called everybody "lad." Hartigan knew that even if today had been a normal day and they had just been responding to a normal job, the sergeant's reaction would have been the same.

As Lanoce was putting on his gear he glanced behind his truck and saw a police officer standing there with a video camera. He was dressed in jeans and a T-shirt, and wore a baseball cap and a jacket with the letters "NYPD" printed in white across the front. His name was Glen Pettit and he was from the Photo Unit at the Academy. After the first Tower was hit, Pettit and a few of his co-workers jumped into a police van and raced from the Academy at 20th Street and down to the Trade Center. He screeched to a halt on West Street, bailed out of the van and began filming the cops in action. This irked Lanoce. He was never shy about having his picture taken. He was always the first guy to jump in front of a camera. But right now, he wasn't in the mood. He turned his back to the camera and thought *Guy, this isn't the time for pictures.*

Brink was feeling nervous, just as everybody else. Once out of the truck, he was rushing to get his gear on and at the same time making sure Garcia had *his* on correctly. He watched him put on his harness and double-checked the buckles and then gave it a tug to tighten the slack. Suddenly, in the middle of his concentration, Brink felt a hand touch his left shoulder. Unbelievably, somebody had to pick this moment to ask a stupid question. He got ready to swing around with a snap answer and say something as, "I have no time for questions," when he looked back and saw Mayor Rudolph Giuliani and Police Commissioner Bernard Kerik standing there with their entourage of aides.

The Mayor said, "Be careful."

He patted the officer on his back.

"We will," said Brink, blankly. Then he turned back to thread the loops to his harness.

Then in the middle of all the confusion, Coughlin walked over to Giuliani and Kerik and, in his proud Marine manner, he said, "Don't worry, Mr. Mayor; Commissioner. We can handle this."

The Mayor had been uptown attending a breakfast at the Peninsula Hotel at 55th Street and 5th Avenue. It was the mayoral primaries, and Giuliani's two-term reign was about to come to an end. He was enjoying the morning with his staff, when a female member of his security team received a phone call. She listened quietly. Then suddenly her expression became very serious and her complexion grew wan. She leaned carefully over the white-clothed table and, in a near whisper, she informed the Mayor there had been a plane crash at the World Trade Center. Giuliani immediately jumped to his feet and, with his staff, climbed into a van and drove down to West Street. Here the Mayor and his entourage exited the van and began a walking tour of the disaster site.

After Giuliani had a good look at the carnage, it was time to move him and other VIPs to a safe location. The only problem was his multi-million dollar armored, post-Apocalyptic, equipped and stocked "bunker" on Vesey Street in Building Seven, was smack in

The First Responders

the middle of the attack. For the next hour, nobody in charge of the Mayor's protection had any idea where to hide him. They took him to 75 Barclay Street, to a firehouse on Houston Street, and to the Police Academy, before settling at Pier 92, a cavernous warehouse situated about two miles north from the Trade Center on the Hudson River. Ironically, the pier had already been book-marked as the command center for a bio-terrorist practice drill scheduled for the next day, on Wednesday, September 12th. It would have been the first time in New York City an exercise simulating a terrorist attack of weapons of mass destruction would have taken place. The drill was to have involved hundreds of personnel from FEMA, the federal government, the state Office of Emergency Management (OEM), and both the Fire and the Police Departments.

After Coughlin and McCormack had finished putting on their rescue gear, they headed towards the Mobilization Point. They crossed West Street and walked east on Vesey. The remaining six men from the two Bronx commands had taken an extra second or two to gear up, and by the time they were ready to roll, the sergeant was gone.

Lanoce, Schwerner, Brink, Garcia, Hartigan and Steinman tried to catch up with Coughlin. They followed the same route across Vesey. It was a long walk, and this gave them time to take in everything that was happening around them.

Vesey looked as a battlefield. There were plane parts, building parts, and body parts, hitting the pavement. Police, fire, medical, and civilian vehicles were parked haphazardly at the curb or on the sidewalk. Their windows smashed and the metal frame dented by falling debris. A plane's engine laid in the middle of Vesey: A 747 turbo jet engine, a thousand-pounds of metal about the size of a Volkswagen beetle so badly twisted by the explosion, as a wad of tin foil crumbled in a ball and tossed away. Brink looked in amazement at the size of it and tried to imagine how big a plane would have had to be to hold it.

To avoid getting hit by the falling debris, the men walked under the scaffolding hanging down from the Verizon Building, on the south side of Vesey, and directly across from the Customs House. The protection only extended from West Street to West Broadway, one city-block. Under the scaffold, the men saw a small group of four or five office workers walking towards them. What caught their attention was the office workers were laughing and joking and sipping their Starbuck's coffee, strolling down the street as though it was a Sunday afternoon in the park. They were completely oblivious to the smoke, fire, and all the screaming people around them.

The cops were stunned. They yelled, "Are you fuckin' kiddin' me? Get outta here! Run!"

The people couldn't understand why the cops were excited. They were looking up in the air and down the street trying to figure out what was so dangerous. A second or two later, they finally saw the seriousness of the situation and, with horror on their faces, ran out of there.

As the Bronx cops continued down Vesey, they looked up at the North Tower and saw people in the windows above the 94th floor. They were hanging blankets and white sheets out the windows, waving them around, signaling for help. They saw people looking down on the ledges and suddenly someone pushed off and began to fall. Then a body engulfed in flames plunged to earth in a fiery somersault. A couple holding hands took the next leap. The man and the woman held onto to each other for several stories down until some cruel force pulled their hands apart. It was a horrifying sight to see. The people were so high up there was no sound, and when they fell it looked as though they were moving in slow motion.

What could they do for these people? They were jumping from above the 94th floor. They knew the air bags would be useless because it wouldn't be able to handle the velocity impact of a jumper above the 10th floor.

There was a horrible feeling of helplessness. Brink thought to himself, "I wish I could help you; I wish I could help you, *right now*." But first, he'd have to get to the buildings and then climb the stairs. "It's going to be awhile. Hang on! We're coming!" he screamed inside his head.

The Bronx cops were approaching Church Street when they heard Central burst over the radio with an urgent transmission: "*All units be advised: JFK is tracking a third plane inbound at a high rate of speed.*"

Everybody thought this was it: the one that was going to take them out of the picture. It ate them up. They listened for the roar of an engine echoing off the buildings. They watched the sky for a giant T-shaped shadow to sweep over their heads.

At approximately 9:25 AM, the distant rumble of a jet engine was overhead and it was getting closer, but then Central radioed that it was one of our military jets and there was a sigh of relief. The unidentified plane turned out to be, not one, but two F-15 Eagles in pursuit of the two hijacked commercial airliners. The silver bird was the crème of the crop of first-strike fighter jets, with its 23,450-pound static thrust twin engine, forty-three feet wing span, an internal 20mm Gatling gun in the ring wing root, and eight external air-to-air missiles mounted on its lower fuselage corners. They were scrambling up from Otis Air Force Base in Falmouth, Massachusetts, 153 miles away from New York City, and were moving at mach-two. Better late than never.

Brink felt the knot in his stomach loosen a bit, but he still felt sick He turned to his teammates and said, "We're all goin' home tonight. We're all gonna make it out in one piece." The others silently nodded in agreement

One minute later, the Bronx cops arrived at the command post. They saw other ESU cops rushing to get ready. They saw Winkler busy on the radio, and they saw Coughlin was already gone. He didn't wait for his men. He had been given a team and an assignment and was making his way to the South Tower. The next boss in line that needed a team was Lieutenant John Murphy. Winkler assigned Brink, Garcia, Hartigan, Lanoce, Schwerner, and Steinman to Team Five and gave them to Murphy.

Murphy had "time" on the job, that meant he had more than fifteen years as a cop, but he didn't have "time" in ESU. In 1998, he was first assigned to the unit as a sergeant and worked at Four-Truck, in the Bronx. He had recently been promoted to lieutenant and left the unit for a short while to get indoctrinated into his new rank and had just returned about a week ago. Murphy was a man of a few words. He was quiet and kept to himself, and that made it hard for the men to get to know him. And because they didn't know him they didn't know how to describe him. They'd have to think for a second, and then they'd say, "he isn't forceful." What they meant was, he knew he was a new boss in ESU and when he showed up at a heavy job he didn't bark orders, as "You do this! You do that!" not as some new bosses who take the required two weekend supervisory Special Training course and then think they know it all. Instead, he'd always look to his senior men and be guided by what they were doing.

This morning, Murphy had been scheduled to go to the range, but because of the mayoral primaries he was reassigned to patrol. He was driving with Lieutenant Stephen Reardon, from Six-Truck in Brooklyn. Reardon was showing him the ropes and orientating him to his new duties as a lieutenant. These included general administrative oversight of the different Commands in the unit.

When the two lieutenants arrived at Church and Vesey, Reardon stayed with Winkler at the command post and Murphy volunteered for the Towers..

Winkler gave Murphy a choice. He told him there was an even number of teams in each Tower. Since there was an equal amount of work to be done at each site, he left it up to him to pick a Tower. Murphy picked the South one.

EAST NEW YORK

At 9:03 AM, as the South Tower was struck, Seven-Truck was racing over the Brooklyn Bridge into Lower Manhattan. They were driving from the 7-5 Precinct in Bedford-Stuyvesant, an urban neighborhood in East New York, Brooklyn, and eight miles south of the World Trade Center.

There were only three men working in Seven-Truck that morning: Billy Beaury, Santos Valentine, and Ronnie Kloepfer. The fourth man, Dennis Sheehan, was sent to Headquarters to drive First Deputy Police Commissioner Joseph P. Dunne. Dunne had snapped his Archille's tendon during a July 4th game of volleyball at a police department picnic. His foot was wrapped in ace bandages and he had to walk with crutches. The injury kept him on restricted duty inside his unmarked office on the 9th floor at Headquarters. Dunne didn't like being confined to a desk and he wanted some fresh air. So, he needed a driver, and besides Sheehan was dating his daughter, Danielle.

Getting back to Seven-Truck. A fly guy was sent to work with Beaury: Steve Blihar from Ten-Truck in Queens. After Blihar arrived, he wasn't there ten minutes before the news of the crash came screaming over the radio.

The traffic in Brooklyn was horrid. Beaury was driving the Big Truck, and in front of him were Kloepfer and Valentine in the smaller truck, the REP. Kloepfer was driving. He cleared the way through Brooklyn, starting from Atlantic Avenue to Flatbush, over the Brooklyn Bridge, and down to Liberty Street, west along the south perimeter of the Trade Center. At Liberty, they made a right turn onto Church Street, a southbound lane, and drove north, against traffic, to Vesey.

Beaury squeezed the big pig through traffic and drove the wrong way down Church Street. There was no way to avoid the debris in the street, so he just rolled right over it. By the time he reached his destination, the truck had three flat tires and not much control. People were jumping out of the way and putting their hands over their eyes so they wouldn't see the disaster that was about to happen. But, when the Big Truck got to Church and Vesey without major mishap, Beaury hit the brakes and, on the one remaining good tire, swerved to the curb and stopped on a dime right in front of the command post. He took a quick look in the mirrors and double-checked to make sure he hadn't run over anybody (he could have sworn he saw Dennis Sheenan fly up in the air to get out of the way!) and then jumped out. His partner, Blihar riding shotgun, exited at the same time.

Beaury ran around the truck flinging open every door bin and compartment. It was an open invitation to grab the equipment stored inside. He had no intention of baby sitting the truck's contents. If anybody wanted something, they could come and get it. In the 1993 bombing, the unit lost a lot of equipment and the Department replaced it. In Beaury's mind, they could replace it again.

Beaury saw Winkler running around with a piece of paper and writing everybody's name down trying to pull a roster together. Beaury caught his attention and said, "Kenny, if you need anything, it's right there." He pointed to the open bins of his truck. Then he nodded towards the three flat tires and the air brakes hissing as a deflating beach ball and said, "I don't think it's goin' anywhere."

However, Beaury did keep his eye on the last Scott-pack, hanging in the back of the truck. Usually the Big Truck carried four packs and the smaller trucks carried two, but today they were short. Most of them had been sent to the shop for repairs, and what remained behind had to be divided between the three trucks. He was hurrying to buckle his harness so he could grab it, when Sergeant Gillis walked up and took it for himself. Beaury saw this and he was ripping. He wanted to say something as, "Why don't you go take one off your own truck?" but he stayed tight-lipped under his walrus mustache and hunted down another Scott-pack from one of the other trucks.

Gillis was going from truck to truck taking equipment. He grabbed a helmet and a radio out of One-Truck and then, after taking the Scott-pack from Seven-Truck, he walked over to Kloepfer and Valentin, who were gearing up on the corner of Church and Vesey, and told them they were on his team.

QUEENS

Sergeant Paul Hargrove from Ten-Truck was just now pulling up to the command post. The sergeant was riding the ladder at the back of his truck. He had given up his seat to the Chief of Patrol, William Morange, who was riding shotgun with his driver, Officer Peter Appice. They had picked up the Chief somewhere north of the Manhattan end of the Battery Tunnel where he had abandoned his own car, frustrated with the traffic.

Hargrove had been racing down the FDR Drive when the second Tower was hit. It was fifteen miles from Ten-Truck's command in Flushing, Queens to Lower Manhattan. The Long Island Expressway was backed up with stalled traffic, and the Mid-Town Tunnel had only one lane open at the booths to let police and fire through to the city. This gave the sergeant plenty of time to rehearse in his mind what his plan would be. This was all déjà vu to him. He and his four cops, Appice, Steven Stefanakos, Richard Winwood, and Tommy Langone had responded to the bombing of the Trade Center in 1993, and on that day they had gone up in the helicopter and rappelled down to the roof of the North Tower. Hargrove figured they'd be doing that again, but he wanted to do it differently this time.

In 1993, they used the ballpark on West Street to land the helicopters, but he remembered how crazy it got down there trying to clear the field of spectators. He could eliminate that problem by using the downtown heliport. The second part of his plan was to take people off the roof and fly them across to buildings that were safe. He felt this would take less time than flying the ten blocks down to Battery Park. So, he got on his radio and told Central he'd respond to the Wall Street Heliport to set up the helicopters.

It seemed as a good plan, but then somebody, who sounded as though he was of a higher rank, transmitted to the Ten-Truck's supervisor, "They'll be no rappelling onto the buildings." The transmission turned out to have come from the Chief of Police Joseph J.Esposito.

At 9:06 AM, Hargrove was ready to turn off the Wall Street exit when the cancellation of the helicopters came over the air. Before his driver could turn the wheel, he said, disappointedly, "That plan is over. Let's go in."

They bypassed the ramp and continued south down the FDR. The next exit was Battery Park. They took it and drove north passed the Brooklyn-Battery Tunnel, that opened at the tip of Broadway. The tunnel was a quagmire. Trucks and cars were at a standstill. Traffic agents standing at the mouth of the tunnel were desperately trying to move the cars.

Once again, Hargrove was reminded of the 1993 bombing. On that day the police department had cleared all traffic out of Lower Manhattan. Hargrove wanted to do that again. He got on the radio and told Central to dispatch police vehicles to the Brooklyn side of the tunnel and have them stop traffic from entering Manhattan. He transmitted, "Slow down traffic. Get as many people out of Manhattan as possible—and, keep them out!"

Then Hargrove yelled out to the traffic agents by the entrance to the tunnel, "Loop them out of the City and back to Brooklyn! Only let emergency vehicles through!"

Every street north of Battery Park was congested with traffic and people. Wall Street, Canal Street, Broadway were packed with spectators. Businessmen with briefcases, cooks in greasy aprons deserted eggs and bacon sizzling on the grill, cabdrivers left fares sitting in the back seat, and deliverymen dropped their load— to climb poles, scaffold supports, steps, garden walls, and stand on park benches—all to find a view to watch the Towers burn.

Hargrove's truck crawled as a snail through the streets—at every turn was another obstacle. It was at this point that Chief Morange pulled up in his unmarked police vehicle and bailed out. He gave up on the traffic, ran over to Hargrove, and asked for a lift. He knew he'd have a better chance cutting through the cars and spectators in a marked police vehicle with turret lights and a siren. Hargrove gave the Chief his seat and climbed the ladder at the back of the truck. Finally, after what felt as an eternity, they arrived at the mobilization at Church and Vesey.

At the same time, Ten-Truck's two patrol units, the Adam-car, with Winwood and Stefanakos, and the Boy-car, with Langone and Paul Talty, arrived at Church Street.

Stefanakos and Winwood had been in quarters in Flushing, Queens when they heard Hollifield's transmission come over the radio. They looked at each other in disbelief and gave out an "Oh, shit." It wasn't clear by that transmission what kind of a plane it was. They wanted to believe it wasn't going to be that bad. But whatever it was, they began to brace themselves for the worst. They ran downstairs to the garage and jumped into their Adam-Ten truck. They raced down 37th Avenue and then ripped a right turn into traffic. This brought them directly to Union Street, a major commercial strip in the middle of Flushing's Chinatown, and a tangled mess of cars and buses no matter what time of the day it was. They plowed through traffic until they reached Northern Boulevard and then cut a left turn at the intersection and pulled into the westbound lane. As they drove they looked up through the window of their REP and saw something that made them gasp: it was the smoke from the North Tower stretched across the blue sky. They were 15 miles away from Lower Manhattan and they couldn't believe what they were seeing.

Winwood was driving and he said, "How should we do this? We can't take the LIE." He wanted to get into Manhattan through the Midtown Tunnel, a direct extension of the Long Island Expressway, but he knew it would be backed up with rush hour traffic.

"Take the GCP to Hoyt," said Stefanakos. "We'll cut across Two-One Street and go right to the Tunnel. We'll bypass the LIE and we'll bypass the traffic."

Winwood stepped on the gas and grabbed the Grand Central Parkway under the overpass of the Cross Island Parkway. On the GCP, traffic started to slow down as they approached Hoyt Avenue, the last exit in Queens before the Triborough Bridge. They got off here and zigzagged through the back streets of Queens, taking red lights and blowing stop signs until they found 21st Street. Stefanakos was concerned about the traffic at the Tunnel. He radioed ahead to the Bridge and Tunnel Authority. He said, "Shut down one full side of the tube! Get us a lane for emergency vehicles only! Stand by!"

At the same time, other ESU trucks were coming over the radio saying they were clearing lanes for emergency vehicles from the other boroughs. The guys in Six-Truck, who were responding from Brooklyn, were calling to close down a lane on the Brooklyn Battery Tunnel. And, One-Truck, who were first on the scene at the Trade Center, were giving the location for ESU's mobilization point at Church and Vesey.

Adam-Ten pulled off 21st Street at the LIE and drove to the mouth of the Midtown Tunnel. All traffic in the Manhattan-bound lanes was at a standstill. The police at the tollbooths weren't letting any cars through. All traffic—going to and from the City—pulled off to the side of the expressway. The people stood outside their cars and watched the smoke rise above Lower Manhattan.

Adam-Ten crashed through the orange plastic traffic-barriers, used as lane-dividers for the tollbooths, and entered the tunnel. Then Winwood suddenly thought of something and he said, "Holy crap! I don't think this is a good idea."

Stefanakos was thinking the same thing, and what they were thinking was the tunnel wasn't the best place to be in the middle of a terrorist attack. If the tunnel blew up the truck would be torpedoing through the East River. But they were already here—so lets get this over with, ASAP! Winwood pushed the pedal to the floor and flew in the high-80s. Nothing was going to make him slow down until he was on the Manhattan side of the river. They exited the tunnel and swung a left on 34th Street. Then another left across Second Avenue and drove a beeline to the FDR Drive. Adam-Ten continued on the FDR and turned off at South Street, to Dey Street. They'd have to drive west about six blocks to reach the mobilization point at Church and Vesey. The streets were packed with emergency vehicles and waves upon waves of people were coming towards them. Winwood kept hitting his siren to get their attention. If that didn't work, he stuck his head out the window and yelled, and if that didn't work, he got on the truck's PA and yelled louder, "Let's go! Everyone keep moving!"

Surprisingly, this bit of crowd control didn't slow them down. The whole trip from the tip of North Queens to Lower Manhattan was accomplished in an amazing fifteen minutes.

As they approached Church Street, they started to make a left turn but quickly caught the eye of an ESU cop standing in the middle of the street. He hand-signaled to turn right. Stefanakos yelled to Winwood, "No! No! Turn right! Turn right!" The sudden change of direction kicked the truck half way up on the sidewalk, slam-dunked their REP at the top of the stairs of a subway station, and then jolted them to a sudden stop in front of a post office. They left their REP tethering on the sidewalk and jumped out.

The Boy-Ten car was Tommy Langone and Paul Talty. When the first Tower was struck, they had been at Queens College running an errand for Talty's wife, Barbara. She had called him at work around 8:15 AM and asked him to stop by the college's bookstore to pick up her books. His wife was a teacher and was returning to school to accumulate credits towards a Master degree.

It's unknown what route Boy-Ten took to get to Manhattan but, knowing Langone, the minute he heard the emergency transmission come over the radio he'd have shifted the gear into mach drive and raced as a madman all the way down. The Long Island Expressway ran along the campus of Queens College, but he knew every short cut in the City and he could have overridden the expressway in favor of some route nobody else but Langone knew about. Langone's driving scared the pants off Talty, and he probably sat there with his fingers clutched as hawk talons in the truck's upholstery.

Langone and Talty rarely worked together. Talty was a new guy in the unit and had only been in the Third Squad for about nine months. He didn't have a partner and most of the time he was an extra guy used to fill-in for manpower. Langone's steady partner was Randy Miller, but he had taken the day off. He was home and asleep in his bed when his fiance, Kim, a nurse in a hospital in Suffolk County, called at around 9 AM, and said, "Turn on the TV. Something bad's happening." Miller took one look at the smoking Tower, got dressed and rushed to work. He knew Langone would be in the thick of it, and he wondered what his partner was doing and whom he was working with.

In any case, Boy-Ten arrived at Church and Vesey about thirty-seconds after Stefanakos and Winwood. Langone parked his REP in the middle of the block between Church and Barclay, and on the same side of the post office.

THE HELICOPTERS

Hargrove wasn't the only one thinking about helicopters. Winkler wanted an air rescue team, too. He was pissed somebody canceled the helicopters. Winkler was thinking, "Let the pilot make the call—not somebody standing on the ground who can't see the conditions on the roof. In moments like this you need to have faith in the specialist."

Winkler wasn't going to give up on getting an air rescue team off the ground. He looked for someone who would agree with him, and one block down from Church and Vesey on Vey Street was where the big bosses from One Police Plaza were assembled.

Dressed in their stark, gold-star uniforms, were the Chief of the Department, Esposito; Chief Thomas Purtell, head of the ESU/Special

Operations Unit; the Police Commissioner Bernard Kerik; and First Deputy Police Commissioner Chief Dunne, propped up on a pair of crutches and a bandaged foot.

Winkler went over and conferred with Chief Purtell, and he agreed with Winkler's assessment. The Chief gave his blessing for air rescue.

Now Winkler had to find a team he could send up in the helicopters. He saw Sergeant Hargrove pulling up to Church and Vesey and he knew his wish was answered. Winkler ran over to Hargrove and said, "Sarge, instead of taking a team into the building, why don't you go down to West Street and set up the helicopter in case we need it?"

Hargrove thought, "This is ironic." That had been his original plan. But now, instead of using the Wall Street heliport, as he suggested, Winkler had them go to the grassy area over by River Terrace and use the ball field right off West Street, the same location they had used in '93. Winkler said the heliport was in a bad spot. It sat in the direct line of the smoke and debris.

Hovering above Lower Manhattan there already was a police helicopter. A small Jet Ranger had taken their position outside the perimeters of the financial district. They had been on routine patrol early this morning when the first Tower was struck and arrived on the scene at 8:52 AM.

The Jet Ranger had had a close encounter with one of the hijacked planes. As it was circling the building to try and get a visual fix on the damage, the pilot looked to his right and suddenly saw a large, low-flying plane moving towards him. It was coming in fast, and at that trajectory, it would take everything in its path to get to its target. He yelled out to his co-pilot, "Oh, my god! There's a second plane!" He pulled up on the control stick and pressed down on the throttle. He cut the blades and in a frantic, spilt-second, near-miss maneuver, the helicopter climbed. The plane passed underneath and crashed into the South Tower.

A Bell 412 helicopter was now responding from Floyd Bennett Field, in Flatbush, Brooklyn. Floyd Bennett was known simply as "the Field." It was built in 1928 with the idea it would become New York City's first municipal airport. But the idea was abandoned a few years later in

The First Responders

favor of a new airport in Queens, which was LaGuardia. During World War II, the Navy used the airstrips to test proto-type planes and the nearby bay to test submarines.

Now it was a park off the Belt Parkway. It had an empty guard booth at the front gate and narrow tar-paved roads that abruptly switched to pebbled paths winding through the rows of rusty, dilapidated old hangars, sand dunes, and overgrown yellow cattails.

There was one area in the rear northeast sector of the Field that was off limits to the public, and where the Emergency Service headquarters and their training school occupied several arched-truss barrack buildings. Also located here were the NYPD's Aviation Unit and their fleet of helicopters: two Jet Rangers, one Long Ranger and three Bell 412s.

The Bells are larger than the Rangers and can carry a crew of three plus room for seven to fourteen passengers. The large sliding doors make a good launch pad for rescue work. It also has spotlights, a Doppler weather/ground mapping radar, and pop-out floats.

Police Officer Donald LaSala was an instructor at the Emergency Service training school. He normally worked nights, but on 9/11 he had to change tours to accommodate the maintenance man who was coming in this morning to do repair work in the building. He sat waiting in the kitchen, watching TV and having a cup of coffee, when the news flashed on the screen. LaSala and the other instructors couldn't believe what they were seeing and they all ran outside to check if this was really happening. They looked north towards Manhattan, and in the distance they saw the Twin Towers and the massive cloud of black smoke.

LaSala ran back inside to change. The school had a very nonchalant atmosphere: the dress code wasn't enforced, and he needed to get from his jeans and sweatshirt into his uniform. As he came through the kitchen again, John Brown, who was out on a line-of-duty injury, was sitting at the table watching CNN. LaSala had his hand on the door and was ready to run outside when a live shot of the second plane hitting the South Tower happened before millions of viewers' eyes. He stopped to look. He took in the horror and he knew it was a terrorist attack. He continued out the door and to the garage.

Sergeant Billy Kennedy ran to the garage looking for LaSala. He found him loading up his REP and told him to drop everything and to get over to Aviation and rig a helicopter for air rescue. LaSala's initial response was he didn't want to do the helicopter. He wanted to be on the street where he could do something useful, and the idea of getting stuck in a helicopter wasn't his idea of helping out. He told the sergeant to go find somebody else.

"There's nobody else," said Kennedy. "Me and you are the only ones here right now that are Rappel Masters."

He couldn't argue with that. The Rappel Master has an important job. He's the "Safety Line" and is responsible for hooking up the ropes so a team of cops can drop down and do the work. He does the rigging by connecting mantle ropes (these are five-eighths of an inch thick with a nine thousand pound capacity) and then threads them through steel loops mounted on the ceiling of the helicopter. Then the ropes are thrown out the doors and the men put on a harness and a carabineer in a figure-eight descender, hook themselves to the rope, and rappel down.

The landing pad sat on the marshes of Jamaica Bay on Runway 30. Looking north, they could see the lower portion of Manhattan from Battery Park to the Brooklyn Bridge. They had a clear view of the burning Towers.

As they sat there waiting for the co-pilot to get on board, LaSala asked the pilot if he had time to grab his camera bag out of his car. Photography was his hobby. He had gone fishing that weekend and his photo equipment was still packed in the trunk. The pilot practically insisted on it, and LaSala made a quick dash to his car, grabbed the video camera and his digital camera and rushed back. In the interim, the co-pilot had climbed into the cockpit, and once the seat beats were fastened and the doors were shut and secured, the helicopter lifted off.

At approximately 9:09 AM, the Bell helicopter arrived at the Trade Center. They circled the buildings to check the roofs to see if anybody had made it up there. The wind was blowing in from the north and the smoke billowing out from the burning upper floors was leaning towards the south. The massive black cloud pouring out from the North Tower looked as a tornado lying on its side. It covered the roof of the South Tower, smoke over smoke. There was no point in even looking there; they couldn't see a damn thing.

But the North Tower had an opening. The wind had cleared the north side corner of the roof, and they could look down and practically count the number of small antennas sitting row after row as reeds poking through a thin mist. The chopper did one fly-pass around the building, and the crew decided that an air rescue was a possibility. There wasn't anybody on the roof—but maybe, just maybe—if they kept watching, somebody would appear.

Back at ESU's command center on Church and Vesey, Hargrove raised Kennedy on the radio and they synched their response to the ballpark on West Street. Hargrove knew he'd need specialized equipment to rig the helicopters, but Ten-Truck's Big Truck was out at the shop for repairs. He looked around to see whose truck he could grab, and he spotted Franco Berarducci, the chauffeur at Four-Truck. He was standing with his Big Truck handing out equipment. Everybody from his command had been placed on teams, including his partner, Steve Driscoll, who was on Coughlin's team. Hargrove ran over to Berarducci and told him he was now with him, close up the bins, and get ready to roll. Then Hargrove ran over to where everybody was gathered in a group, found his two men, Stefanakos and Winwood, and told them to get their equipment and meet him back at the Big Truck.

As Hargrove was climbing aboard the Big Truck, a fire captain came running up from behind. He was out of breath and in civilian clothes. "I'm from Rescue. I'm off-duty," said the fireman. "My guys are going in the building. Can you lend me a Scott-pack?"

The sergeant jumped back down and pulled a mask and an air tank off the back of the truck and gave it to the fire captain. The fireman thanked him profusely, but Hargrove didn't think twice about it and said, "No problem. We'll catch up later."

At 9:25 AM, just as everything was getting organized, there was one minor interruption. Stefanakos and Winwood had just finished hooking their gear together, when suddenly they saw Chief Esposito come running up the block and into a covey of ESU officers. He had a very distraught and urgent look on his face, and he warned, "We have a third jet and it's inbound. They have no identification on it and it's coming up really fast." And then he added, "Be safe."

For one second of suspended animation everyone stopped what they were doing and looked at each other. They were under the impression a third airliner was heading straight for New York City and was about to hit another target. In the stir of excitement Winwood heard someone behind him call out, "Put your helmets on!" And that started a chain reaction of helmets being scrabbled for. Just thinking about that comment would have made him laugh if he hadn't been so busy putting on his own helmet. Any other day he'd have turned around and given the guy a shocked look and rolled his eyes, thinking, *Yeah, right. Like that tin bowl is going to deflect airplanes off your head. Just keep on doing what you're doing and hope for the best.*

It was one "oh shit" after another. Now a radio transmission came over the SOD radio nobody thought they'd ever hear in their entire career: "Central, inform the White House that New York City is under attack. Send air support."

Everyone's heart leaped into their throat. The cloudless blue sky had looked so calm and beautiful this morning and was probably the last warm day of the summer was suddenly a panorama of kamikaze pilots. It felt as if every man and woman scrabbling around was a bit player in some goddamn awful B-movie. How could something like this be happening? But it was happening, so deal with it.

The "third plane inbound" was the same radio transmission the Bronx cops had also heard. The instant Central identified the plane as military jets, two F-15s appeared above the buildings, so close, weaving in and out as a video game sneak attack ready to strait the people running in the street

After that scare was over, Stefanakos and Winwood ran back to their REP. As they stood there pulling out equipment for the helicopter they saw Tommy Langone shoot around to the other side of their truck. He was opening bins and pulling out rope. The day before, he had put together a High-Rise Rescue Kit, a combination of a large number of carabineers, ascending and descending equipment, and a Haul System of pulleys. Langone was very proud of this accomplishment and was excited he was getting a chance to use it.

Stefanakos and Winwood were watching him raid their truck.

"Tom, what're you doin'?" said Stefanakos, quizzically.

"We're goin' in! We're in Tower Two! We're goin' in with Coughlin!" said Langone, in that machine gun speed rap he was famous for. "And, besides, I took your High-Rise Rescue Kit."

What Langone was talking about was that Sergeant Coughlin had requested him for his team. The sergeant had already grabbed Brian McDonnell, Joseph McCormack, and Stephen Driscoll, and he needed two more guys to fill out his team. They had already gotten their assignment to the South Tower and were waiting for Langone and Talty to catch up with them.

"You wanna do the helicopters?" asked Stefanakos. "We've been redirected to fly up to Tower One to start air rescue."

It didn't matter one way or another who got what assignment. They could easily have switched. Watching the swollen plumes of black smoke engulfing the top floors was a frightening sight, and the thought of flying to the roof made the strongest heart pound. And to be perfectly honest, they were thinking that going in the Tower looked a whole lot safer than being lowered into the mouth of a high-rise fire-breathing furnace. But that wouldn't stop them, for they had flown to the roof in '93 and they could do it again.

"No, don't worry about it, Cocko," said Langone. "I'll see you in a little while. Be safe." He gave him a half-cocked smile and whipped his hand in the air and off he went.

Sergeant Hargrove didn't know Langone and Talty were assigned to another team—not until Winkler came over and asked him if it was okay if they went with Sergeant Coughlin.

"They're suited up and ready to go," said Winkler. "They'll fill out his team."

But before Hargrove could give an answer, Langone came flying around his vehicle. Paul Talty was with him, and the two of them were lugging ropes and the High-Rise Rescue equipment over their shoulders.

"I got it, Sarge," said Langone. "They're calling for high-rise rescue."

What could Hargrove say? So, he said, "Okay. I'll catch you later."

They didn't look back at each other. They didn't even give a slight shrug of their shoulders or a thumbs-up. It wasn't as if they were doing anything different than they have done a hundred times before. Even if they had both known this was a final farewell, he probably wouldn't have done anything different. You couldn't have told Tommy Langone otherwise. He was the type of guy who'd cut his vacation short just so he wouldn't miss anything. It was two weeks ago, on one of his very rare vacations, he took his wife, Joann, to New Orleans, but after a few days he wanted to get back to start his counter-sniper training. The job always came first. When he walked into work, Hargrove looked at him in disbelief, shook his head and said, "Tommy, you didn't?"

"Ah, Sarge," he answered, embarrassed but apologetic. "I didn't wanna miss the sniper training. I promised Joann I'll take her back to New Orleans."

"Just as long as you promise," said Hargrove, sounding more as an approving father than his supervisor.

But nobody thought those buildings would collapse. As far as they knew, they'd follow the same scenario they went through eight years before at the first terrorist attack. It would be a tough and long day. It would be exhausting. But there would be no doubt in anybody's mind at the end of the day or night they would all go home.

4
9:03 AM: Eight-Truck

Now, it was time to move into the Towers. Winkler assigned numbers to the teams, with even numbered Teams going to the South Tower—Tower Two, and all odd numbered Teams going to the North Tower—Tower One.

Sergeant Gillis was Team Two—the South Tower. None of his cops from Eight-Truck were present at the command post, so he had to grab men from the other trucks. He had Santos Valentin and Ronnie Kloepfer (from Brooklyn) on his team, as well as Walter Weaver and Jerome Dominguez (a fly car from the Bronx working in Two-Truck).

At 9:03 AM, Adam-Eight was still at Cedar and Broadway, and the men knew they had to make a move and find their unit. But where? They never heard the transmission telling where the mobilization point was. They didn't know that all of the ESU units had assembled at Church and Vesey.

"What'd you want to do?" asked Nessenthaler. They had already tried to find Sergeant Gillis, but he wasn't answering the radio, so he was open for the next best suggestion.

"I don't know what we're goin' to do, but I do know what we're not goin' to do," said DeMasi. "We're not goin' to run in there blind."

This was a big job. It was bigger than anything they had ever seen or done. Never in a million years would anybody have guessed suicide pilots would attack New York City. Even in your wildest dream, how could you plan for it? DeMasi needed to hear a plan was being drawn up. He suggested they grab all the gear they could carry and look for any Emergency Service boss and be guided by what he said; but the instant DeMasi and Nessenthaler turned around, they saw swarms of people coming at them from all directions, battered and covered in blood. With panic in their faces, the people scrabbled against each other to show the officers their injuries. DeMasi and Nessenthaler didn't know where they had come from—maybe from the Tower, or maybe they had been walking on the street when the plane crashed and were struck by falling debris. One man held up his limp arm and pointed to a bone sticking out through his flesh. A woman with a bloodied face, her hair matted in a mess of wet clots, had a deep gash across the top of her head.

DeMasi turned to open the bin in the truck to get the first-aid kit. As he leaned in to grab the bag, he heard a loud booming sound that made him jump back. Then a wave of hot wind rushed over him.

"What the hell was that?" said DeMasi, astonished.

Nessenthaler doesn't remember having heard the impact, but he did feel the blast of heat. Both men looked down Broadway and saw a large crowd of people pointing up to the sky and screaming, "O, my God, it's another plane!" It was indeed the second plane, smashing into the South Tower.

Things were getting worse by the minute, but the two men didn't have time to think about the knot in their stomachs growing tighter and tighter. Now they had all these people pleading for medical attention. They tied a splint on the man's broken arm, and DeMasi grabbed a passerby who wasn't hurt and pointed to an ambulance across the street and commanded, "Take him to the ambulance." Then they bandaged the woman with the gash on her head and grabbed another passerby to escort her to the ambulance, and things went on like this until they had everybody patched up.

Now, it was time to get to the Trade Center.

They walked down Broadway to Liberty Street, south along the perimeter of the Trade Center, and then turned west. As the two officers were walking, DeMasi stepped on something soft and wet that instantly slipped away from under his foot. He looked down and stared at it for a second. "What the hell is that?" Then he realized it was a human organ. And now, everywhere he looked—on the sidewalk and in the street—there seemed to be body parts. Right in front of him was a woman's severed arm lying by the curb. It was in perfect condition, as though detached from a mannequin. It had a wedding band still on its finger. He pulled his eyes away and he caught sight of a skull whose face had been blasted off. The face was lying beside the skull, as a mask that had slipped off its wearer. He could only guess these body parts had shot out of the buildings at the moment of impact and were now sprawled out as far away as four blocks in all directions. The streets looked as an anatomy class. And the closer they came towards the Trade Center, the worse it got. It reached a point where they were literally jumping over human remains.

The two officers kept walking west towards West Street where they made a right turn and then walked straight until they passed under the South Bridge—the walkway connecting the Trade Center to One Financial Center—and then continued on under the North Bridge, connecting with the Winter Garden. As they passed the plaza, DeMasi was surprised to see a large congregation of firemen corralled at the base of the Towers. It felt as though thousands of them were standing around waiting for something.

"Why are all these firemen standing here?" DeMasi asked Nessenthaler. He could feel in his gut an uneasiness that's a cop's instinct telling him things could take a turn for the worst. What that turn could be had not manifest. It did not occur to him the Towers would soon collapse. What was in the back of his mind was if two planes could hit the Twin Towers, why shouldn't they expect a third or a fourth? And if that was the case, why would anyone want to be standing directly under the World Trade Center?

"I don't feel good about this," said DeMasi. "Let's keep walking north."

They squeezed their way through the firemen and followed a straight path up West Street that brought them to the corner of Vesey and right in front of the Customs House. Here they found the Emergency Service bosses they were looking for: Sergeant Tom Sullivan of Brooklyn's Six-Truck, Sergeant Tommy Urban from the A-Team (Apprehension Team), and the ESU Commanding Officer, Inspector Ronald Wasson.

DeMasi's gut feeling was right. At 9:30, ten minutes after he and his partner walked through the crowd of firemen, a jumper fell from the North Tower and landed on firefighter, Danny Juhr, from Engine 216, who was standing on Liberty Street and killed him.

Some of the units didn't make it to the designated mobilization point. For instance, Six-Truck from Brooklyn had entered Lower Manhattan through the Brooklyn Battery Tunnel and ended up on West Street, and this placed them on the opposite side of where they wanted to be: Church and Vesey, ESU's Mobilization Point. The criss-cross of narrow streets had been a snarled mess of people and cars. Instead of trying to fight traffic, Sergeant Sullivan decided to put down stakes at West and Vesey. It wasn't long after that Sergeant Urban and Inspector Wasson joined Sullivan and his men at the corner. They formed their own mobilization point and were picking up cops who, for whatever reason, didn't hear the initial transmissions giving the location of ESU's Command Post.

There were already fifteen other ESU cops at that corner, including Curtis Garvey and Pete Linarello from Eight-Truck, and Bob Brady and John Gilliam from Nine-Truck. DeMasi and Nessenthaler started hooking up their Larakus belt and Scott-packs and threw a hoop of rope over their shoulders. Now it was "hurry up and wait," as the three bosses tried to make a decision as to who was going with whom and where.

As they waited, Nessenthaler was looking up at the North Tower. He suddenly saw an object falling from a window around the 90-somethingth floor. The object disappeared for a spilt-second as it passed through an opaque cloud of black smoke and then reappeared on the other side. As it continued to fall, Nessenthaler stared hard at it until he could make out what looked as a human form.

It took so long for the person to hit the ground that Nessenthaler had enough time to reach over and tap DeMasi on the shoulder and DeMasi had enough time to turn to his partner, and say, "What?" Nessenthaler pointed up and said, "Look." DeMasi still had time to catch a glimpse of the body before it hit the ground.

Team Three, headed by Sergeant Curtin, consisted of John D'Allara, Joe Vigiano, Vinny Danz, Mark DeMarco, and Steve Blihar. Curtin had added Billy Beaury, but Winkler hadn't wanted Beaury to go inside the Tower. He wanted him outside at the command post to help him out. But Billy Lutz, who worked at One-Truck, just happened to be off-duty and working in the area at his side job as a security guard in the federal courts. He had run over to the command post and volunteered to be Winkler's second pair of hands, so Beaury was free to join Team Three.

Now everybody began to roll out. The teams—Two, Three, Four and Five—were on their way to the Towers, and Team Six was heading to the ball field to wait for the helicopters.

As each Team passed the corral of gold stars and white shirts, the Chiefs and the Deputy Commissioner saw their men off, as generals standing on the sidelines of a battlefield. Dunne gave his blessing as he watched them head out towards the plaza destined for a burning Tower.

"God Speed," he told them.

9:25 AM: Team Three Inside The North Tower

At around 9:20 AM, before the warning about a possible third attack, Vinny Danz and Joe Vigiano of Team Three ran down Vesey Street. They didn't wait for their team to catch up with them. They kept going until they had a half-block lead and were making their way up the escalators to the plaza. The way they were hurrying it looked as though they couldn't wait to get to the bedlam. The confusion was relentless: radio calls, men shouting, women crying, people running by, ambulances pulling up, things falling out of the sky and crashing onto the sidewalk or smashing car windows. There was so much going on they didn't know which of their senses to use, their eyes or their ears. It was sensory overload. By the time Sergeant Curtin and the rest of Team Three climbed the long flight of stairs to the plaza, he had lost sight of the two cops who had run ahead.

Sergeant Curtin and the four men who were still with him—D'Allara, DeMarco, Beaury, and Blihar—had walked down the alleyway between Building Five and the Customs House. They saw carnage up ahead, and this made them stay close to the rows of large cement planters of manicured shrubs that ran along the wall of Building Five. It wasn't much protection, but it made them feel less out in the open.

They began to hear loud thumping noises coming from the plaza, and that made them stop abruptly half-way down the alleyway. When they looked to see what it was, they saw large pieces of debris falling from the burning Towers and crashing into the plaza. Then suddenly, the next falling object they saw was a body. It landed with such force it exploded as a pitched watermelon. Seeing jumpers isn't a new thing to a cop, but this was different because there were so many. First, they'd see one person jump and then fifteen seconds later they'd see another and then thirty seconds later it would be three bodies in a row. It looked as though it was raining people. The whole scene had this wild, too-real unreality of a suppressed dream.

They'd have to pass that area of the plaza to get to the North Tower, and right now it looked as an exploding minefield. Bodies and debris kept crashing down, and kept everybody pinned close to the side of the building.

The First Responders

Curtin turned to DeMarco and Beaury and said, "Hold on here for a second." He wanted them to stay put in the alleyway, next to the cement planters on the side of the building. Then he told D'Allara and Blihar to follow him. Curtin and the two men ran about ten yards down the alleyway to the southwest corner of Building Five. Here, they stopped short and took cover at the edge of the building.

DeMarco and Beaury lowered the bags to the ground—the tools clanked. The medical bag didn't clank, because there was nothing inside that was made of metal, except for the oxygen bottles but they were nestled between the rolls of bandages and the sealed squared-shaped packages of sterilized glazes.

They didn't know why Curtin had told them to wait. DeMarco thought it might had something to do with the heavy equipment he and Beaury were carrying. They both had two bags and each bag weighed forty pounds. He thought maybe the sergeant scouted ahead to confirm a clear passage before proceeding with the equipment. There was a lot of debris blocking the plaza. If they couldn't get in that way, they'd have to drag the equipment back and look for another access route.

But Curtin appeared to be waiting for something. He was looking attentively out across the plaza—was somebody coming? Maybe he was looking for Vigiano and Danz. They were his guys for the day, they had already passed the plaza and moved on, but they were nowhere in sight.

What DeMarco liked about Curtin was here was an experienced Emergency Service cop, well-respected for his leadership, but no matter who you were or how long you had been around, he was always open to suggestions. DeMarco remembered being on jobs where Curtin would come over to him, and just because he was the senior guy, he'd ask, "What do you think?" And DeMarco, who had a modest, low-keyed way about him, would say, "You don't need to ask me. You know what you're doing." But this was something DeMarco appreciated, and it always meant a lot to him that someone he respected, respected his seniority.

All of the men had similar stories about Sergeant Curtin. He was an All-American guy who loved the job and wanted to keep the *esprit de corps* alive. He wasn't gung-ho, but he believed in discipline. Nobody lagged behind and nobody came unprepared. Any time one of his guys got depressed about the job and complained it wasn't like it used to be, and anytime the white shirts made you feel dispensable, unimportant, and worthless, Curtin would get everybody together for some training exercises. There was nothing as getting your brain to secrete endorphins for forgetting the humps that were making your life miserable. They'd go find some stripped down, burnt out, abandoned car and pull out the "Jaws of Life," rev up the motor, and practice cutting the metal apart as piranhas chewing up bones and spitting them out again. It was an opportunity to blow off steam and at the same time to get their rescue skills well oiled.

But today, Curtin was doing it on his own. He moved silently, not really telling his men what he was doing or thinking. Still, they trusted him, and they knew they'd follow him to hell and back if they had to.

A half a minute later, Curtin left the corner of the building. He ran back up the alleyway with D'Allara and Blihar still tagging behind him and returned to DeMarco and Beaury. Apparently he had given up on whatever it was he had been waiting for. "The heck with this," he said. "Lets go."

As Beaury bent down to pick up his equipment, a frantic transmission burst over the radio: "Get out! Get out! There's more planes coming! Kennedy Tower is reporting a third plane coming into the World Trade Center!"

The four cops ducked and looked around. They were ready to tear ass down the block when Curtin, listening intently to the distant rumble in the sky and cradling an MP-5 semi-automatic submachine gun in his arms, calmly said, "Those aren't civilian planes. Those are F-14's; or, F-15's."

They took his word for it. If there was anyone who would know, he'd be the man. Curtin was forty-five-years old and a former drill sergeant in the Marine Corps. He spent twelve years on active duty, met his wife, Helga, a fellow Marine, then joined the reserves, became a police officer, worked in the 7-5 Precinct as a cop, got transferred to ESU, took the sergeant's exam, got promoted, and then, just as he was about to return to ESU, his reserve unit was deployed to Kuwait to serve in Desert Storm. Because of his military background, he thought in a tactical way. As the team leader, he also thought of the safety of his men. He was the only ESU cop responding inside the Towers who had armed himself with any kind of heavy weapon. He told another sergeant before departing for the Tower he suited up this way because of "the nature of the job." This was a terrorist attack and they didn't know what they'd find inside.

A few seconds went by and finally a transmission came over the radio that said the inbound plane were military jets. That was a relief. Curtin knew his jets—it was no wonder he was as cool as a cucumber. And because nothing blew up, Beaury and the others were glad they hadn't embarrassed themselves by running for the hills!

Everybody pulled their rattled nerves together and waited for the sergeant's next move. He led them around the back of the Customs House. They stood under the awning and paced the seconds between falling objects and no falling objects. When it was safe, they ran across the short, open space to the Tower. They weren't familiar with the Trade Center, and they didn't know which Tower was which, but here they were, sprinting across a courtyard, hoping they were heading toward the right building.

They entered the mezzanine, looked around, and caught the attention of a few Port Authority cops standing off to the side. They asked, "Is this Building One?"

"Yes," the Port Authority cops answered.

"Where's Stairwell C?"

The PA cops pointed to a door off to the rear left-side of the mezzanine. Here, the team walked around the balcony and took the stairs that stopped at the 3rd floor. From there they needed to walk across a hallway to another door that picked up where Stairwell C ended and started again. The 3rd floor was a maintenance storage area for cleaners and trade workers. There were no people there, just mops and buckets, the smell of cleaning fluids, and machinery with blinking lights. The floor was filled with heavy smoke and they wanted to get out of there as fast as they could.

There were two things Curtin did before he and his men started to climb the stairs. First, he told DeMarco to dump his equipment. After lugging it this far, it seemed ridiculous to not go any further, but they could move faster without it, and time wasn't something they had plenty of. The only thing they kept was a few lightweight tools and the medical bag DeMarco had slung over his shoulder

Next, Curtin turned to Beaury and said, "Listen, shut off your radio." Then he looked to DeMarco and Blihar and repeated the same order.

Curtin, just as D'Allara, Beaury, Blihar, and DeMarco, had been on the job long enough to remember the World Trade Center bombing back in 1993. On that day they were stuck in the Towers for so long the radios went dead, and everybody was walking around saying, "Hey, your radio work?" The sergeant didn't want a repeat of that situation. Curtin figured if he and D'Allara kept their radios on while the others kept theirs off—and, if and when the radios died—they'd still have three fresh ones.

The smoke continued up the staircase and gave the lights on the wall a hazy glow as headlights in a fog. In spite of the smoke, they didn't put on their Scott masks but let them dangle off their hips. They'd save their air tanks for when it got really bad. They were walking in water funneling down from the upper floors. The water, either from sprinklers or busted pipes, rolled down from step to step in a slow and steady cascade. They turned the first landing and were met by a long stream of office workers coming down the stairs, walking in a calm and orderly fashion. Nobody was in a panic and nobody was in a hurry. The people kept to their right side and the cops kept to their right side. For Beaury, it was a flashback to his old Catholic schools days as a kid growing up on Long Island. He remembered how the nuns would monitor the halls and stairwells and keep everyone quiet and walking to their right. And God forbid if anyone tried to walk in the middle, because they'd be immediately jumped and beaten up.

The people were helping one another, holding onto elbows and shoulders, the younger or more fit kept the older and weaker of heart moving along. Some of them had climbed down fifty, sixty, seventy floors.

The First Responders

"Just pull your T-shirts over your noses," said Beaury, as the people passed. The smoke in the stairwell started to become more and more irritating, and there was a sickly odor of jet fuel. Somewhere around the 9th floor, Beaury looked into the crowd and caught a woman's eye and asked, "What floor were you on?"

"Ninety-first," without breaking her stride, she looked back over her shoulder to answer. "Whatever it was it was just over our heads."

When the airliner crashed into the building it sliced through the building from the 93rd floor and severed all the elevators and stairwells clustered in the center. Anybody above those floors were doomed with no way to escape. Beaury thought it was incredible this woman had just walked eighty-odd floors. But she was a big woman and she looked strong. He looked back at her and gave her an amazed look.

TEAM ONE: Inside The North Tower

Lieutenant Hollifield and Sergeant Amendolare and his four officers had already reached the 21st floor in the middle of the North Tower. They had received a transmission there were injured firefighters at that level.

The cops went in and out of the offices and down the aisles calling, "Anybody here?" But, the floor was deserted. The offices had a suddenly abandoned feel. A suit jacket still hung on the back of a chair, a computer screensaver still pulsating with its colored geometric swirls, and there was paper work, folders and a fresh paper cup of coffee, still warm, with one spilled package of sugar surrounded by several other unopened ones.

After they determined it was a false call, the team returned to the stairwell and continued their climb. On the staircase they found a fireman's helmet. Thinking that it might have something to do with the injured firemen they couldn't find, Hollifield made inquiries over the radio. After an exchange of mundane questions and answers, the owner was found, and the helmet was put back on the stairs exactly as they found it.

As Cliff Allen walked up those stairs, he started to think back to the bombing on February 26, 1993. On that day, Islamic extremists drove a van loaded with explosives into the Secret Service section of the underground parking lot underneath the North Tower and blew a hole three floors deep in a concrete wall above the PATH trains. The explosion set off a fire that sent smoke billowing up through the building. Allen had been on one of the first rescue units to respond. He and the team that he was on climbed so high in the Tower they actually met the ESU cops that had rappelled from a helicopter to the roof and then walked down the 110 flights of stairs. He remembered how smoky the stairwells were and how difficult it was to breathe. The fire was below him—in the basement—and all the smoke was rising to the top. This time, on September 11th, the fire was above him, burning out of control on the 93rd floor. Allen thought it wasn't that bad. There was hardly any smoke in the stairwells, only in the lobby and on a couple of the lower floors. The only thing really annoying was the water slowly rolling down the steps, as an overflowed bathtub flooding the apartment of the neighbors downstairs. But the building did reek of fuel. It had a gas station smell, except it was heavier and less sweet.

Winkler's voice came on the radio and sent Team One on a new rescue mission. He told them to go to the forty-somethingth floor and check on a man dangling a woman out the window. Allen didn't quite catch the floor number, but he knew they didn't have far to go. He had been counting in his head, and he knew they were getting close to the 30th floor. "Looking back," Allen would say, months later, "there was only one transmission that came over Tac-g about the jumpers. And it said, *a jumper.*" Allen and his team had no idea what was going on outside. They never knew the sky was full of falling people.

Then, somewhere around the 26th floor, they looked up and saw a fireman standing at the top of the staircase. His name was David Weiss and he was from Rescue One and he yelled down, "ESU, do you have any medical gear?"

"Yes, we do," Norman yelled back up.

Weiss recognized the police officer as the brother of a Fire Captain from his own company and he said, "Dave Norman? Is that you?"

"Yeah."

"Listen," said Weiss. "I have firemen down with chest pains on the thirty-first floor. Can you get up here?"

"We got a report of firemen down on twenty-one."

"No, it's thirty-one," Weiss corrected.

They followed Weiss to the 31st floor, and in the foyer were a dozen and a half firemen sprawled out across the floor and propped up against the walls. They were in bad shape. It was a combination of heat exhaustion, middle age, the weight of heavy turnout coats, and the long haul of gear up thirty-odd floors.

The men got to work. Norman, Allen, Mack, Amendolare, and Hollifield moved into the room, dropped the medical bag to the floor, and pulled out oxygen masks and canisters of O2. Morley, who had been tagging along with the ESU team, was a narcotic detective and wasn't a qualified EMT—not as ESU—he didn't know CPR and some of the firemen looked as if they were on the verge of a heart attack. But he didn't want to stand around and do nothing, so he got down on one knee so he'd be at their eye level and talked to the firemen. It was just small talk. A word or two to comfort them.

Norman turned to Weiss and told him this was as good a place as any to set up a triage and if his firemen on the upper floors found any injured people they should bring them to the 31st floor..

Hollifield walked to a water cooler at the end of the foyer. Next to the cooler were plastic, ten-gallon bottles of water packed in wooden crates. He began pulling apart the crates. When he looked up for a second, he saw Morley trying to help one of the fireman loosen the collar to his turnout coat. Meanwhile, there was Morley himself, in his white, tailored shirt with his tie pulled up around his neck tighter than a hangman's noose. To Hollifield, it was the funniest thing he'd ever seen.

The lieutenant laughed and said, "Timmy, do me a favor and take that fuckin' tie off."

"I can't take this tie off. It's a Nicole Miller tie," said Morley. He kept a straight face and played along with the lieutenant's ribbing. "My wife bought it for me for our anniversary."

Morley was getting a kick out of busting Hollifield's chops. He looked back at him, grinned, adjusted his tie, and made himself look even more prim and proper. It was gray silk with silver stripes and it went with his gray suit. It was the first chance he'd had to wear it.

Morley was your typical NYPD detective. He was burly and tall and as Irish looking as they come. He was thirty-three years old, with short-cropped ginger hair, and bright blue eyes. He got his gold shield following the Department's career path. Morley did his rookie years in the 4-1 precinct in the South Bronx, and when it was time for a change of scenery, he transferred to City-Wide Street Crime at Randall's Island, and then later, to Manhattan North Street Crime Gang Unit. But he wanted a detective shield and he knew the only way he was going to get it was if he did time in Narcotics; so he made his move to Manhattan North Narcotics, MNI, and then Brooklyn North Narcotics, and after eighteen months of sitting in SUVs with blackened windows watching street-corner nickel-bag buys, and sometimes money laundering cases, and sometimes breaking up big time *Miami Vice* Colombian drug dealing rings, he got his gold shield.

Weiss stayed out of everybody's way and took a position on the staircase. In the Police Department, when a police officer is injured, another cop will stay with him throughout his medical treatment, and this is also true in the Fire Department. Weiss's assignment was to stand by his men. His company was one or two flights up. He was missing all the action upstairs.

It's unknown how far up the North Tower the firemen had climbed, but they never reached the fire. In the oral histories that FDNY had complied from the five-hundred men interviewed describing their actions on 9/11, some had reported they climbed as high as the 35th floor. A civilian named Adam Mayblum, who worked on the 87th floor of the North Tower, wrote in an Internet blog he'd seen firemen as high up as the 44th floor. Also, there had been a radio transmission from a firefighter from Ladder 3 who reported a collapse on the 65th floor. That still left twenty-eight flights before the fire. However, in the South Tower Fire Chief Orio T. Palmer from Battalion Seven in Manhattan and some of his men had reached the skylobby on the 78th floor. He was one flight down from the impact area and he could see the fire from the stairs. He also saw near the elevators numerous charred bodies. Palmer climbed that high because he had the help of an operable freight elevator located away from the impact on the southwest side of the South Tower that took him to the 40th floor. From there, he hiked the rest of the way.

Now, that fire department personnel had made it to the fire it was unclear how they'd put it out. Water can't be pumped up more than a few stories. Fighting a fire in a high-rise would have had to rely on hoses fed by a standpipe system situated on each floor. The water would have then been gravity-fed from the bottom. Firefighters would carry three lengths of hoses to the floor below the fire, hook the hose to a standpipe and stretch the hose up one flight to the fire floor. But since seven floors of the North Tower had been severed by the impact of the plane, the pipes had probably been severed too. If they were going to do anything, hopefully, they'd have tried to do a horizontal trench cut and let the fire burn itself out.

In the book *Fire Fighting Principles and Practices*, by former New York City Battalion Fire Chief William E. Clark, he wrote: "when an airplane crashed into the Empire State Building in 1945, the standpipe was sheared in two, but because the New York City building code required shutoff valves at 150-foot intervals in the riser, fire fighters were able to bypass the break with three-inch hose from an outlet below the lower point of shutoff to one above the upper shutoff."

If the system is completely unusable, Clark suggested an alternative would be to stretch hoses all the way up the face of a high-rise building. This is accomplished by threading hoses in and out of windows every fourth floor, or so, to take the weight off coupling ("coupling" are hoses linked together, and each 50-foot length and 2 ½-inch hose filled with water could weigh as much as 175 pounds).

It didn't take long for the Fire Department to realize they didn't have so much as a spitball to put out the fire. Ray Downey, the Fire Department's Deputy Chief of Special Operations, was heard in the uncut version of the tape by the French filmmakers, telling the other chiefs, "We're not going to put this fire out. Move the command post out of the building. Get as many people out and limit the number of men going in."

They were in the process of doing just that when the first Tower fell.

Meanwhile, Cliff Allen was down on one knee on his side of the foyer trying to assist as many firemen as he could. As he leaned in to place an oxygen mask over the face of one of the firemen, he heard an urgent transmission come over the radio. It was the warning of a third plane inbound. The message first came over the Fire Department's radio. Then he heard Winkler shouting over Tac-g, "There's another plane heading for the Towers!"

The First Responders

The message hopped down the foyer from radio to radio, man to man. They turned up the volume and tilted their heads closer.

The time was now 9:25 AM. A firefighter from Ladder 1-5 who was in the South Tower could be heard transmitting to his unit. In an animated but calm voice he said, "We got reports of another incoming plane. We may have to take cover. Stay in the stairwell."

Another firefighter from Ladder 1-5 Roof, answered, "Ten-four."

Everybody in the foyer held their breath. There was nothing Allen, his team, or the firemen sitting incapacitated on the floor could do. There was nowhere to run. All they could do was sit tight and wait for impact.

After a fifteen-second pause of radio static, the firefighter from the South Tower transmitted, "One-five to one-five-roof. The plane is ours. I repeat. It's ours. What floor are you on, Scotty?"

"Fifty-four," said Ladder 1-5 Roof.

"All right. Keep making your way up. We're behind you."

"Ten-four."

Then from the police radio, Winkler said, "Disregard. It's a military plane."

Everybody in the room gave out a big sigh of relief, but the fireman sitting on the floor with his ear to his radio had more bad news. He tilted his mask off to the side of his face, looked at Allen and said, "The Pentagon's been hit."

The Pentagon had been struck by a third commercial airliner at 9:37 AM. The fireman heard somebody say it over his radio, but Allen didn't hear the news over Tac-g. The two men talked, trying to make sense of not knowing who or why we were being attacked, but all the talking in the world couldn't get rid of the feeling of doom or dissolve that hard lump stuck in their chest.

The fireman began to get upset. He squirmed and rubbed his hand across his forehead. "I'm a week away from retirement," he said. "What the hell am I doin' here?"

"Don't worry," assured Allen. "You'll get out." He didn't know what else to tell him. He was nervous, too.

Allen never got his name. The fireman was older, maybe in his fifties.

When the officer looked around the room, he noticed the different numbers on each of the firemen's helmets. The men were not from the same company. For some reason the number seven stuck out in his mind.

7
9:45 AM: Team Five On The Plaza

Lieutenant Murphy felt the safest way to get to the South Tower was to go under it. He'd do this by going through the concourse shopping mall beneath the Trade Center. There he thought he'd find the escalators down to the PATH trains and the escalators up to the plaza and inside all the buildings. It was easy access, and Murphy knew by taking that route he'd find elevators and escalators to get inside the Tower. He also knew by walking under the plaza he and his team could avoid the falling debris.

Team Five walked up some steps behind the command post at Church and Vesey, and that brought them up to a landing just below the plaza and on the same level of Border Books, connected to Building Five and faced out to Church Street. Then they walked along the eastside wall of Building Five and towards a wide, rectangular-shaped entrance with stairs and escalators leading down to the concourse. There were thousands of people exiting the stairs and pouring out to Church Street. Office workers evacuating from the Towers were using the concourse as an escape route. Port Authority and NYPD police officers, fire wardens, and Trade Center security guards, were posted at various strategic spots throughout the underground corridors and exits to keep the calm and direct the civilians to the street.

Murphy came across a gray-uniformed security guard standing by the exit where the people were streaming out. He was an older, white-haired gentleman in his sixties. Murphy called over to him, "Hey, which way to the South Tower?"

"Oh, well, it's down this escalator," said the guard, casually pointing his finger downward as if he was giving directions to a tourist attraction. "But, you don't want to go down there."

The guard was cautioning the lieutenant about the large number of people hurrying through the corridors and stairs. The escalators were also not an option. They were inoperable, and escapees from the Towers that were impatient with the all the people trying to squeeze their way through the stairwell were using the "down" escalators to walk up.

The concourse was a bad idea. Trying to fight against a mob with heavy equipment on their backs would be an impossible feat. Murphy realized the plaza and the falling debris and bodies were unavoidable. It was the only viable route to the South Tower. At this point, he decided to change initiatives. Instead of going to the South Tower, the furthest from where they were standing on the northwest side of the plaza, they'd go to the North Tower, which was much closer.

Murphy turned to his Team and asked, "You guys wanna go to the North Tower?"

The men looked around at each other to see if everyone was in agreement. Murphy was the team leader and, if he wanted to switch Towers, well, it was fine with them.

"Yeah," said the guys. "We might as well."

Murphy asked the guard how to get to the North Tower. The guard said he'd show him, and he led Murphy and his team back towards Border Books. There was a double-glass door just before they got to the bookstore and that led into the lobby of Building Five. They entered and passed a Port Authority Police substation. There was no one there, but the surveillance cameras pointing down from the ceiling kept an eye on them as they walked through the empty corridors.

As they walked through Building Five, there were large glass plate windows that opened onto a view of the plaza. The building was deserted and it was very quiet. There wasn't any of the usual chatter normally heard on a busy Tuesday morning.

The guys on Team Five were a pretty tight crew. They had known each other for years, and that made them familiar with each other's personalities and senses of humor. You could make a fool of yourself and the guys wouldn't flinch. It was all part of the camaraderie of working in a small unit. So, as they filed pass the large window, Brink looked out at the wrecked plaza and thought of a line from the film, *Ghostbusters*. He said, "Boy, is the landlord goin' to be pissed."

A collective groan rose up from the Team. Apparently, his gallows humor had struck a wrong chord. He was trying to lighten up the serious mood, but the guys rolled their eyes, told Brink to shut up, and then went back to their sullen silence.

They were just coming to Building Six at the end of Building Five.

The First Responders

Right between the two buildings was a small alleyway or airway they'd have to cross. It was approximately two stories high and looked as if it was cut into the building. But there was only one problem: people were still leaping from the Tower. At one point the men looked up and saw two persons jumping and then four people holding hands and floating down as a string of paper dolls.

To get safely to the other side, a Team member would step to the edge, glance upwards, and if he saw nothing was falling, give the thumbs-up-coast-is-clear signal, and in one quick rush, each man would take his turn to run across the alleyway. Once on the other side, they stood against the wall of the Customs House. It looked as a street-fighting scene in an old World War II film, but instead of dodging bullets, they were dodging falling debris and jumping bodies.

Sergeant Coughlin was on the 20th floor of the South Tower. He radioed back to Winkler and told him he was having problems getting up the stairs. Evacuation wasn't going smoothly. The staircases in the Towers were not very wide, and they only had enough room for one person to go up and for one person to go down. The onslaught of people rushing down the stairs made it look as though somebody had opened the floodgates. It wasn't they were pushing or shoving—there just wasn't enough elbowroom. It was one big, sweeping wave of bodies pushing back the team of cops. The cops were packed in a narrow staircase with hundreds of people rushing towards them. All that Coughlin and his men could do was stand back on a small corner of a landing with their backs pressed to the wall as people swooped down the stairs and passed them as a herd of cattle on a drive.

Winkler raised Gillis, who was climbing the South Tower in an opposite staircase. He was having the same problem.

"We're on the twentieth floor," said Gillis. "We're meeting some resistance."

Suddenly, Winkler looked back over his shoulder and saw McCormack strolling pass the command post. He had gone back to his REP. It was parked all the way over at West Street, three blocks west. He was now walking down Church Street towards the South Tower. Winkler couldn't believe what he was seeing. He turned to Billy Lutz, pointed McCormack out to him, and said, "What da'fuck?"

Winkler stopped McCormack and asked him what he was doing and told him he was supposed to be on Sergeant Coughlin's Team. The officer replied the sergeant had sent him back to the truck to get a piece of equipment. Winkler got flustered for a second: this was messing up the tracking he was doing in his head!

"Who's on your Team?" said Winkler.

McCormack gave him a quick run down of the names: Langone, Talty, McDonnell, and Driscoll.

It suddenly occurred to Winkler, if McCormack was walking around loose, it meant others could have walked off their teams too. Winkler got on Tac-g and raised Coughlin, Curtin, Gillis, Murphy, and Amendolare. He double-checked what officers they had with them. Now, he was writing it down on paper. Before, he had been keeping a mental checklist. The teams were small and he thought he could keep track, but now he felt he needed to have the names right in front of him.

Winkler didn't let McCormack return to his Team. Instead, he told him to stand by.

"You're never gonna find Coughlin. He's already on the way up," said Winkler. "I'll get you on another Team."

The First Responders

TEAM SIX: *Waiting For The Helicopters*

When Sergeant Hargrove was redirected to West Street to set up the helicopter for air rescue, he still had clearance. It was a five-block ride to the ball field: three blocks west across Vesey, then a right turn two blocks north up West Street. Two straight lines. But before Hargrove and his team were half way there, this transmission came over their portable SOD radios: *"Central, advise those units that there will be no roof operations. There will be no rappelling from the helicopters. The conditions on the roof are too dangerous."*

Everybody was bouncing around in the back of the truck, and because of the din of the clank and rattle, they weren't sure whose voice it was. It was First Deputy Police Commissioner Dunne canceling air rescue for the second time.

For years, the Police and Fire Departments had always had a High Rise Rescue Plan in effect. The plan was so old and went back so many years, that a lot of the guys couldn't even remember when it was first implemented. The way it was supposed to work was a battalion fire chief would go up in the helicopter to survey the fire. This had been done in the past with major brush fires and other high-rise fires. Based on the fire chief's assessment, the police helicopter would then shuttle firefighters to the roof. But in the case of the Twin Towers, a landing pad would have to be prepared. The South Tower had a ready-made heliopad, but the North Tower, did not. The roof of the North Tower was covered with antennas. To take care of this, an ESU team would have to rappel to the roof, cut down the antennas, and break open any locked doors.

In the 1993 World Trade Center bombing, an air rescue was utilized, but it didn't quite follow the letter of the plan. The Fire Department alone was supposed to be allowed to put it in effect, but on that day, Louis R. Anemone, a four-star police chief, activated the helicopters, and twenty-five ESU police officers rappelled to the roof of the North Tower.

This made the Fire Department a bunch of unhappy campers. They don't like it when the police do things on their own, nor do they appreciate it when the cops take the glory away from them. To add insult to injury, after the ESU teams landed on the roof, the police officers walked down and met the firemen who were walking up, on the 75th floor. The firemen were exhausted from their climb, and they were surprised to see the police.

The firemen said, "How'd you guys get here?"

"We took the elevators," said one of the cops.

"You took the elevators?" said the firemen, flabbergasted. "All the elevators are out of order."

"Not ours," said the cop, facetiously. "We have our own elevators."

The Fire Department hadn't been happy about the police rappelling to the roof *then*, and they weren't happy about it *now*. On September 11th, at 9:35 AM, the Fire Department simply canceled air rescue and passed this order to the police brass.

Another thing about the roof on September 11th was the doors were locked. It had always been the Fire Department's policy to discourage people from climbing to the roof during a high-rise fire. The danger was to be trapped above a fire. After the '93 bombing, the Port Authority and the NYFD decided to lock the roof doors to keep people from going there. Another reason for locking the doors was because of structural and radiation hazards and to secure the communication antennas on the North Tower.

However, on September 11th there were people trying to get to the roof. At 9:00 AM, on the 98th floor of the South Tower, Sean Rooney, a fifty-year old insurance salesman who worked for AON, made a phone call to his wife, Beverly Eckert. She didn't pick up, and Rooney left a message on her voice mail: "Hey, Beverly, this is Sean, in case you get this message." He told her he was all right and he could see the burning North Tower from his office window. The minute he hung up the phone, the South Tower was struck. The impact swayed the building. The second airliner had crashed through the 73rd floor—twenty-five floors below his office.

Immediately, Rooney left his office and walked down the staircase, but for some reason he couldn't get passed the 78th floor. He turned around and walked back up the stairs with the intention of going to the roof. At the 105th floor he was stopped again because of a large group of about two hundred people packed in the staircase. They, also, wanted to get to the roof and were waiting for somebody to unlock the roof's door, five flights up. In order to access the roof it required passing three doors, one leading from the stairwell onto the 110th floor and two leading from the floor to the roof. Within the group, there was a window washer named, Roko Camaj, who had a key. But the door was locked by an electronic interlock. The only way he could get through was to be identified by a security camera, and then buzzed in by the command post on the 22nd floor. But the post had been evacuated and nobody was answering the intercom.

When Rooney realized he couldn't get to the roof, he left the staircase and entered an empty conference room on the 105th floor. He found a phone and made a second call to his wife, and this time Beverly answered. Rooney told her where he was in the South Tower and the door to the roof was locked. He asked her to look at the TV news and tell him if she could see where the fire was in the building. She said he was far from the fire, and she would dial 911 and ask the operator what staircase was safe to climb down. Rooney said while she made the call he'd try the roof door again. He put down the phone and left the conference room, and went back to the staircase. A few minutes later, he returned to the phone. He told his wife the roof door was still locked. Beverly said the 911 operator didn't know what staircase was safe. Rooney started to panic; he was worried about the flames. She said there wasn't any fire near him. "But the windows are hot," he said. His breathing became labored. Ceilings caved in. Floors were buckling. The phone call was cutting on, and off. They said goodbye, then there was a loud explosion, and the phone went dead.

But even if Rooney and the others had been able to open the door to the roof they would have made a deadly discovery: The roof of the South Tower was completely engulfed in dense, black smoke. Not only would the helicopter hovering near by not have been able to see them, but smoke inhalation would probably have overcome the people and killed them.

Team Six was still heading to the ball field. Air rescue might be canceled now, but that didn't mean at a moment's notice the smoke couldn't shift, the firefighters would get the fire under some kind of control so the choppers could get up there. As far as the cops were concerned, they were still on stand by.

As they reached the ball field, the Big Truck pulled up in front of the gate, that opened through a chain link fence. They parked outside and along the construction trailer, propped up against the fence and a utility pole.

As soon as they rolled to a halt, everybody exited the rear of the truck, made a visual sweep of the ball field, and confirmed it was clear of civilians. The only people around were in the street: small groups, here and there, standing and watching the chaos they'd left behind.

Sergeant Kennedy radioed Team Six. He wanted to double-check that Hargrove and all of his men were at the ball field. He also wanted to round up the same guys that had rappelled to the roof in 1993. Kennedy was there that day; so was LaSala. But, there was one guy missing and that was Tommy Langone. Hargrove informed him he was with another sergeant. So, Kennedy radioed Langone and asked him to respond to the ball field. Langone transmitted back and said he wouldn't be able to comply because he was already in the South Tower.

Not everything was the same as it was in '93. This time the condition on the roof was perilous, and because of the way the north wind was blowing, only a small section of the northeast corner of the North Tower was clear. It was that corner that would be the drop zone for a team of rescuers. Hargrove wanted to get his men in by a technique called "fast roping." Fast roping is very similar to the way firemen slide down a pole in a firehouse, except the rescue workers use a three-inch wide nylon rope thrown out of a hovering helicopter. This technique is deployed to insert men inside a tight area whenever it is impossible to land or bring the helicopter down to ground level.

Fast ropes come in lengths of sixty and ninety feet. The officer places his hands around the rope and free falls to the ground. Just before hitting, the officer grips the rope to break the descent. This allows for a very rapid descent with a momentary stop before hitting the ground. If gripped too soon, he risks burning his hands. If gripped too late, he risks breaking a leg.

In this scenario, the helicopter would be hovering only twenty-feet above the area of insertion. Low flying insertions are called a "touch and go" operation. Stefanakos, Winwood, and the others would fast rope to the roof, cut down the antennas, break open the emergency doors, and start an evacuation from the top down. Any civilians trapped on the upper floors would be brought to the roof, placed in vests and harnesses, and airlifted to a safe location.

In 1993, ESU didn't fast rope to the roof. Instead, they lowered themselves by using a harness with carabineers on a figure-eight. Fast roping is a good idea only when you want to get men in very quickly, such as, in a combat zone under heavy fire. Although Hargrove was thinking fast roping, the truth is this technique is far too dangerous for an operation as this. If, while you're fast roping, the helicopter veered off, you're not going to be able to support your own weight for very long and would fall off the rope. It could happen just as it did in the film, *Black Hawk Down*, when the young soldier lost his grip and fell forty feet to the dusty, embattled street of Mogadishu.

The helicopter started to make its descent, gliding in towards the ball field. It hovered momentarily above the ground and then slowly touched down. With the rotors still whipping up the wind, the helicopter sat there as Kennedy got out and ran over to Hargrove and his team.

"This one's already rigged and ready to go," said Kennedy, yelling over the repeating whoosh of the rotors slicing though the air. "We have a second chopper coming in."

Hargrove didn't want to break up his team again, and he told the sergeant he'd wait for the second helicopter flying in from the Field. They had already pulled six hundred feet of rope off the truck and had everything ready for their own rigging, but they wanted to know what the conditions on the roof were like, so Kennedy gave them the latest news flash:

"I can get you in," he said. "But I can't get you out."

He went on to say the smoke and the heat were so severe on the roof that once they were dropped in, there was no way the helicopter could come back for them. This wasn't good news. The way Kennedy was talking, it sounded as though he didn't know about the cancellation. Hearing they'd be dropped in and left to fend for themselves was a big reminder somebody better tell him the deal.

"They don't want us going up," said Winwood and Stefanakos, simultaneously. "They want us to standby until the condition changes."

Kennedy gave this a two-second thought and said, "We're not going to stay on the ground." As far as he could see, there was no reason for the helicopter to be a sitting duck in the middle of this ball field. "When you get a team in place, call us back."

Kennedy climbed back in the helicopter and lifted off. It was safer in the air. The pilot was concerned about a secondary attack and, if there were going to be anymore surprises, they didn't want to take the chance the chopper would be either grounded or crash during take off.

Kennedy and LaSala weren't happy about their rappel team being scrapped, and it wasn't going to stop them from making a rescue attempt if they saw an opportunity. They went back up with the intention if they saw anyone on the roof, they'd go against orders and use the hoist to lower LaSala down with a harness and airlift that person out of there.

As they passed close to the top floors, they could see, high above the smoke, people hanging out the windows waving to them. It was killing them there was nothing they could do. They could only hope the firefighters or the ESU teams would be able to get to them.

Hargrove watched the helicopter swing out over the Hudson River and slide back towards its position hovering close to the roof of the North Tower. The whole scene looked ominous, as if it had been plucked out of a Tom Clancy novel. From his position at the ball field, he could only see the Tower from the 80th floor up. His view was partially blocked by other high-rise buildings in the area of West Street and Vesey. The sergeant was looking for the second helicopter flying into the area from the south. He saw Kennedy's chopper hovering semi-circle around the west wall of the North Tower just above the

The First Responders

rising black plumes of smoke. To Hargrove it looked as though it was the second chopper coming in.

"Here comes our helicopter," said Hargrove.

Just as he spoke, there was a rumbling. Nobody standing at the ball field knew where it was coming from. It was loud and started to pick up speed. It sounded as a thousand freight trains crashing together in a horrific train wreck. Everybody stopped what they were doing, looked towards the Trade Center, and watched as an eruption of smoke and thick gray dust hurled upward where the South Tower stood. The smoke and debris began to peel back as a banana skin. The floors were collapsing one after another, one floor onto the next, and to the next after that, and they could actually hear each individual floor hitting the floor below. It began to build in a terrifying momentum that finally brought all 110 stories to the ground.

Radio traffic became a sputter of incoherent, panicking voices. What they were screaming into the radio didn't make sense. They knew guys were in trouble, but it was hard to make out what they were saying. Then, a hot wind came rushing down the street, preparing the way for the next wave of devastation.

To the guys on Team Six it looked as though there had been a partial collapse. They thought only the top portion of the South Tower had fallen onto the Marriot Hotel. But there wasn't any time to investigate what had really happened, because roaring down the street was a ten-story high cloud of debris, smoke, and dust. The dust cloud was moving at fifty miles an hour. It traveled through the canyons of streets carrying burning rubble, knocking down poles, transporting stones and pulverized cement. Everything in its path was rapidly and completely interred. Nobody could out run it. Everybody was racing for cover.

Hargrove, Appice, and Berarducci jumped inside the back of the Big Truck, while Winwood and Stefanakos ran inside the trailer. After securing all windows and doors, they watched as the dust cloud consumed everything around them. For the next seven minutes the world outside went to total darkness.

"The whole Tower is gone! Holy crap!" screamed the helicopter pilot.

"They knocked the whole friggin' building down!"

LaSala squirmed out of his seat belt and swivelled around to get a better view of the collapsed. He couldn't believe what he was seeing. The Tower had plummeted to the ground in a near perfect column of smoke. Simultaneously, the smoke rolled out in all directions and covered the streets. Suddenly LaSala remembered his video camera. He had been holding his digital camera but he didn't want to take stills. He swung around and grabbed the video camera out of the bag, aimed it down and photographed the rolling plume of smoke heading out towards the river. He was amazed at the speed of the dust cloud.

"We got outta there at the right time!" said the pilot, shouting over the loud cranking noise of the helicopter's blades.

"What?" said Kennedy.

"We got outta there at the right time!"

The pilot was referring to the ball field they had just lifted off from. It was now a blanket of black smoke.

A voice came over the pilot's radio and ordered them to land. The helicopter had been in the air for forty-five minutes. The aviation base wanted them to conserve fuel in the event they might be needed to med-vac injured people out of the devastated area. The helicopter glided west across the Hudson River and landed on a pier in New Jersey. The instant they touched down, LaSala, Kennedy, the pilot, and the co-pilot ran down to the end of the dock. Below them was a boat basin, and standing next to them were a few New Jersey State troopers. They all looked across the river and watched the tip of Lower Manhattan disappear under a cauldron of black smoke. The only building they could see was the mid-to-top portion of the North Tower, still standing, smoking, and reflecting sunlight off its aluminum exterior.

The pilot looked over at LaSala and saw him holding his video camera. He said, "Did you get the Tower coming down?"

"No," said LaSala. He was too stunned by what he saw that he couldn't bring himself to film the collapse.

LaSala switched back to his digital camera and photographed the stillness of the smoke. Then thirty minutes later the North Tower collapsed. Once again, he was too overcome with shock to hold up his camera and take a picture.

9:59 AM: Team Five On The Plaza

When the South Tower fell, everybody was so caught up in their own situation, the crash came as an incredibly unexpected shock. The collapse was so fast Winkler barely had time to take cover. He ducked behind a truck, and in complete darkness, got on the radio and tried to raise the two teams that were in the collapsed building. He knew it was futile, but he had to try. The last transmission from Coughlin was, "We're on the opposite staircase from Gillis, heading up."

Winkler knew you didn't have to be a rocket scientist to know that whatever had happened to the South Tower could and probably would happen to the North Tower. In the minutes before the collapse, he had gotten the rundown from all the teams, so he knew where everyone was. There were three teams inside the North Tower, and he had to get them out. Immediately, Winkler ordered his teams to evacuate the building.

Team Five never made it to the North Tower. Moments before the collapse of the South Tower they were still in the alleyway on the plaza. The last guy had just finished running across the walkway and they were now all lined up against the southwest corner wall of the Customs House. They gave themselves a two-second breather—just enough time to catch their breath and psyche themselves for the march to the North Tower.

Suddenly, there were three loud explosions in a row. Boom! Boom! Boom!

Brink winced and waited for the shrapnel to hit him. He didn't feel a hit, but he did feel the ground rumbling under his feet. He saw Steinman standing in front of him with a startled look on his face. His head was tilted back and his eyes were transfixed on something. Brink was too afraid to turn around to see what he was looking at. It had to be horrible.

"What is it, Bobby?" said Brink.

"The building's comin' down."

"You're fuckin' kiddin' me?" said Brink.

The rest of the team—Murphy, Lanoce, Schwerner, Hartigan and Garcia—turned and saw across the sixteen-acre plaza, and on the very spot where the South Tower stood, a giant compression plume shoot straight up in the air. As if in slow motion, the cloud started to roll towards them. They moved quickly, bracing themselves for impact. There was only seconds to find cover. Ten feet away from the southeast corner of the Customs House was a three-foot concrete extension jutting out from the wall. They dived inside the small space and grabbed onto one another as they waited for whatever it was that was going to hit.

It hit hard. There was a crash of metal. It was the loudest noise they had ever heard. It sounded as a large empty dumpster truck hitting a pothole with the bang echoing off all the buildings around them, only a thousand times louder. Bah-bah-bah-boom!

Brink closed his eyes and dropped to his knees. He didn't want to know what was coming. He didn't want to see his own death. He was facing a wall in a praying position, and all he could think was, *This really sucks. I'm gonna be buried under a hundred and ten stories and no one is gonna know where I am.* He didn't think about his family, he didn't think about his four-year-old son. There was no "My life flashing before my eyes" revelation. It was all about survival and gut instinct

There was a shock wave of hot air. It felt as standing on the edge of a subway platform waiting for the local as an express train rushed down a tunnel. The heat was immediately followed by an avalanche of steel and concrete poured down and filled the alleyway between Buildings Six and Five. Team Five was in this alleyway and the dust cloud pounded them with full force. Then it became very dark. The bright sunlight and the clear blue sky disappeared. Brink thought even though his eyes were shut, he could sense the darkness, as if a heavy blanket had been thrown over his head.

Hartigan, Schwerner, Lanoce, Murphy, and Steinman grabbed for their Scott masks only to find they were now useless pieces of apparatus, as dust filled the interior-breathing regulator. Brink deliberately did not put his on. He'd have had to remove his helmet to pull it down over his face, and he didn't want to risk the chance of getting hit on the head by hurtling debris, so he covered his face with his heavy, work gloves and let the mask hang down by his side. As the men crouched in the blackness, flaming pieces of paper were flying by as dry leaves blown off a bonfire. They landed in the street and on cars, setting them on fire.

Suddenly, the deafening noise stopped and there was silence. The end of the world kind of silence. For a moment, they weren't really sure if it was silence or not. They thought they were dead, but that wasn't right, because you can't "think" you're dead, if you're dead. Instead, they were surprised they were alive.

They tried to open their eyes, but it was too painful. Their eyes were tearing, and if they opened them, their eyeballs were seared by the ground glass and silica that filled the air. It felt as if somebody was slicing them with a razor.

Their mouths were filled with powdery dust, as a box of pancake mix had been poured down their throats. It mixed with their salvia and turned into a gritty paste. Brink reached into his mouth and pulled out a large, wet glob of cement, the size of a golf ball. Steinman had it the worst. The dust was lodged in the back of his throat and he was dry heaving and his face turned bright red. He coughed it up as a cat choking on a fur ball and then caught his breath.

They continued holding onto each other, although no one could see who it was he was holding on to. Then Steinman yelled, "Everybody sound off!" One by one, he called for each of his teammates to answer up:

"Schwerner, you there?"

"Yeah."

"Lanoce?"

"Yeah, I'm here."

"Brink, Hartigan, Murphy?"

They all answered up.

"Garcia?"

No answer.

"Garcia? Garcia?"

Brink's stomach turned over. The rookie was his partner for the day and he was responsible for his safety. *Shit, the guys are gonna be pissed that I got him killed.* Then he heard that Darth Vader heavy breathing—

the loud, sucking inhale and exhale. It was the unmistakable sound of a Scott-pack. Garcia was the only one fast enough to put on his Scott mask. So, while everybody else was gagging on the smoke and spitting up charcoal biscuits, the new guy was breathing in and breathing out his fresh air. Brink was so happy to know Garcia was okay he wanted to smack him in the head for scaring the beJesus out of him.

They used their fingers to dig the dirt out of their Scott masks. Then they purged the breathing tubes and put the masks on. Finally, they opened their eyes, and all they saw was dust and total darkness. But the darkness wasn't black; it was a white opacity, as a blizzard. Steinman tried to move his arm and a jolt of excruciating pain shot up from his left elbow to his shoulder. When he ducked for cover he had thrown his arms over his head and dropped to the ground with such force he banged his elbow. It felt broken, though he couldn't properly evaluate the injury because of the darkness. Touching it was painful, and bending it was almost impossible. He suffered calmly, and reassured the others he was fine.

Murphy's radio was in a leather case on his gun belt that had a wire that ran up to a speaker-mike clipped to his shirt's left epaulet. He yanked the mike off his shoulder and yelled over it they were trapped. "Team Five! We're alive! But, I don't know where we are!"

Winkler transmitted back, "Okay. Sit tight!" He was going in himself to retrieve the trapped men. Winkler rushed to get a team together. He grabbed every blue uniform he could see in the dusty fog. He found Sergeant Paul Buscemi from Nine-Truck, and police officers, Rowe, McCormack, Facara, and Kurt.

Half of Team Five's equipment was gone. The ropes, the first aid kit, the Hurst tools had all been knocked out of their hands. Garcia had managed to save one bag of rope, secured under his arm and across his chest, and Brink had held on to a bag of halogen tools.

Because of the blinding smoke, Team Five couldn't see how they were trapped. They thought they were under a collapsed lean-two. Just before the dust cloud rolled in, they remembered seeing the large glass-plate windows of the Customs House. Half-blinded and stumbling over the debris, they reached out to feel for the windows. They decided if worse came to worst, they could use the tools they still had to break down the glass; or they could do what cops and cowboys do in the movies: use their guns to break the glass by shooting it out.

Then the dust settled a bit and the darkness began to lift. They removed their Scott masks to save oxygen, just in case something else happens and they might need them again. Now they saw a small ragged opening of light breaking through one side of the pile up, and began to crawl towards what they thought was a way out.

"I see light!" shouted Murphy over the radio. "We're getting out!"

Team Five climbed single-file over the uneven heap of rubble until they reached the opening. They stooped down and squeezed out. Now they found themselves standing outside on the plaza. They looked up, but the sky was shut out, and all but the nearest objects faded from view. Anything further than a few yards away was still hidden behind thick, gray smoke. Even the ground had disappeared. But they could see the buildings because they were all on fire. Flames shot out from the roof of the Customs House; and Building Seven, sat directly across from the plaza on the other side of Vesey Street, and the Chase Bank Building were both glowing orange from the firelight. Behind them was a wall of rubble that blocked the alleyway. They had just escaped from a smoky cavern only to be trapped on the plaza.

They felt like trapped rats. Every corner they ran to was blocked. Then they saw the enclosed Plexiglas walkway that connected Building Seven to the plaza and decided to see if that could serve as their exit. The idea was if they could get inside the building, they'd make their way down to the street. They walked across the walkway, but when they came to the rotating-glass doors that led into Building Seven, it was locked. Why anyone would lock a door under these circumstances was anybody's guess.

"Break it," somebody said.

Brink and Schwerner were down on their hands and knees scrambling through the one equipment bag they still had to get a halogen tool, but Lanoce had another idea. He took out his 9-mm handgun and, without giving anyone the heads up, fired a shot at the bottom-glass pane of the door.

Schwerner threw his hands over his head and yelled, "Shit! They're fuckin' shootin' at us!"

"No," said Lanoce. "It was me."

"Son of a bitch!"

The gun had gone off near Brink's right ear, and he felt the blast pierce through his eardrum. He recoiled from the pain in his head and yelled, "Steve, you dummy!"

Murphy winced and pressed the heel of his palms to his ears and shouted, "God damn it, couldn't you've warned us?"

What made matters worse was the bullet didn't even break the glass—it was bulletproof! The glass cracked, and triggered the burglar alarm to Building Seven. So, on top of everybody's ears ringing from the gunshot, they had a siren wailing around them that wouldn't shut up.

"Oh, great, Steve!" said Steinman. "I'm outta here."

Right. Out to where? He stomped off as a kid who tells his parents he's running away from home, but only goes around the block because he's not allowed to cross the street! Steinman walked to the end of the walkway and conducted a private search for a way out. The rest of the team decided to finish what Lanoce had started. With their heavy boots, and in unison, they kicked in the broken glass. The instant the glass dropped, leaving an opening wide enough to crawl through, flames whipped out from the building and shot at them. They jumped back as the fire singed their skin. The team quickly retreated and started working on a Plan B. The only way out now seemed to be to rappel forty feet down to the street using the one rope Garcia had saved. They took it out of its bag and began to tie it around the railing, but Steinman interrupted their preparations to rappel with a discovery.

"Hey, guys!" he shouted, "I've found something!"

What he found was the top of an escalator, just coming into view after having been hidden beneath the smoke. The smoke now was lifting as if the result of a magical invocation and the escalator steps appeared. It was not operational. The blast from the collapse had jammed the motor. But, nonetheless, it was intact and led down to Vesey Street and West Broadway.

The First Responders

As the team regrouped and started to position itself at the top of the stairs for self-evacuation, something suddenly caught their eye. An opening in the dust settling on the plaza appeared, and moving through a rocky pathway, was a long procession of people stumbling out of the North Tower. They were bloodied and battered and coming towards them. The cops knew they couldn't leave. All plans for personal escape were instantly abandoned, and they instinctively went back into rescue mode.

In order to mitigate the situation and move the people out quickly and safely, the lieutenant had his men set up a human chain. Schwerner went to the head of it with Hartigan standing next to him. Brink and Garcia were third and fourth, and Steinman and Lanoce rounded out the end of the line. As the people emerged from the plaza, Schwerner grabbed them one by one and passed each person down to Hartigan, who passed them along to the next cop, and so on. Because debris was still falling from the sky, they kept the people against the building line and under the protection of the overhang. Then they had to help them walk a thirty-foot path to the escalators.

The people just kept streaming out of the North Tower as a mass exodus from a sinking ship. The path to the escalators was littered with boulders of cement. The men had to run back and forth, alternately rolling the debris out of the way and going back to the people to show them how to get to the steps. It was starting to get grueling.

"You gotta help us help you," the cops pleaded to the people. "If you can walk, help the person next to you."

There were all types of people on the line. Of course you expected to see civilians—office workers, and such—but there were also City firefighters stumbling out, and tagging right behind them was a motley volunteer fire company from the South Bronx. They were wearing dark blue jackets with yellow lettering that said, "Aviation Volunteer Fire Department." Although, New York City employs a full-time, professional fire department, the "vollies" (a nickname for volunteers) were from Glason Point, on the edge of the East River in the Bronx, and is one of the few communities in the City with a volunteer fire department. The word "aviation" in their name didn't mean they had planes, but because their firehouse sat on a deserted pre-WW2 air field.

The cops couldn't believe they were seeing volunteer firemen. They rolled their eyes and gave them a good tongue-lashing: "What the fuck are you guys doin' here? You're volunteers! You have no Scott-packs, no rescue equipment, no protective gear! You guys aren't gonna help anyone! Get outta here!"

The vollies stood there with their mouths hanging open with a blank stare—stunned that they were yelled at. Then they quickly recovered and followed the firefighters down the steps.

Then a man with caramel-colored skin, black hair, black eyes, and Arabian features came passing down the chain. In front of him was another office worker, a black man in a suit and tie. Suddenly, the black man hurled around and punched the Middle Eastern man in the head and shouted, "It's because of you, motherfucker!"

The Middle Eastern man stumbled from the blow. His attacker came at him again and punched him a second time. He would have hit him a third time but the cops jumped in and blocked him. They screamed, "Get the fuck outta here!"

They didn't need this. Now all the assholes were starting to show up. The cops separated the two men. That gave the Middle Eastern man a second or two to regain his balance and then scurry down the escalator stairs as a spider in a drainpipe.

Murphy stood directly across from his men and continued to maintain radio contact with Winkler. He confirmed his Team was all right, Winkler should cancel the rescue, and his men were extracting civilians from a building. Then the lieutenant switched his radio over to SOD and asked for a medical team to help carry out some of the injured.

"Central, we need EMS up here," said Murphy. He held the hand-mike in the air about eight inches away from his mouth. "We need stoke baskets."

As Murphy was talking into his radio, he saw a shadow falling towards him from the sky. He moved back to get out of its way, but he wasn't fast enough. The shadow was a long, sharp piece of debris. It hit him and sliced off his left index finger. Then it continued down the back of the hand and removed the skin off the bone, as a potato peeler. Hartigan looked up to say something to the lieutenant at the precise moment he was hit. It happened so fast he couldn't tell whether the object was made of glass or metal. The radio went flying. He thought Murphy's hand had been severed. The radio laid in the alleyway, but no hand was on the ground. The lieutenant keeled over, clasping his good hand over his injured hand.

Murphy's finger was hanging on by a thread. He took a handkerchief from his pocket and wrapped it tightly around the hand in an attempt to keep his finger from falling off and to hold the flap of skin on the bone. Then he walked over to Lanoce, at the end of the human chain and near the escalator. Lanoce was the designated medic on the team. Even though all ESU cops are certified EMTs, Lanoce had more experience because he had once been a medical technician on an ambulance prior to becoming a cop. When he looked up from moving the civilians down the line he saw Murphy standing in front of him. The lieutenant was holding his injured hand in the air. His other hand was cupping the elbow to give it support. It was bleeding as Niagara Falls. The handkerchief he used as a bandage did little to slow it down. It was soaked red with blood. Lanoce grabbed the lieutenant and steadied him. He pressed his fingers down on the brachial artery in Murphy's left arm, a major blood vessel inside the arm above the elbow. Then he turned around to Steinman, who was standing behind him on the human chain, and yelled, "I'm takin' the lieutenant to a bus!" A "bus" is cop-talk for an ambulance—and, then he escorted Murphy down the escalator steps.

Coming up the escalator were four Bomb Squad detectives: Claude Richards, Danny McNally, Mike Oldnixon, and Joe Nolan. Nolan had once been an Emergency cop before joining the Bomb Squad and he knew Lanoce. He stopped and went to the other side of Murphy and helped carry him down the steps. The three remaining Bomb Squad cops continued up the escalator to the plaza. Lanoce yelled to them, "My team's up there! They're evacuating civilians! Tell the guys I'm takin' Murphy to the hospital!"

10
9:59 AM: Team Three Inside The North Tower

Before the first Tower fell, Sergeant Curtin and his Team had gotten as far as the 11th floor (it could have been the 9th floor. The surviving members of the Team don't all agree about how high they climbed). They were still passing people on the stairs when, just as they stepped up to the floor's landing, an office worker ran out from the foyer and told them there were some people inside that couldn't get out. The man wasn't clear about the situation, but who had time to hear the details? Somebody was in trouble. That was information enough.

The cops entered the floor and found two women sitting at a desk. They were so petrified they couldn't move. They sat huddled together as two scared rabbits. As soon as the women saw these larger-than-life, strapping cops in their blue helmets, yellow air tanks, and guns, they began to shake and cry. It was as though the presence of rescuers confirmed the danger. There were two coworkers standing with the women. They had been trying to persuade them to leave with them to no avail. But as soon as the cops walked in, the two coworkers couldn't get out of there fast enough. As far as they were concerned, the two women were now the cops' problem.

Curtin, D'Allara, and Beaury stayed with the women and tried to comfort them, and Blihar and DeMarco spilt off and did a sweep of the floor. They went in and out of offices, bathrooms, and closets to make sure no one else was left behind.

When they were satisfied the rest of the floor was empty, the two men walked back to the Team. As DeMarco came around from the back offices, he saw that Blihar had returned a few seconds ahead of him. Curtin was already leading the two women towards the stairs, and Blihar was holding a coffeepot of clear water. He was about to pour some of it into a glass for one of the women, when suddenly there was a rumbling. It got louder and louder. The guys were looking at each other with a *what the fuck is that?* expression on their faces. The coffeepot was shaking in Blihar's hand. The water swished back and forth. Whatever was rolling towards them sounded as though it was aiming straight for their heads. Everybody nose-dived to the floor. Whatever was going to

The First Responders

happen, it was going to happen *now*. With a crash, the rumbling and shaking brought ceiling tiles and walls down on top of them.

The power shut off and the emergency lights kicked in. There was only enough light to outline the hallway and show the way to the staircase. Other than that, there was an eerie harsh glow over their heads and dense shadows at their feet. To make matters worse, the air was filled with a chalky dust that smudged out details; it was as viewing light through wax paper.

Beaury was lying in the dark picking pieces of the ceiling off himself. He was getting pissed, and he was thinking, *I could have left last month and I didn't.* He had completed twenty years on the job and was supposed to have retired this past summer, but his friend, Ronnie Kloepfer, had talked him out of it. Kloepfer had this great idea if Beaury could hold out another eighteen months, they'd retire at the same time. They had all these plans to go into business together—open a restaurant, a bagel shop, a plumbing service, a guy thing. And now, here he was, lying in all this crap.

After the building stopped rocking, they grunted, coughed, and swore—just to confirm they were still alive. There's no better way to get your adrenaline flowing than saying *holy shit* a few times.

Everyone did a quick look around and got to their feet, dusted themselves off, and then clicked on their porta flashlights. It was at that moment a frantic voice started shouting over the radio: *Everybody in Tower One evacuate! Tower Two just came down!*

It was Winkler ordering all the teams out of the building. Little did the men know he was getting bombarded by a dust cloud roaring through the canyons of streets as a tsunami on a rampage. He was still out in the open, crouching down behind the tire of a parked truck. It wasn't much protection, and the smothering dust and debris were hitting him hard. Every time he opened his mouth to speak he inhaled a lung full of dirt, but he kept on transmitting and made sure everyone heard his warning.

Came down? Team Three was sure they were hearing this wrong.

"How much of the Tower came down?"

"The whole fuckin' Tower!" Winkler yelled over the radio.

"What do you mean the whole fuckin' Tower came down?" They all answered at once, looking at each other with incredulous expressions. They were far from any windows, and there was no way they could look out to see what had happened. They thought maybe it was the top of either the North or the South Tower had tipped over and fallen off. But, whatever it was, it sounded as a wave building in a storm, climbing higher and higher until it peaked. A wall of kinetic energy. It crashed so hard they thought the earth would spilt in two.

The First Responders

9:59 AM: Team One Inside The North Tower

They say when the South Tower fell, it went down with such power it registered as a two-magnitude earthquake at an observatory in Palisades, New York, twenty miles away. Considering the Twin Towers stood only twenty-two yards apart in its cramped five-acre plaza, imagine what it must of felt like to the people who were still inside the North Tower!

It took eleven seconds for the South Tower to fall—all 110 stories and 1380 feet of it—moving in an unstoppable free fall. In the North Tower, on the 31st floor—the five ESU cops and one detective—plus the twelve firemen, didn't know what was happening. The tremendous roar and the violent shaking made them think a bomb had exploded over their heads, or another plane had crashed into the building. They thought the roof was about to cave in and crush them. The ESU officers and the firemen gave each other a split second look of horror, then dove for cover. Whoever was standing dropped to the floor. They pinned themselves against the wall, threw their hands over their heads, and curled up as armadillos.

The building swayed back and forth as a forty-one footer on a rough sea. It started off fast, but then gradually the rocking slowed until it stopped. The overhead florescent lights flickered but didn't go out. The walls cracked and sheet rock fell. Then a warm wind swept up the long stairwell and flooded the room.

Somebody shouted, "Flash over!"

Morley jumped to his feet and ran to the steel door. It had been tied open with a hose. He undid it and slammed the door shut. At the same time one of the firemen got on his radio and started yelling, "Mayday! Mayday! Mayday on the thirty-first floor!"

Two seconds later, Weiss, the fireman from Rescue One, came bursting back into the foyer, and he didn't look too happy. "Who the fuck is callin' a mayday?" said Weiss. He looked at his firemen lined up against the wall and saw one of them holding a radio up to his face. He had a sheepish expression, as a kid that just got caught with his fingers in the cookie jar.

"Why're you callin' a mayday?" said Weiss, looking straight at him. "Who's goin' to come get you? We're IT! So, shut up and hold on and we'll all get outta this."

After Weiss chastised the fireman, he felt bad. He changed his tone and tried to calm him down. But he was right. Who was going to rescue the rescuers?

Weiss saw the closed door and the fire hose thrown to the floor. Then he looked over at Morley and said, "You did this? Great job. Where do you work?"

Morley was stunned. He couldn't believe the fireman was actually in the mood for small talk, unless, of course, that was just his way of relaxing everybody.

Weiss was a big man, not in height but in weight and muscles. His hair was close-cropped, almost shaved off completely and, when he moved the hiked-up sleeves to his turnout coat, there were biker tattoos on his forearms. He was as tough as he looked, and he didn't seem concerned about the rattling and shaking. He said, "Don't worry, guys. Relax. My father worked on these buildings. I'm from Staten Island. I used to be an iron worker in the seventies."

That assurance didn't make Morley feel any better. The way the building had rocked from the explosion made him really nervous. He said, "I don't know. That didn't sound too good."

Weiss smiled sympathetically. It was obvious the detective in his white shirt and gray, silk tie wasn't an Emergency cop. Morley didn't have the training that Rescue and ESU had. He didn't know about prying people out of high-rise elevators or the twisted remnants of a car wreck. He didn't know how to handle heavy-duty Hurst tools. ESU and Rescue were the guys that were into swinging from bridges. They often had practiced rappelling and other training exercises right there in the Twin Towers. For them, this was just a practice drill being played out for real.

Hollifield, Amendolare, the three ESU officers, and Weiss stepped out into the staircase and discussed the situation. They were all in this together and they needed a plan.

"The core of the building is the strongest part," said Weiss. And, that was true. The engineers had built the center with massive vertical columns and cross-bracing steel cables that made it strong enough to hold most of the building's weight and absorb the sideways shaking of an earthquake. It contained the elevator shafts, staircases, bathrooms, and utility spaces.

The Twin Towers were built as no other buildings in the world. They were the first skyscrapers to use floor sections that consisted of trusses instead of the typical hung steel. Truss construction allows expansion at a much greater distance, and this often eliminates the need for interior beams, columns, or footing. With hung steel there are columns every few feet. Removing the columns created an open-space atrium and, this was a big selling point for the Trade Center.

Structurally, truss construction is stronger than high beams when it's put together as a team system. It creates a domino effect where each truss relies on another to support its strength. If one of them fails, it pushes a load onto the next. When two or three start failing, the load doubles, then triples, and as dominos, it moves down the line.

In a fire, however, trusses perform poorly. All it takes is a little heat for the bottom chord of a truss to buckle and fail and this will cause the roof or floor to drop. Architects try and get around this by covering them with a fire-protective coating or by doubling up the sheet rock to give it a better burn time; but firemen say that in a hung-steel building or even in an old wood-frame, heavy-duty timber building, when the frame fails, it gives a warning: the wood starts to creak and groan, or the steel bends. That can give the firefighters the heads-up to get out of the building. With truss construction there is no warning. It catastrophically fails without so much as a whimper.

Suddenly, Winkler's voice came shouting over Tac-g. He was ordering his teams to evacuate and, to the men of Team One, he sounded as though he was saying something completely crazy: the South Tower had fallen.

Cliff Allen turned to Amendolare and said, "Sarge, ask Winkler what part of the Tower fell." It seemed as a reasonable question. They weren't near any windows, and they couldn't see what was happening outside.

"There is no fuckin' South Tower! It's gone!" Winkler shouted back. "Your building is in immediate danger of collapse! We're callin' a total evacuation. Get the fuck outta there right now!"

Dave Norman thought this was unfathomable. Before September 11th, if he had heard a radio transmission that said New York City was under attack, he'd have laughed and said, "Quick! Somebody psyche-service that cop and take his guns away!" And if it had been anyone but Winkler yelling the Tower had fallen, he and the others probably wouldn't have budged. But he knew Winkler was a levelheaded guy who never over-reacted. To hear *him* get excited was unnerving.

In any event, police do follow orders. If Winkler said, "Evacuate," then they were going to evacuate.

Norman turned to Weiss and said, "They're callin' us out of the building."

Just as he said that, the fire department's radio started to pick up speed. The volume was turned up and the room was bustling with crackling voices. The radios were screaming, *"Evacuate! Imminent collapse! Imminent collapse!"*

Weiss put his radio an inch away from his ear and listened to the hurried voices stepping over each other. Amendolare then asked Weiss what he was getting on *his* radio and Weiss reported the fire units were also being ordered out of the building.

The first thing they had to do was to get the twelve firemen who were suffering from heat exhaustion up on their feet and ready for the walk down. The ESU cops—Mack, Norman, and Allen—cradled the 0-2 cylinders in front of each fireman, put the oxygen masks on their faces, wrapped electrical tape around the bottles, and taped them to their bodies as a sling.

In order to lighten the load, they started dumping some of their equipment. They got rid of the medical bag, Hurst tools, and everything else they thought would slow them down. The only equipment they kept was the ropes and something they called "rabbit" tools. They had no idea what was happening on the floors below them, and the ropes might come in handy if they encountered broken or missing staircases. Then they could use the ropes to lower themselves down. The "rabbit," a Hurst tool with a hydraulic pump and spreaders, could be used to open jammed doors manually.

By this time, the word to evacuate must have spread, because there were firemen coming down the stairs. Weiss stopped them and told them to go inside the foyer and get the firemen that were being treated for heat exhaustion and chest pains. They went in, lifted the men on their wobbly feet, and carried them out to the landing. Dave Norman handed them all the extra oxygen bottles and said, "Stay on oxygen and go!"

The firemen didn't hesitate. They turned on their heels and, with an injured man under each arm, they started the walk down. Then the cops delayed a second or two to have a last few words with Weiss. .

"Okay. You guys are leavin'?" asked Weiss. He wanted to make sure the 31st floor was clearing out so he didn't have to look for them or any of his own men.

"Yeah. We're leavin'," said Amendolare. Then he asked Weiss the same question, "You guys goin'?"

"Yeah. We're gonna go."

Then Weiss said he had to run back up to his rescue company—one or two flights up—and tell his supervisor, Captain Terence Hatton, about the evacuation, in case he didn't know already. He also said he wouldn't be able to leave immediately because his men were separated. The firemen were spread out over acres of office space and he'd have to go floor to floor in order to round up everybody.

Now that everybody knew what everybody was doing, it was time to get the hell out of there! Amendolare did a quick head count and ordered his men into line formation. The sergeant took the lead followed by Hollifield, Allen, Mack, and Morley. He put Norman in the rear and told him to make sure nobody was left behind. Then the men spilt off. Amendolare and his team started the walk down, and Weiss started the walk up.

When Weiss got to the top of the staircase, he stopped for a second, turned around, and yelled to the men disappearing down the stairs, "I'll be right behind you!"

12
9:59 AM: Down On The Streets

The two teams inside the North Tower couldn't have imagined in their wildest dreams what was happening on the street. The world outside was a disaster area. The dust cloud had chased everyone—the firemen and the police—far away from the site. The entire perimeter of the Trade Center was a ghost town. Only moments before there had been dozens of ESU officers teaming up and preparing to go into the buildings, but they never made it inside.

At 9:56 AM, three minutes before the collapse of the South Tower, Sergeant Sullivan and Sergeant Urban were at the corner of West and Vesey getting ready to take two teams into the buildings. They were geared up and ready to go and, just as they were trying to decide which team was going into what Tower, and just as they were about to take the first step to cross the street, news of the attack on the Pentagon came over the police radio.

"Screw rescue!" said Sullivan, with alarm and anger in his voice. The sergeant pulled his men back and announced all teams would be going in tactical. "I want heavy vests, helmets, rifles, and machine guns."

Everybody started stripping off their rescue gear. They took off the blue safety helmets and replaced them with ballistic helmets. They took off their air tanks and placed them down on the sidewalk. They unbuckled their Roco harnesses and put them back in the bin. And even though they were already wearing bulletproof vests under their uniform shirts, they added more body armor—double-Kevlar ballistic vests—and tightened the Velcro straps across their chests. They unlocked the gun bins and removed the Ithaca 37-pump-action 12-gauge shotguns, the Heckler & Koch MP-5 9mm submachine guns, and the Mini-14 5.56mm assault rifles.

Some of the guys were grumbling under their breath. They were pissed at Sullivan for holding them back. ESU cops were used to showing up at a scene and getting straight to work. They didn't like wasting time fiddling around with equipment. They were pumped and ready to go and this sudden switch interrupted their adrenaline momentum.

Then, right in the middle of switching from rescue to tactical, the

South Tower collapsed. They heard the tremendous roar and saw the huge cloud of dust leaping into the air and rolling towards them. They dropped everything—the eighty-pounds of Hurst tools, bags of rope, the heavy vests—all except the guns, that stayed glued to their hands. A cop never lets go of his gun, no matter what. This was more than just plain, old common sense—dropping your firearms was sacrilegious! If you're a cop it's always in the back of your mind that not only could someone pick up the gun and use it on you, but you could loose thirty vacation days!

Inspector Wasson, DeMasi, Garvey, Linarello, Sergeants Sullivan, and Urban, and four other cops, dived under one of their trucks. They were packed in as sardines with the rifle butts and machine gun barrels poking them in the ribs. One of the guys, Nessenthaler, chose to run rather than dive. When the dust cloud hit him, he was hanging off of a chain link fence some two blocks away.

DeMasi wanted to turn off the ignition. He figured if they were going to go under the truck they didn't need their faces burnt off by hot exhaust fumes. He charged towards the driver's door and shoved aside Sergeant Urban.

"Get outta my way!" shouted DeMasi. "We gotta turn off the truck!"

Urban couldn't believe DeMasi had just pushed him. The whole time Urban was crawling under the truck and holding his breath with debris rushing around him and the hot wind up his nose and down his ears and in his mouth, he couldn't stop thinking about DeMasi pushing him.

Anybody who was unlucky enough to get caught in the dust cloud without their Scott masks was feeling a lot of pain, but the tanks were sitting on the sidewalk and beyond arm's reach. The smothering sensation was unbearable. If they tried to breathe there was no air. Mouth and nostrils filled up with soot and debris. It clogged the ears and the only thing they could hear was their own thoughts inside their heads. Everyone started coughing, and it felt as though their lungs were going to explode.

"If you have a helmet put it over your face!" yelled Wasson. He had his helmet in front of his face, and it made his voice sound deep and hollow, as talking through a cardboard tube.

DeMasi heard the inspector and he unstrapped his ballistic helmet and rolled it down in front of his face. It provided some relief. But there was something clogging his throat that felt as a nasty ball of phlegm. DeMasi let out a big cough into his helmet and brought up all the mucus packed deep in his throat. He felt better; but he was afraid to take another breath.

When the roar stopped and things seemed calm—or as calm as it could be under the circumstance—everybody started to climb out from under the truck. It felt as though they had just survived a nuclear blast. They looked around, and the whole world was covered in a powdery gray snow. So this was what a nuclear winter looks like! Everybody was feeling numb and hyper at the same time, and nobody was talking much.

Curtis Garvey was having a problem. He managed to crawl out from under the truck, but he couldn't get to his feet. He tried to stand, but he lost his balance and fell back against the truck. It was a hot and humid morning, and the combination of his heavy gear and the excitement of the collapse had begun to overcome him. His head was swimming, and he could feel himself blacking out. He bent over and tried to keep the blood circulating in his brain.

DeMasi saw that Garvey was in distress and he grabbed him. The other officers ran over and helped lower him to the sidewalk. They ripped off his heavy vest, his uniform shirt, and stripped him down to his undershirt. They grabbed containers of bottled water from the truck and poured it over Garvey's head and down his back. It took a long time to cool him off. By the time they were finished, they must have gone through twenty bottles of water. His clothes were soaking wet and he was sitting in a pool of gray mud. The water turned the dust on his dark brown skin into long, gray lines that ran from the top of his head and down his face and neck. Garvey was starting to come around. He was groggy and his eyes flickered open.

Stefanakos and Winwood had been going nuts listening to the radio.

They felt trapped and helpless inside the trailer while their friends were in the Towers. They could only imagine what was happening to them, and it wasn't good. During the collapse and the dust cloud all transmissions had stopped. The radio seemed to be in suspension mode. There was just the dead quiet of radio static.

The silence was frightening, and when something as frightening as this happens, most people start to think of their loved ones. Winwood immediately grabbed a phone inside the trailer. It was still working, and he called his wife, Jeanine. This was the third call he had made to her this morning. The first call was back in quarters right after Hollifield's emergency transmission came over the radio. Winwood told his wife, "A plane just hit the Trade Center. Call your sister (who worked at the Trade Center) and tell her I don't know what's going on, but something's wrong. Get outta work!" Fortunately, his sister-in-law was late for work and was down on the street with the spectators. Then he called Jeanine a second time when he got to the command post. He borrowed somebody's cellphone and told her he'd be flying to the roof of the South Tower. He knew she was probably watching the events on TV and wondering where he was in all of this. And now that the Tower was no longer there, he thought he had better call her one more time and let her know he was okay.

Winwood and Stefanakos had been partners since 1993. They were originally Housing cops who worked vertical patrols in Queens housing projects. They hooked up when they both joined the Housing Police Department's Emergency Rescue Service (ERS). In 1994, Housing PD merged with the NYPD, and everybody in ERS was brought into ESU. Stefanakos and Winwood were assigned to Three-Truck in the Bronx and then later, in 1998, transferred to Ten-Truck in Queens.

Their long partnership made them friends, best men at each other's weddings, and godfathers to each other's first born. They were truly as brothers and they looked after each other's family. When the shit hit the fan this morning, they promised to keep an eye on each other.

The dust cloud ran its course and began to settle, and the radio came back to life. Once again, urgent calls were coming over Tac-g. One of them was from Lieutenant Murphy. He said his team was trapped on the plaza.

Without thinking twice, Stefanakos and Winwood put on their Scott masks and jumped out of the trailer. They ran south on West Street towards the Trade Center. It was only a two-block run. As they ran, they were putting together in their mind a plan of rescue, but that was until they saw what had actually happened to the South Tower. It was an unrecognizable massive heap of twisted steel and rubble. Stefanakos and Winwood were mortified. The locations the guys were screaming out over the radio wouldn't put them where rescue looked feasible—at least, not for two men alone. They stood with their mouths hanging opened, and tried to piece the Trade Center back together in their minds, just to figure out what they were looking at.

What are these guys talking about? Stefanakos was thinking. *They're giving out locations that aren't there anymore!*

While Stefanakos was thinking this, he and Winwood were catching up with two or three other ESU cops who were emerging from the dust cloud. They were in one piece, understandably shaken up, but ready to turn right around and dig out their friends.

"Have you seen anybody?" asked Stefanakos.

"No."

"Where was our last command post?" asked somebody.

The command post was at Church and Vesey, and since the South Tower was now lying all over it, they knew nobody would be there. They tried to think of the next strategically logical place the command post would be moved to and they came up with West and Vesey. They ran to the intersection but there was no one there. The streets were abandoned except for the firemen scrambling under the North Bridge, just off the corner of West and Vesey.

They stood at the corner for a long time. They thought if they waited long enough, the bosses from their unit would show up and put a game plan together, or else they'd see their friends coming out of the Towers, that everybody would be alive and retreating to the command post, but none of this was happening, and Stefanakos and the others were worried. Finally, they heard some good news. On the radio, Lieutenant Murphy was shouting, "We see daylight! We're workin' towards the light! We're goin' to make it out!"

The First Responders

Then there was nothing from that team for a few minutes. Whatever was happening in those moments caused a lot of anticipation, for everybody who was listening. At last they heard the voice of one of the men on Murphy's team, saying the lieutenant was injured and they were carrying him off the plaza.

At 10:12 AM, somebody in authority was giving orders over SOD: "We want people on West Street! Get additional manpower on West Street! Have them muster on Vesey and West!" The only problem was the North Tower was looming over that corner as Colossus in a thunderstorm.

Hargrove was still at the ball field. His two men, Appice and Berarducci, were assisting civilians staggering up West Street. The dust had blinded the people and the two cops were flushing their eyes with water. But Hargrove was concerned about the order to pull equipment and personnel back to West and Vesey. He didn't have a good feeling about it. He transmitted back: "Don't put anyone on Vesey and West. If we had a collapse of the first Tower then we're going to have a collapse of the second."

Some big boss that didn't like being challenged rescinded the sergeant's warning and repeated his order to mobilize police personnel to West and Vesey. Hargrove was frustrated. There was no way in hell he was going to send his men to that corner. He'd find out later the men did hear his transmission and stayed off that corner, but there were some that criticized him and said, "You were a coward to not go down to West and Vesey after the Towers collapsed." The sergeant defended himself and said, "No, I don't think so, because, we were alive to do the work that had to be done after the second collapse. What would we have gained losing fifty, sixty, a hundred more people?"

Hargrove fought back his feelings of futility. He felt if his radio transmission was going to get squashed, then if he had to, he'd pass his warning from man to man. He saw a fire chief running down the street. Hargrove reached out and stopped him.

"Chief, I don't know what's coming over your radio," said Hargrove. "But, don't commit your men to West and Vesey."

The fire chief nodded. His expression was anxious, as though it was a nuisance to stop and talk. He didn't look at the sergeant, he looked pass him and down towards the bottom of the street where the firemen were assembled under the North Bridge.

"I saw the collapse of the first Tower," said Hargrove. He wanted to emphasize his own personal concern. "And I'm telling you there's going to be another collapse."

"Okay," said the fire chief. Then he took off as though someone had suddenly released him from a trap. His turnout coat flew open, and the thudding steps of his rubber boots echoed behind him as he ran down to West and Vesey.

Hargrove could only hope the fire chief was thinking the same thing he was thinking and that he was running back to get his men off the corner.

Inspector Wasson looked north down West Street and couldn't believe his own eyes. He saw, coming up the block, a small platoon of patrol officers marching towards the North Tower. There were about ten of them, and they were being led by a plain-clothes police inspector. The inspector wore a blue nylon jacket with the initials "NYPD" in white letters on the back. His shield dangled from his shirt pocket and showed his rank, but there was nothing to indicate what command he came from. He had been on the West Side Highway when the South Tower collapsed.

The West Side Highway is an elevated structure that runs eight miles along the shoreline of the Hudson River, and ends at the Brooklyn Battery Tunnel. At the West Street exit it was bumper to bumper with emergency vehicles. There were ambulances, fire trucks, police vans, and police cars, all trying to squeeze down the exit ramp at the same time.

When the South Tower fell and the dust cloud rolled out, it rolled over the highway and down to the river. Everybody immediately bailed out of their vehicles and ran. Somebody was hollering, "Stay away from the cars! Go towards the water!" as if they were afraid the cars would flip in the air and burst into flames.

One of the police vans stuck on the West Side Highway was from

The First Responders

the 1-15 Precinct, in Queens. Inside were: police officers, Jimmy Berg, Patrick Donnelly, Jim Kadowski, Kevin Williams, MacKenzie, Ann Morrison, Lisa Cordero, and Sergeant Evelyn Varella. When they saw the dust cloud coming in their direction they flung open the sliding doors of the van and jumped out and ran. A helmet rolled from the seat and dropped to the pavement. Williams ran back and picked it up. It wasn't his helmet; it was someone else's. It was an automatic reflex to pick it up. Then he looked over and saw MacKenzie standing by the van watching the collapsing skyscraper turn into a giant stack of smoke. It was the most fascinating thing he had ever seen in his entire life and he couldn't take his eyes off of it. Williams grabbed him by the arm and started to pull him. "Come on!" he shouted. Finally, MacKenzie snapped out of his trance and ran.

As Cordero leaped out of the van her uniform pants ripped open at the seams. She had a gapping hole from her knee and up her thigh. Donnelly kicked open the rear van doors and took off as a bat out of hell. He dropped his cellphone. Cordero stopped and picked it up. Then she kick-started her run and blended in with the fleeing crowd. They were all running down the highway with their arms outstretched in front of them, and their heads looking back over their shoulders at this huge monster cloud. It looked as Godzilla chasing them down the street. Cordero wasn't scared. She felt exhilarated, as an electrical charge pumping through her veins. Williams and Donnelly were running together. They ran down a bicycle path along the West Side Highway and then down to the street. They stopped running on Chambers Street to catch their breath. Williams wanted to go back to find his sergeant and the other cops from his command, but Donnelly refused. He wanted to stay as far away as he could from the Towers. Thirty minutes later, when the second Tower fell, he jumped in the back of a fleeing ambulance, and Williams was left standing by himself. He was still holding somebody else's helmet.

Back on the highway, everybody stopped running. Then the dust settled, and the Citywide-radio began popping with one "10-13" after another (a "10-13" is a NYPD radio code for "a cop in trouble"). A female officer was calling for help, saying she was trapped, but her transmission was so garbled nobody could understand where she was or what had happened to her. She was frightened, and that made everybody listening to her frightened too.

Radio dispatcher Modesto Muniz transmitted, "Try to talk into your radio. What was your last location? What was your last location? Talk to us."

"I think she said the second floor of the South Tower," said a cop over the radio. Then, in his next breath, he tried to raise her on the air. "Where are you?"

She replied, weakly, "Help me."

The inspector in the blue nylon jacket (whom we last saw with his battalion back on West Street) could no longer stand by and do nothing. He ran up and down the highway and grabbed every cop he could find. He grabbed some Task Force cops and he grabbed six more cops from the 1-15 Precinct: Sergeant Varella, and what was left of her crew: Cordero, Morrison, Berg, MacKenzie, and Kadowski, and, gathering them into a group, said, "We gotta go in and help these people." Everybody was in agreement, and every second of listening to those calls for help was making them crazy.

The inspector lined everyone up and marched them across the West Side Highway and down the exit ramp to West Street, and when they hit the street, they broke into a run. They raced towards the North Tower, their adrenaline pumping, their minds focused on rescue, and their hearts blind to fear.

As they got closer to the Trade Center, they looked up at the incinerating North Tower and something suddenly clicked in their heads: *This don't look too good. This don't feel too good. My God, this is how the first building looked before it came down.*

Their run slowed down to a walk. This was *definitely* a bad idea. But they didn't want to look as cowards, and they didn't want to disobey the inspector, so they kept on walking and they kept on looking up and, when they reached the corner of West and Vesey, one of the police officers, Morrison, stopped dead in her tracks.

"We can't go in!" said Morrison, nervously. "We shouldn't go in!"

Everyone stopped and looked at her. She was panicking. The Task

The First Responders

Force cops kept walking, but her fellow co-workers from her command, Cordero, Berg, MacKenzie, Kadowski, and Varella, stayed with her. And right behind them was the inspector in the blue nylon jacket, and he was shouting at them to keep moving, "Get in there! Get in there!" Nobody wanted to move. Suddenly, a large ball of smoke rolled towards them and out stepped Wasson waving his hands and shouting, "Go back! Go back! That building is going down!"

At that very moment, the North Tower began to tilt, recover, and tilt again, and in an eleven-second clash of thunder, it disappeared from the skyline in a free fall of dust, steel, and human beings.

13
Team Three: In The North Tower "We Can't Get Out!"

At 10:02 AM, three minutes after the collapse of the South Tower and twenty-seven minutes before the collapse of the North, in Staircase B of the North Tower there were no more civilians walking down the stairs. The only people evacuating were firemen, a few Port Authority police officers, the five ESU officers, and one narcotic detective from Team One. In Staircase C, Sergeant Curtin and his men of Team Three had their hands full. They were trying to remove the two women who had been sitting in an office immobile from fright, getting more scared-to-death as the minutes ticked by. There was no time for sympathetic coaxing now. Curtin and his team forced the women to the staircase. When they stepped out to the landing, they saw a large crowd of people coming down the stairs.

The staircase was dark and the emergency lights in the stairwell did a poor job of guiding the way. The five men moved quickly down the stairs, spreading themselves over the length of the human line. Their flashlights led the way—five circles of light jumping around in the dark. Suddenly the flashlights fell on the faces of people bunched up at the bottom of the stairwell. Everything had come to a halt. There was some murmuring coming up from the front of the line, as a kind of a discussion. When the people at the back of the line realized the people at the front of the line were no longer moving, they turned around and walked back up the stairs.

What the hell's happening? If the officers didn't *say* that then, the expressions on their faces did. They stood dumbstruck as they watched two hundred civilians now passing them in the opposite direction.

"What's wrong?" asked one of the officers.

"We can't get out!" the people on the stairs anxiously called up. "There's no where to go!"

They weren't specific about the conditions. The collapse of the South Tower could have done several things: the debris could have blocked all the exits around the north and east side of the building, or the staircases could have broken loose from the impact, or a door might simply have jammed. Which was it?

The First Responders

Okay, somebody think fast! We have an x-number of minutes to get out of here and an x-number of civilians waiting for us to come up with a plan.

Curtin moved closer to the front of the line somewhere near the first floor while the officers spread themselves up the staircases covering several flights. Blihar was at the top of the stairwell as far back as the 9th floor taking up the rear. DeMarco was one flight in front of him. Beaury was a flight or two ahead of DeMarco, and D'Allara was another two flights ahead of him. The three men in the rear couldn't see what Curtin was doing, but they heard someone yell up from the bottom, "I found a way out!"

Then there was an order, "Okay, everybody to the third floor!"

Whoever was shouting at the bottom of the stairwell was getting the stagnant crowd moving again. Now, on those orders there was another about-face. The idea was to go back to the maintenance level on the 3rd floor and hook up with one of the other staircases. Since Staircase C was blocked, they had two other main staircases to choose from.

Everyone merged forward and followed the four officers to the 3rd floor. D'Allara stayed with the people in Staircase C as DeMarco, Beaury and Curtin went out on the 3rd floor and scouted for another exit. They found a staircase that led down to the same door Team Three had originally used to enter the building (the staircase was probably A, because it ended on the mezzanine level. Only Staircase B went directly down to the lobby situated at street level). Curtin took a position on the stairs around the 2nd floor, and Beaury stood at the bottom of the stairwell as DeMarco waited in the mezzanine to direct the civilians out of the building. This made a chain for the people to follow.

The bottom stairs and the mezzanine were a wall of smoke. In order to see where they were going, the police officers swung their porta-lights back and forth as ushers in a darkened theater. The people ran from man to man. DeMarco yelled and told them to keep their hands on the wall and to feel their way down the corridor that curved around as a crescent-moon.

"Don't panic," he said, as the constant flow of people passed him and then disappeared inside the smoke. He told them there was a fireman at the end of the corridor who would point the way out.

But the people still had a long way to go. They couldn't just run out through the glass-plate doors bidding their freedom just a 100 feet away. The exit would take them to the plaza and to the air outside that was alive with crashing debris and bodies. Instead, they'd have to take the escalator down to the concourse level and then walk under the Trade Center through the corridors of the shopping mall to find the exit to Church Street.

"And when you get outside—just run!" shouted DeMarco. The mezzanine was filled with dust as thick as green pea soup and they could barely see the outline of the fireman at the far end of the corridor directing his flashlight towards the escalator stairs.

During the turn around on the stairs, Blihar somehow had gotten cut off from the team. He was taking a small group of civilians from the rear end of the line back up the stairs and across the 9th floor.

Nobody noticed he was gone. It wasn't until he zigzagged and found another staircase and was making his way down that Blihar realized nobody was following him. The way they had positioned themselves on the stairs had kept everyone out of eyeshot of everyone else. He couldn't see Curtin. He didn't hear the order to go to the 3rd floor. All he saw were people walking back up the stairs, and he just automatically assumed they were all going to the 9th floor to find an exit there.

Instead of turning around and going back, he switched on his radio and tried to raise Curtin. When the sergeant acknowledged, he explained to him what had happened. Curtin instructed him to continue what he was doing, and he and the rest of the team had found a way out on the 3rd floor. This made Blihar feel better. Everything was going to be okay. The rest of the team would get out and he'd hook up with them in the lobby.

The First Responders

Team One: Strange Encounter In The North Tower

Team One felt no urgency. They weren't rushing and they didn't feel any panic. They walked down the stairs at a steady pace and kept in radio contact with Team Three. They knew Sergeant Curtin was in the building and they wanted to confirm he was leaving. "I'm on the 9th," said Curtin. Team One answered back, "We're just passing 27th." Back and forth over the radio they shouted out their floor numbers as the two teams descended the staircase.

On every flight down, Team One saw dozens of firemen resting on the floors. Some were standing in the stairwells and some were sitting in the foyers, backs against the wall, legs extended, completely exhausted, taking a "blow" from their air tanks. Since the firemen didn't look as though they were going anywhere soon, the cops, Amendolare, Hollifield, Mack, Norman, Allen, and Morley, asked them if they knew about the "imminent collapse" and the order to evacuate. All the firemen said they knew about the evacuation. They didn't act surprised by the news or give the cops a shocked look, they just gave a conceding nod and a quick, "Yes, we know." At one point on the stairs, Amendolare ran into a fire lieutenant whom he knew. He asked him if he was evacuating. The fireman said he'd be leaving as soon as he gathered all of his men.

Morley didn't have a radio, but he could hear the transmissions coming over the firemen's radios as he passed them on the stairs. He heard bits and pieces from a fire chief talking about "a suspicious man on such-and-such floor that wasn't listening to FD's orders," and this man was "talking gibberish on his cellphone." Morley couldn't catch everything being said, but the fireman sounded scared.

It didn't take long to find out what the firemen were worried about. Just as they were approaching the 21st floor, they saw something peculiar. They were making a turn on the landing when they noticed a dark-haired man in a dark suit sticking his head out from around a door. Everybody stopped to see what this man was doing. The cops stood very quiet. All they could see was the back of his head. He was watching a group of firemen go down the stairs, and when he saw them turn at the bottom of the stairwell and he knew they were gone, he slowly skulked out into the stairwell. It looked very suspicious. This was a building that was being evacuated, it had been checked and cleared of civilians, and now, here was someone sneaking back in. Immediately, they followed the man on the stairs, and Morley called out to him, "Hey! What're you doin'?"

The man stopped and turned around, and now they could see that he was carrying a leather valise. He held it in front of him with both hands and let it dangle against his knees. He was well-dressed in a suit and tie, about forty years old, with an olive complexion and dark eyes. If they had to pick a nationality, they would say he looked Middle Eastern.

"Do you work here?" questioned Morley.

Morley knew a felony shuffle when he saw one. His experience as a narcotics cop made him an expert on everything the streets could dish out. And this man was acting just as the street punks who pull an arrogant attitude and give a defiant look when they want to stand up to a cop that stops them and asks about the dope they're selling. But this was a man in a business suit; he wasn't some kid on a street corner, caught between a buy and a bust. As far as they knew, there was no obvious reason for him to be unhappy to see the cops.

The man just stood there. His back stiffened and his chin jutted out. His face was emotionless and stern. He refused to answer the question.

"Who are you?" asked Morley.

But the man wouldn't say a word. You'd think a civilian would say something, anything, even if it were just to tell them he was going back to his office to get his coat.

Suddenly, the man snapped open his valise and pulled out a white and fluffy object about twelve inches long and shoved it in the cop's face. For a spilt second nobody knew what it was. Norman knocked it out of his hand. When it fell to the floor they saw it was a stuffed toy bunny rabbit!

That had to have been the most sinister looking bunny rabbit since Monty Python went looking for the Holy Grail. If they weren't all in

The First Responders

such a serious mood the whole scene would have been comical.

In the interim, a few firemen came down the stairs and stood behind the cops. They saw the man with the valise and the diabolical bunny rabbit on the stairs. They got a little excited. "What is he? What'd we got? A terrorist?"

Norman darted a glance back at the fireman as a signal to be quiet. They didn't know what they had; maybe he was just a nut. Lets not give this guy any ideas, okay?

"You want to know who I am?" said the man, balefully. "Let me show you."

He reached for a cellphone hooked to his belt. Was he actually going to make a phone call? His fingers were an inch from the touch pad, when Morley shouted, "You're not pressin' any buttons!"

Simultaneously, Morley, Allen, and Norman reached out and grabbed the cellphone and tossed it onto the floor. Whoa, that was a close call! Everybody was thinking, it could have been a detonator device.

By this time, traffic was snarled on the staircase. All the firemen and Port Authority cops that had been walking down stopped to watch the commotion on the stairs. There were two civilians that came from the 65th floor and they were standing at the back of the line. Someone yelled up and asked them if they knew who this man was. They squeezed through the crowd, poked out their heads, gave the guy a good look, and said, "He's not from that floor," indicating the 21st.

That was all the information Hollifield needed to know that this man didn't belong in the building. "Get this guy outta here," said Hollifield, fumed. "We'll find out what he is, and who he is, later."

A Port Authority sergeant standing with the crowd on the stairs began to collect the man's belongings. After all, he thought, it could be evidence. He gathered up the man's valise and then he picked the cellphone off the floor and dropped it inside the valise. Next, he reached out to grab the toy rabbit but Morley quickly put his hand up and stopped him. "Don't touch that fuckin' thing," he said. "Leave it."

The sergeant backed off, and the bunny rabbit was left where it had fallen, sitting lopsided on the stairs. Now, the line started moving again. As each fireman passed the bunny rabbit, he cautiously stepped over it as though it was a sleeping rattlesnake with one eye opened.

Hollifield had the man walk ahead of the team as they escorted him down the stairs. About two flights down, the man stopped dead in his tracks. He swung around and began to curse in perfect English, flailing his arms and punching and kicking the cops.

"Fuck you!" he said. "Get your fucking hands off me!"

In his rage, he tried to break through the barrier of cops to run back upstairs. He was a slight man and quite outnumbered. They grabbed him and pulled him back without much effort.

A newly arrived group of firemen walked onto the scene just in time for the tail end of the scuffle. One called out, "Hey, what'cha think ya doin'?" in a tone of voice that implied he thought the cops were unduly picking on this man. That really stuck in Norman's craw. He shot a dirty look back at them as if to say, "Gimme a break."

At this point, Hollifield ordered Morley to arrest the man. The man's refusal to leave a dangerous condition was about all the aggravation they were going to take. With every passing second, the man with the valise was raising the police's level of suspicion up a notch. The idea that he wanted to go up the building while everybody else wanted to go down didn't make sense. If nothing else, handcuffing him and forcing him down the stairs was for his own good. Plus, his disruptive behavior was blocking the staircase and slowing down the evacuation.

Morley's handcuffs were in his suit jacket, now obliterated somewhere back on the plaza, so he borrowed a pair from Roger Mack and handcuffed the man behind his back. Once the cuffs went on, the man shut up.

Morley searched the crowd packed on the staircase for the two civilians from the 65th floor. When he saw them again, Morley gestured and said, "Okay, you have to come with us." He wanted to get statements from them for the arrest report, and he figured he could do that when they got outside.

With the man safely tucked away, everyone was able to continue the walk down in peace. Every once in awhile the mystery man (lets call him, Mr. X) would make some wild statement, "I was a soldier in my country." *That's nice; what country was that?* "The Ukraine." *That's funny, you don't look Ukrainian.*

The First Responders

Morley was falling behind the team. Mr. X was dragging his feet, and Morley was taking his time bombarding him with questions, trying to get him to utter more spontaneous statements. Plus there was a constant stream of people coming down the stairs, who wanted to move faster than Morley was walking. Hollifield looked back to take a quick head count of his men and saw Morley lagging behind. He shouted, anxiously, "Timmy, hurry up!"

Morley was about to answer when he noticed Fire Chief Pete Ganci walking up the stairs. He was the main man, the Chief of the Department. As he passed the team Hollifield said to him, "Chief, you gotta leave. Everybody's leaving."

Ganci gave Hollifield a you-got-to-be-kidding look and kept on climbing.

Again, the lieutenant said, "Come on. Come with us."

The Chief stopped just long enough to turn around and said, "I'm not leaving. I'm going to get my men." Then he resumed his walk up the stairs.

Morley was impressed. He thought, *wow, this is a leader. He doesn't leave his men.* He watched the fire chief walk by, decked out in his turnout coat and his white helmet. He looked as an old time war hero returning to the front line.

When they finally reached the plaza level, they could see the devastation through the mezzanine windows. Everybody was startled. They stopped and stared at the mountain of debris and at the opaque fog of dust that hid everything but the fires burning in the background. As they were taking all of this in, Mr.X snickered and said, "Look at the fire. Nice, nice fire."

Everybody within earshot of that comment gave out a growl of disgust. What kind of a person would find this so funny?

Hollifield wanted to step things up. The rubbernecking on the stairs was wasting time and this made him nervous. He yelled at everyone to look straight ahead and keep walking.

Looking back over the past twenty minutes or so, it seemed to Hollifield they had all been walking down the Tower as if they had all the time in the world. Hollifield wished he had known it was that bad before; he'd have had himself and his men walk a hell of lot faster.

As they continued passed the mezzanine, they found themselves standing at the very spot from where they had started. They were back at the Fire Department's command post under the North Tower. It was now abandoned. Fire Chief Pfeifer and his men had long since run for cover. All that was left was two inches of gray soot all over the floor that must have blown in through the broken windows. They could see the street outside. It looked as a freak snowstorm had just passed through New York City. It was a weird sight to see gray "snow" on a muggy, eighty-four-degree day.

While they were standing in the abandoned command post, they overheard Curtin on Tac-g asking Winkler for assistance. He said he had a fireman on the 6th floor trapped in a hole and he was going to need help getting him out. Winkler raised Team One to direct them over to Curtin. But Cliff Allen and Dave Norman were already on top of it and immediately they radioed back, "Mike, its Cliff and Dave, do you want us to respond with the Roco gear?"

Allen had a rotten feeling they were running out of time. After seeing the plaza, the seriousness had finally registered in his head. They really weren't sure exactly where Curtin was. They'd have to walk back, then up and forward again, just to get within the general vicinity of where Curtin and his team might be on the 6th floor. Looking for him would waste time, so Allen asked Amendolare to ask Curtin for his exact location, but as soon as Amendolare radioed, "Hey, Mike, where are you?" Curtin came back on the radio and told Team One to disregard.

"No, no. Forget it. We got him out," said Curtin. Then he went on to say he and his guys were getting out of the building. He was right above them on the mezzanine and racing for the doors. He added, "Get yourselves out of the building."

To this very day nobody knows what Curtin meant when he said he had a fireman down in a hole. Curtin had been killed in the second collapse and the surviving members on his team had been out of visual contact with him a couple of times as the excitement of the evacuation began to escalate. If he had gotten involved in something for a few minutes, they hadn't seen it.

The First Responders

There was a possibility it might have had something to do with some trapped firemen and police officers on the 5th floor. The story was Lieutenant Daniel O'Keefe from the 6th Precinct and a few Intel (Intelligence Unit) cops and five firemen couldn't get off the floor because the door was jammed. Then one of the firemen went up the stairs to look for help and ran across "rescuer workers" that were able to get the door opened. The details are sketchy, because O'Keefe never saw who these "rescue workers" were. He was so grateful to escape with his life that he never looked back to see who had helped them.

Team One gathered around to discuss their next move. Believe it or not, they felt they were safe underneath the North Tower and weren't eager to go into the war zone outside. The debris was still falling and visibility was down to zero, but Hollifield and Morley wanted to get Mr. X out of there and into the hands of federal agents or to anyone who could find out who or what he was. Morley collected his two civilian witnesses and the Port Authority sergeant carrying the valise and the cellphone and turned to the ESU team and said, "I'm gonna take this guy and hand him over to the first FBI agent I see." With that, Morley, Hollifield, and their small entourage walked out through the tall, broken windows and headed towards West Street.

When Morley walked outside, he made a wrong turn, and a man standing on the walkway—somebody who probably worked for the Trade Center—raised his hands and told him to go the other way. Morley stopped briefly to let some water rippling off a ledge drip down the back of his neck. The water felt good. Then he heeded the man's warning and went the other way.

Morley and Hollifield led their posse north on West Street, and when they reached the corner of Vesey, they found Police Chief Allen Hale. He was from Manhattan North—a tall, distinguished looking man in his sixties, who had been around in the police department for three decades. Hollifield spoke with the Chief and told him about Mr. X and his strange behavior on the stairs. There were some Intel officers standing with Hale, and they took out pen and paper and spoke to Morley and the Port Authority sergeant and the two witnesses, and wrote things down.

Morley saw Port Authority Police Captain Kathy Mazza standing on the same corner. He noticed her because she was a bit of a celebrity. She was the first woman in that department to rise to the rank of captain. Morley had seen her on the stairs coming down the Tower and he was thinking *what a small world it is*. Just a few days ago he had spoken to his mother-in-law's neighbor, a retired nurse, and Mazza's name came up. The neighbor had once been a teacher at a nursing college, and she had taught Mazza nursing.

Suddenly, there was an explosion a third of the way up the North Tower. It looked as though a section of the outside wall blew away. There were giant chunks of debris about the size of a Lincoln Towncar flying through the air and aiming towards the very spot where everybody was standing. Morley heard Hollifield shout, "Move!" and everyone ran for cover. Morley grabbed his prisoner by one arm, and the PA sergeant grabbed the other arm, and they tried to run, but Mr. X dug his heels in the ground and pulled a tug o' war. They had no time for games. The two cops gave him one good yank and sent him into an aerodynamic spin. Now he was up on his tiptoes, sandwiched between two cops, running, whether he wanted to, or not.

Morley led the run, pulling the prisoner and the sergeant towards a row of fire trucks. He thought they'd make a good buffer against the falling debris. Then he looked back to see where Hollifield went; he wanted to make a mental note on which way he ran so when this was over he'd know the general vicinity to look for him. Instead, he saw Captain Mazza running back inside the North Tower. He didn't think anything of it at first. In housing projects with tall buildings and delinquent kids throwing objects off the roof at cops and firemen, it wasn't unusual to run back inside a building to avoid getting hit. Mazza quickly disappeared, her back, her white shirt, her dark hair moving further, in the wrong direction, away.

Two seconds after the explosion, the Tower began to crumble and the huge cloud of soot and ash immediately started rolling out. Morley was still running, going north towards West Broadway. Then the Port Authority sergeant let go of the prisoner's arm, leaving him to Morley by himself. Morley watched the sergeant fall back and then run down a different street. There were things flying in the air, swept off the ground and spinning above their heads, and Morley saw something fall and hit the sergeant. He doubled-over from the blow and collapsed to the sidewalk. Morley thought he was unconscious and was going to run back to him, but the sergeant suddenly came back to life, rolled off the curb, and then under a truck.

Morley could sense the wind. It felt as though he was at the ocean and running in the water away from a big wave. It was on his back and it was coming and it was crashing and he was trying to run faster, but Mr. X didn't want to move and he was yelling at him to hurry. Morley wasn't thinking about living: he was thinking, *I better hang onto that prisoner or I'll loose ten days.* He couldn't believe he was thinking this. All those years of working in Brooklyn had him brainwashed. Departmental procedures, Patrol Guide 210.00, section three: *failure to safeguard a prisoner will result in immediate disciplinary action.*

He dragged his prisoner up Murray Street where he saw a line of fire trucks and he watched people dropping to the ground and rolling under them. Morley ran to one of the trucks and stuffed Mr. X underneath, and then he dropped down and squeezed next to him. There was a man lying under the truck somewhere behind Morley and he heard him yell, "We're goin' to have rockets of debris and a sea of ash! Be prepared to hold your breath 'cause here it fuckin' comes!"

The dust cloud rolled out as a hot, desert sandstorm. Morley could hear it hit the short, skinny trees planted in the rows of square-shaped dirt in the middle of the block. He heard it pounding the truck and made it rock and bounce. He was afraid the truck was going to fall and crush everyone, so he pressed his back against the undercarriage and tried to hold it up! He heard the windshield smash. A tire popped on a fire rig parked next to him. Then the light closed down, one click at a time, as the aperture of a camera lens, and then it was all dark.

Morley didn't pray, he was too angry. He squeezed his eyes shut and thought to himself, "Fuck you. I'm not gonna go like this."

15
10:29 AM: Team Five On The Plaza

In the last fifteen minutes before the North Tower fell, Winkler was juggling radio contact between Sergeant Amendolare, Sergeant Curtin, and Lieutenant Murphy. He was right in the middle of directing Team One out of the building when Curtin made his call for assistance. Now he directed Team One back inside to help Team Three. But before Team One could respond to Team Three's location, Curtin canceled his call. Winkler had to go back to directing Amendolare's team out of the building. At the same time, he was putting a rescue team together to go in and retrieve Team Five, but Murphy radioed back and said they had forced their way out, to cancel self-rescue and they were evacuating civilians.

While he was making all these transmissions back and forth between the three teams, Winkler turned around and saw that Lieutenant Murphy was injured and being led out by two of his men. Winkler watched Lanoce and Nolan carry Murphy to an ambulance parked near the command post at Church and Vesey. It was never a good sign when a team gets separated. There could be men unaccounted for.

The ambulance was packed with injured civilians—no room for Murphy. He stood in the street while the medics removed his Scott-pack and wrapped compressing bandages to his mangled hand. The medics stopped the bleeding, but the lieutenant couldn't stop worrying about the five men he had left on the plaza. He became agitated and he kept saying, "My men! My men are on the plaza!"

Lanoce's face was plastered in gray soot. It was packed over his eyes as a heap of donkey's dung. Nolan saw how pathetic Lanoce looked. He grabbed a plastic bottle of Poland Spring water out of the hands of a passerbyer and poured it over Lanoce's face and scooped in with his fingers and cleaned his eyes. He was relieved to see again.

Lanoce had to find another ambulance. He saw several parked in the middle of the street, one block down from Church. He grabbed Murphy's arm and started leading him, heading east on Vesey. The black iron fence that surrounded the graveyard to St. Paul's Church was to their right, and straight-ahead was Broadway. But before they could get half way down the block a fire department Chevy Blazer pulled up in front of them. A fireman stuck his head out from the driver's side window, and yelled, "Get in the back!"

Lanoce grabbed the rear handle of the Blazer but the door wouldn't open. He yelled to the fireman, "It's locked!"

At that moment, they heard rumbling. The second Tower was collapsing and they knew they only had seconds to escape before the debris cloud was on top of them. Lanoce frantically yanked on the handle and yelled to the driver to open the door. Instead, the fireman hit the gas, spun the wheels, and left Lanoce and Murphy standing in the middle of the street. There was no time to cuss out the heartless bastard. The hot wind was already on their backs and they knew the debris cloud was right behind it. Lanoce and Murphy started to hoof it as fast as they could down Vesey Street. They didn't get more than a few yards before they were in total darkness. The pulverized Tower was a storm of tiny pellets. It felt as an entire beach of sand was lifted in the air and dumped on top of them. They closed their eyes and held their breath. Murphy didn't have his Scott-pack since he had removed it moments before at the ambulance. Lanoce was still wearing his and he passed the mask to Murphy. After he took a few breaths, he passed it back to Lanoce. They kept moving forward and passing the mask back and forth. Through the clear plastic of the mask they couldn't see a thing until it was practically on top of them. A piece of debris flying around inside the dust cloud struck Lanoce on the back of his head. It spilt his helmet wide open. He kept on going. Next, he walked into a sign pole and clipped his right shoulder. It hurt like hell. He was sure he had dislocated it, but his adrenaline was pumping hard and he pushed through the pain. Only one thing on his mind: find shelter. Lanoce saw through his Scott mask a police van parked in the street. He picked up a good-sized chuck of cement off the ground and smashed out the glass of the back windows. He and the lieutenant stuck their heads inside the van just to get some cover and to breathe the air inside, but they kept on buddy-sharing the Scott mask until the dust cloud stopped rolling and thinned to a hazy fog. Lanoce pulled his head out of the window. There was a man standing by the van, covered with dust, who might have been in a uniform but it was hard to see who or what he was, except he was pointing to a building across the street and shouting, "In that building! There's EMS in that building!"

Lanoce and Murphy crossed to the building and in the back lobby there were paramedics treating firemen and civilians sitting on the floor and leaning against the walls. Lanoce passed the lieutenant to the medics. Then he stepped back, turned to place his hand on a wall, and blacked out.

The next thing Lanoce knew he was lying on his back looking up at a plain white ceiling. His head was on fire and his shoulder throbbed with pain. The second his eyes popped open he yelled, "Where's Murphy?"

"Don't worry," said a voice. "He's in another ambulance."

Lanoce tried to make out where he was. He saw the cabinets with bottles and bandages, and the dials of an oxygen tank. He saw the medic patches on the arms of men leaning over him. He thought, *yeah, I'm in an ambulance*. He felt the rocking back and forth and the bumps and turns in the road. They were driving him to Beekman Hospital on Williams Street, south of City Hall, and three blocks east from the Trade Center. They wheeled him into the emergency room. He was disorientated. Ceiling lights were spinning and the faces of people standing in the hallway were a blur. Suddenly, he remembered where he was and what he was doing last. He had left his team on the plaza and the North Tower came down and all he could think was that his buddies were buried under a ton of rubble.

Lanoce sat up and tried to get out of his hospital bed. He yelled, "My team is trapped! I wanna go back! I wanna go back!"

The nurses and the doctors held him down, but he was fighting as a madman. They strapped his arms and legs to the bed rails. They cut off his clothes and put an oxygen mask over his face, and the nurses stuck needles in his arms and pumped him full of Valium. But after all that, he was still fighting. The doctor left the room and then came back with a captain from Internal Affairs—who just happened to be an old friend of Lanoce's that he hadn't seen in years—and three sergeants. They surrounded his bed and told him he was in no shape to go anywhere. Lanoce cussed and fought the restraints and told them to go fuck themselves. Finally, the sedatives kicked in. He went limp as a jellyfish. His mind wandered off and the faces looking down at him bled into shadows and light.

When Murphy's hand was degloved by the falling piece of debris, it was about fifteen minutes before the collapse of the second Tower. The other men—Brink, Schwerner, and Garcia—had been so busy evacuating civilians and passing them down the line to the escalators they never noticed one of their own was injured. When they looked up, they saw the blood, and they saw Lanoce rushing the lieutenant down the stairs. They heard him shout, "I'm takin' him to a bus!"

At the same time, they saw three Bomb Squad detectives, Danny McNally, Claude Richards, and Mike Oldnixon appear at the top of the escalators. They were so dusty and there were so many small boulders piled up around the entrance of the stairs they looked as miners climbing out of a cave-in.

"You can get out this way!" shouted Richards. He was referring to the escalators. He was standing on one of them and he assumed Team Five was looking for a way to evacuate their load of civilians off the plaza.

Brink was glad to see the Bomb Squad. He had heard three very loud, consecutive explosions just before the South Tower fell. He was thinking there might be more bombs or plastic explosives still inside the other Tower. The Bomb Squad guys were hauling their equipment and looking to get to the North Tower.

"Yeah, guys," said Brink. He pointed back over his shoulder to the path where the civilians were walking out. "Go this way."

Meanwhile, Chief Purtell was standing at the command post outside the ambulance when he saw Murphy's injuries and heard him yelling that his men were still on the plaza. Purtell was a big bull of a man with a shiny baldhead and a thick neck. He looked strong as a wrestler. He was the commanding officer of the Special Operations Division who oversaw the Emergency Service Unit and he felt responsible. They were his men too. He had trained them, he had attended their award ceremonies, put medals on their chest, and listened to their gripes. No cop had been lost in the unit in fourteen years. The last incident had been in January of 1987 when a police officer named Frank LaSala from One-Truck had tried to evacuate a burning building. While he was in the staircase, the fire somehow vented itself and then flashed over him, burnt him, and LaSala died of his burns a few days later. Now one of his guys was already badly injured, the South Tower had come down with ten of his men inside, and he didn't want any more casualties. Without telling anybody where he was going, Purtell walked down Vesey Street and climbed the escalators to the plaza to try and find Murphy's men.

Team Five was still where Murphy had left them. Hartigan, Brink, Steinman, Schwerner, and Garcia were exhausted and beaten up. They had pulled what must have been two hundred civilians from the rubble, and there were still people coming out! Then Purtell appeared out of nowhere. At least it seemed that way. He was standing on the plaza, he was excited, and he was bellowing orders at them.

"The South Tower came down! Get away from the building!" yelled the Chief. "The other one is going to collapse!"

The South Tower came down? Hartigan didn't know what Purtell was talking about. He knew something had come down—he was standing in the middle of it! But, it never dawned on him this massive pile of rubble and the billions of dust particles suspended in the air, and the fire and smoke was the result of a supposedly indestructible skyscraper collapsing to the ground. But he and his teammates were evacuating civilians. Surely Purtell didn't expect them to drop everything and leave?

Hartigan shouted back, "We got people here!"

It was getting close to the end of the evacuation. The number of civilians started to dwindle but, just when it looked as though they had everyone out, a man walked over to Hartigan, pointed down the alleyway, and told him a woman had collapsed. Hartigan looked to where the man was pointing. He could see there was something going on around the bend of the southeast corner of the Customs House. There were people moving erratically inside the dust, and then he saw that one of them was Schwerner. How had he gotten down there? Two seconds before, he was standing right in front of him. He hadn't even seen him walk off the line. Apparently he had gone because of the woman. Now Hartigan followed after him because there is an unwritten rule in the police department and especially in ESU: No man goes off alone. To be without a partner is the most dangerous thing a cop can do: to get involved in something and not have anyone to watch your back. Hartigan knew very well the reason they were all still alive was because they kept an eye on each other, remembered their training, and worked as a team.

When Hartigan caught up with Schwerner, he found him leaning over a heavy-set black woman who was sitting on the ground. The woman couldn't walk anymore; her legs had just given out. He was struggling to lift her, but she wouldn't budge. Hartigan ran over, and together he and Schwerner were trying to pick her up, but the second they got her so much as an inch off the ground, she'd flop down again. It was frustrating. The woman just sat there as a three hundred-pound rag doll. "Leave me," she said, in a pathetic voice.

They weren't going to leave her. They were just as scared as she was and sometimes their language got a little ripe. They screamed and cussed at her. They weren't trying to be mean; they wanted to motivate her. They wanted the shock of four-letter words to make the woman listen to them.

To make matters worst, Purtell had followed them down the alleyway. He was standing behind them and yelling frantically, "Get out of here! Get out of here!"

They struggled to stay calm, but that wasn't easy, with the Chief shouting over their heads. They pleaded with the woman to stand. "You gotta get to your fuckin' feet!" They kept telling her, "You're gonna fuckin' die if you stay here!" It was just as in the film *The Terminator* when the soldier tells the heroine, "Come with me if you want to live."

Finally something clicked in her head and she began to rise. Maybe she got her second wind or maybe her survival instinct kicked in, but whatever it was, she slowly staggered to her feet. Hartigan and Schwerner held her arms and steadied her. They walked her around the plaza, down the alley, and over to the top of the escalator. It was a chore to get the woman to walk down the stairs. The woman cried out and swooned with every step. Hartigan and Schwerner reassured her they had a good grip, but the woman weighed more than both of them together, and one false move would have sent the three of them into a nose-dive.

The rest of the team was still on the plaza. Brink, Steinman, and Garcia were on the northwest corner of Building Five. They had just gotten all of the civilians off the plaza, down the escalators and into the street. Now it was their turn to leave, but suddenly, the now too familiar sound of rumbling started shaking their boots and they knew what was happening. The North Tower was coming down. Brink didn't hear any explosions as he did when the first Tower collapsed. He only heard the sickening crash of metal on metal. Before they had a chance to react, the smoke rolled in and darkness dropped as a lead weight.

Brink wanted to run. He wanted to run with all his strength but he knew he couldn't outrun a thirteen hundred-foot building. He thought, Can I really be lucky enough to survive two collapses? Brink chose to stay and see. He tried to remember how he had stood before, how he had placed his hands, how he had positioned his feet, how close to the building he had been. Had he faced the wall, or did he face out? What did he need to do to get caught in a void again? Then he felt Garcia and Steinman right behind him, and they pushed him against a wall and braced for impact.

Even though Brink knew what was coming, he didn't put on his Scott mask, for the same reason he hadn't put it on the first time. He didn't want to take his helmet off and get hit on his unprotected head by something flying through the air. Once again he pressed his gloves to his nose and mouth and waited for the smoke to roll over him. As the smoke covered his face, he suddenly realized he was looking through a window. Inside he saw a large, dusty room full of children's plastic toys and games and little chairs and tables. It was a deserted day-care center.

From the corner of his eye he saw the smoky shadows of men. A group of probationary firefighters—brand new with baby faces—groping in the dust storm searching for a place to bunker in.

"Stay with us!" Brink shouted to the firemen. "We went through the first one! We know what we're doing!"

Steinman grabbed one of the firemen who was wearing a Scott-pack with a PAK-Alarm system. This meant if he got buried or stopped moving, a loud, annoying alarm that sounded as a London police siren would go off. This was something the fire department used to locate a downed fireman. Steinman thought, *if they found him, they'll find me, too.* He practically had the fireman in a bear hug. They spun and stumbled together until they came to a stop against the wall of the building.

Hartigan and Schwerner were still on the escalators when they heard the rumbling. They had ten more steps to take and then they'd be on the ground. They tried to move faster, but the woman they were carrying walked as rigid and as slow as a mechanical doll winding down on a lose spring. No time to dally! Let's go! They were afraid the second collapse would wipe out the escalator with them still on it. They began to panic, and that caused a rapid descent. They felt themselves stumbling forward as a diver on the edge of a board. A Port Authority female cop was at the bottom of the stairs. She saw the two ESU cops struggling to keep a grip on both their balance and the heavy-set woman. She rushed up and grabbed the woman from the front. Together the three cops carried the hapless woman down the stairs and to the street, just in time for the dust cloud to roar over their heads. Immediately, everyone hit the ground. They bunkered in against the wall of the escalator. The cops shielded the woman with their bodies and Hartigan put his Scott mask over her face and turned on the air. All they could do now was ride the wave as the North Tower collapsed around (or on top of) them.

The Untold Story of the New York City Police Department & 9/11

16
10:29 AM: Team Three Escapes From The North Tower

Just moments before the second collapse, a Port Authority police officer named Jamey Hall was escaping from the North Tower. As he ran through the mezzanine, he caught a glimpse of an ESU sergeant that fit Curtin's description—silver haired and hefty—standing at the bottom of the stairs. Curtin was yelling to a group of rescue workers who were carrying down a heavy-set man. The sergeant was shouting, "Get out! The South Tower came down! Get out! Get out! Get out!"

When they had dragged the heavy-set man outside, everybody started running. Hall ran inside the building and dove out through a window blown out by the blast of the first collapse. From the corner of his eye he saw Curtin running in the opposite direction.

Officer Hall had only been witness to a brief moment. What had happened was: after Team Three had directed all the civilians out of the building, Beaury and DeMarco regrouped on the mezzanine and waited for Curtin and D'Allara to come downstairs. The mezzanine was deserted and, as far as they could see, their work was done. The seconds were ticking away, and they couldn't understand why the delay but, Curtin seemed to be stalling and the suspense was killing them.

DeMarco yelled up the stairs, "What're we waitin' for?"

"Mike, what're we doin'?" shouted Beaury. "Are we gettin' outta here?"

The time was 10:24 AM, five minutes before the collapse of the North Tower. Team Three could feel in their guts they were cutting things too close for comfort. The evacuation had taken nearly thirty minutes, plus, the sergeant had three team members who were missing: Vigiano, Danz, and Blihar; but he made no mention of them.

"Just a second!" Curtin shouted down the stairs. "There's one more!"

Then Curtin and D'Allara came down the stairs and stood on either side of the door looking up the stairwell apparently waiting for someone. Beaury and DeMarco could hear a thump-thump sound and a lot of heaving and grunting coming from inside the stairwell. They couldn't wait to see who was holding them up. Suddenly, ten firemen carried out an extremely obese man sitting on an office chair. The man's large frame and folds of flesh poured over the sides. He was semi-conscious and his head was rolling around as a rag doll's while both his arms hung limp as two old dishtowels. The size of the man was out of proportion to the chair, and it looked odd, as balancing a Butterball turkey on a teacup.

The firemen struggled to navigate the man in the chair out of the stairwell. Once they reached the main floor, they tried to push the chair down the corridor as a sled on ice, but the bottom of the chair's legs weren't smooth, and the chair lurched to a stop. The ten firemen reached under the chair and lifted the man. They looked as a collective hernia about to happen—ten stubby-legged dwarves squatting under the man's weight and running down the corridor behind the cops and toward the plaza doors.

The long row of windows in the mezzanine was composed of forty-foot high Moorish-styled arches. Through them, the cops and the firemen could see everything going on outside including the debris and bodies dropping forever in a panoramic view of the horror. They couldn't see the remains of the South Tower or the plaza through the dust—but it was pretty damn obvious something was terribly wrong.

Beaury and D'Allara opened the plaza doors and waited for a moment nothing was falling from the sky. As soon as it was safe, the cops gave the firemen the "thumbs up," held the doors open, and kept them open by jamming a pry bar into the doorframe. Two firemen darted across the short courtyard to the Customs House and positioned themselves as "lookout." The idea was to signal every few seconds when it was safe to run out in the open. When it was "all clear," the eight remaining firemen picked up the man in the chair again, and under the strain of his enormous weight, sprinted across the courtyard and got under the over hang of the Customs House.

Now the cops followed. One by one they ran between the falling debris and joined the firemen.

D'Allara was the last to run across. When he got to the other side, he suddenly remembered the pry bar stuck in the door. DeMarco told him to forget about it, but D'Allara insisted on going back for it.

"We might need it," he said. Without skipping a beat he raced back across the plaza to the Tower's large glass-paned doors, yanked the pry bar out of the doorjamb, and ran back. This was completely in character for John D'Allara. He was a stickler about his equipment. So, it shouldn't be a surprise to anyone he had to run back and get that pry bar.

The time was now 10:27 AM, two minutes before the second collapse. What was left of Team Three—Curtin, D'Allara, DeMarco and Beaury—and the ten firemen were positioned against the east wall of the Customs House. Squeezed together inside an irregular covey formed by the wall and the lobby doors, with an alleyway to the left, they were looking out at a huge mound of steel and concrete. This was going to be a problem. What was left of the South Tower was lying across the plaza as the Great Wall of China. The only way out was to retrace the same route they came in by, but the entire area was blocked off. The stairs and the way down were on the other side of the heap. The dense fog made it difficult to see more than a few yards in front of them, but there appeared to be a narrow path cutting through the debris between the Customs House and the mountain of rubble. It wasn't certain if it was passable all the way through, but the path was the only chance they had.

Sergeant Curtin had his back to his men as he stood a little out in the alleyway talking with one of the senior firemen. DeMarco watched him as a hawk. He knew at any second Curtin might give the signal to move, so all eyes were on him. Suddenly a body fell from the sky and landed right behind the fireman. Everyone jumped ten feet in the air. The men began yelling, "Get under the overhang!" They dove and scrambled to get against the wall.

Now the passageway looked even smaller. There wouldn't be enough room for all the cops and the firemen to get through at the same time. There was still the danger of getting hit by falling bodies and debris. Curtin decided the firemen would have to leave first, since they'd be moving slower, bogged down with the heavy man in the chair.

The ten firemen heaved up the chair and carried the man through the pathway. It was a tight squeeze and a rocky climb. While Curtin waited for them to get through, he turned to Beaury and DeMarco and said, "Go inside the Customs House and make sure there's nobody inside. If you find anybody, send them out to us, and by the time you're finished," he nodded towards the firemen. "They'll be gone."

Right behind them was the main entrance to the Customs House. It had two big glass doors that led into a huge, open-spaced lobby. Beaury and DeMarco ran inside the lobby. It was deserted, and this was going to be a two-second check. They wanted to get this over with as fast as possible.

Suddenly DeMarco could feel someone walking up behind him. He glanced back over his shoulder and was surprised to see Claude Richards and Danny McNally, the two Bomb Squad cops, entering the lobby. They came in fast. It looked as though they had come across the plaza, stepping out of the thick fog as the "invisible man" from the H.G. Wells story emerging out of nowhere.

As DeMarco and Beaury tried to get their bearings, they saw stairs straight-ahead. There was one set going up and another set going down. To their left were large sliding doors and to the right and in the center were escalators rolling up from the street level. Coming up on those escalators were two Port Authority cops, Ned Beatty and Sergeant Pete Francis.

Sitting in the center of the lobby was a pallet of bottled water that looked as though a deliveryman had suddenly abandoned his load. DeMarco was super thirsty and reached for a twelve-ounce bottle of spring water. From the corner of his eye he could see Beatty walking up behind him. Beatty grabbed a bottle too, but the instant they snapped the plastic with a twist of the cap they heard a rumbling. It was over their heads and getting louder and louder. It sounded as an out-of-control freight train coming down on top of them. No time to think. Impact! As the steel beams crashed through the roof, the concussion of air and solid matter pushed Beaury, DeMarco, McNally, Richards, Beatty, and Frances, to the floor.

The time it took them to run from the North Tower to the Customs House, and the time from Curtin giving the order to the check the lobby to the time the Tower collapsed on top of the Customs House was no more than two minutes. Beaury felt his helmet fly off. Then it was as if everything was moving in slow motion. Every moment lingered in stillness and clarity. In the slow fall to the floor, images began to flood inside his head. In his mind's eye he saw the faces of his wife and four children. For him, it was true your life flashes before your eyes. He recognized he was headed toward death. He recognized you don't get two chances to walk away from a close call. *Living and dying, in a sense, deserve the same respect.*

The First Responders

17
10:29 AM: Team One Escapes From The North Tower

Five minutes before the second Tower fell, Amendolare, Mack, Allen, and Norman were still standing at the abandoned fire command post under the North Tower. They were discussing what to do next. They tried to imagine what was going on outside. They thought there would be hundreds of people wounded in the streets and they'd be better served out there. On the radio, Sergeant Sullivan had ordered all remaining teams to take off their rescue equipment and put on combat gear. They thought maybe martial law was being declared and ESU would now be going into a different mode.

Norman wandered away from the team for a moment. He took a short walk halfway up the stairs and looked out across the lobby floor. Through the tall windows he saw the gothic arches of the devastated South Tower leaning as a giant rib cage in the smoke. Norman said an inaudible "Oh, shit" to himself, did a quick about face and, trying not to get too excited, calmly told Mack what he'd just seen. Mack, on the other hand, let out a perfectly audible "Oh, shit" and interrupted the team's town meeting.

"What the hell are we doing here?" said Mack, impatiently. "Lets go!"

Everybody snapped to attention—as if they'd just received a slap in the face. Unanimously and simultaneously they all agreed it was time to leave. Getting out of the building, however, was going to be tricky. As it got closer and closer to the moment of collapse, the Tower deteriorated faster and faster, with the debris falling harder and harder. It looked as the next-to-the-last scene in *Aliens*, thirty seconds before the nuclear tower blew, where the heroine stood on a platform waiting to be rescued and the debris was crashing all around.

Norman suggested they all line up in front of one of the broken windows and just run for it. There were several broken windows facing in various directions, and it was important they picked the right one. They knew they couldn't go south since the area in that direction laid devastated by the first collapse. Because the streets and the surrounding buildings were hidden under a heavy fog, they couldn't see what areas were safe. Amendolare radioed Winkler and asked, "Which way do we go?"

"Go north!" shouted Winkler over Tac-g. "Don't go east and don't go south!"

The team lined up in front of one of the windows that faced west and out onto West Street. Norman was at the front of the line, with Amendolare, Mack, and Allen falling in behind him. They looked as though they were ready to jump out of a plane.

"Everybody lined up?" said Norman. "Okay. On 'three' we're gonna run out that window! One-two-three! Move your ass!"

The cops dove out the window as ordered. Outside, they kept their heads down and ran for cover under one of the awnings that hung out over West Street.

It was somewhere around this time Blihar hooked up with Team One. He had made it down the stairs from the 9th floor and had, unbeknownst to him, bypassed his own team still on the plaza level. When he got to the lobby, he saw the backs of the men wearing ESU uniforms running out the window and, at first glance, he thought it was his own team, so he linked onto them as a caboose. It wasn't until he was half way out the window he realized he was on the wrong team. Blihar had completely missed Sergeant Curtin.

Team One wasn't out of the woods yet. They had made it to the street, but now they were pinned under an awning. Debris was crashing on the sidewalk and into the street and delaying their escape. Every second counted. They spied another awning about thirty feet north from their position. They'd have to run out in the open to get under it. They figured if they ran fast enough in twos, they could shorten the line and increase their chances of evading the falling debris. They kept their heads down and dashed to the next awning. They got across without anybody getting hit.

Now they were near the corner of West and Vesey. Suddenly they heard the tremendous lion's roar over their heads and ran like hell! They threw to the wind whatever tools they were still holding. Amendolare had been carrying the forty-pound "rabbit" tool all the way up and down the North Tower, and he hadn't put it down once; but as soon as he began to run, he flung it away. The dust cloud from the second Tower's collapse was running along the ground as a flood. It caught up with them in seconds and brought them down. It was every man for himself. They spilt in five different directions and nose-dived for cover.

Norman dove underneath the front of a fire truck but this didn't stop his forward motion. The force of the dust cloud was so strong it pushed his body along the full length of the undercarriage. He kept sliding until his head hit the rear axel and his helmet got caught between the bolts. Then two firemen scrambled under the same truck with him. He couldn't see them; he could only feel them and hear their radios: codes and "fire lingo."

The dust cloud was as thick as mud. Norman thought to himself, *I can't breathe this. I gotta get some air*. It felt as though somebody was trying to push a pillow down his lungs. He struggled to get hold of his Scott mask but only found his porter light. *Not going to get any oxygen out of that thing!* He kept feeling around his legs until he found the mask. He put it to his face and purged the regulator. A flow of pressurized air shot out of the tubes. He took a breath, but the mask was so filled with dirt that when he sucked it in, he gagged and vomited. He tilted the mask to let the vomit pour out. He kept purging and blowing out the dirt, as a vacuum cleaner running in reverse, until the regulator was cleared. Finally, he was able to take a decent breath.

He regained his composure and kept breathing in the fresh air. He listened and waited for the constant roar to stop. Objects were hitting the fire truck, and he could sense it squatting, dipping, and bouncing every time it took another blow. The undercarriage lowered closer and closer to his body until it was almost pressing on his chest. He was afraid he was going to be crushed. He debated whether to stay under the truck, or climb out and run. Both options were a bad idea. He didn't know what would kill him first, being squashed as a bug under the truck, or getting torn apart by the raging dust storm outside.

When the roar finally subsided, it got very quiet. Scary quiet. Norman's immediate reaction was to crawl out. He yelled to the two firemen lying next to him, "We gotta get up! We gotta move!"

But nobody moved. The firemen were motionless, and only the sound of breathing in their masks confirmed they were still alive. Because they wouldn't move it made Norman think they were trapped. The combination of the darkness, the Scott mask on his face, and the truck so low over his head he could barely look up, made him claustrophobic. He had to escape.

He crawled and squeezed his way between the tires. He put out his hand and felt something powdery as snow piled up all around the outside of the fire truck. When he touched it, his hand went right through. He kept pushing forward but felt nothing—just a mass of snow that yielded to him as he moved; it wasn't preventing him from getting out. He kept expecting to hit something that would impede him—there had to be a reason the firemen wouldn't move—but there weren't any obstacles. He broke through the powder and climbed out.

Norman stood up and looked around, but the dust was so thick it blocked out the sunlight and he couldn't see his hand in front of his face. He knew the truck he had just climbed out from under was facing south, but he wanted to go north, so he put his hand on the truck and followed it to its rear end, then let go and tried to walk on his own. He kept his arms outstretched in front of him as a sleepwalker feeling in the dark, waiting to hit something, looking for objects in front of him. Then his hands touched another vehicle—a tow truck. He walked along the side and lifted his mask just long enough to yell out, "Roger Mack!" Mack had been the last person Norman saw before diving for cover. He remembered seeing him running a few feet ahead and he knew Mack had to be near by.

Mack was indeed underneath the tow truck. When he saw Norman's boots come along the side, he grabbed his ankle and crawled out. Together they kept moving, going north, yelling out for the others. They found Amendolare under the next vehicle over, but they couldn't find Allen.

Cliff Allen was lying face down at the curb. He had been running down West Street when the concussion of the collapse knocked him to the ground. He fell next to a truck and tried to crawl under it, but couldn't move. The pressure and the heat of the dust cloud had him pinned. As he fell, he felt a fierce sensation of burning on his face. Tiny pieces of cement were hitting him and they felt as hot coals sinking into his skin and eyes. He covered his face with one arm, and felt around his hips for his Scott mask with the other. When he found the mask he put it on. The moment he inhaled, dirt went up his nose and in his mouth. He caught the dust at the back of his throat and snorted and spat it out.

The roar of the collapse lasted eleven seconds, but it felt much longer. When it was over, the strange silence made it seem as though every living thing, and every human activity that made a noise, had vanished from the face of the earth. Allen looked up to see how bad things were. It was a total whiteout. He couldn't see a damn thing and began to panic. He thought his eyes had been burnt and he was now blind. The truth was, the reason he couldn't see anything was a massive cloud of dust was suspended in the air from the two collapses. A few minutes later, he saw a smudge of sunlight, and objects—cars and buildings—began to appear through the dust, the way an image slowly develops on a Polaroid. He wasn't blind, after all.

Allen heard Amendolare on Tac-g trying to locate his men. Then he heard Norman and Mack on the radio asking for Amendolare's location and then their attempt to locate Allen himself. Allen tried to answer, but his throat was clogged with so much gook that he couldn't get his vocal chords to work. Amendolare must've had a feeling something was wrong. In his next transmission, he said, "If you can hear me, I'm at Chambers Street."

Allen stood up. The dense chalky fog made the streets unrecognizable. He felt disorientated but, in a slow, numb walk, he started heading north on West Street. As he approached Chambers, the dust in the air cleared away, the blue sky appeared, and he saw his teammates, Amendolare, Mack, and Norman, standing in the bright sunlight, waiting for him, on the corner of Chambers and West.

Norman was having trouble with his left eye. He could feel something like a piece of grit floating around on his eyeball and it was irritating as hell. He desperately needed water to flush it out. As luck would have it, a Poland Spring Water truck was driving south down West Street. Just as the truck reached Chambers Street, the driver took one look at what he was driving into: a huge, gray wall of dust, and came to a screeching halt. Then he attempted a wide U-turn in the middle of the six-lane intersection. Norman ran over and commandeered the truck. He told the driver he could leave, but they were taking the water. Norman rolled up the shutters and helped himself to a twenty-gallon, plastic-container full. He held it above his head and let the water gush over his face and down his body. Then he grabbed another twenty-gallon container and poured it over Amendolare. The water soaked their uniforms until they were blue again.

The First Responders

18

TEAM FIVE: Sanctuary

Team Five couldn't believe they had made it through the second collapse. They were closer to the North Tower than they had been to the South when the South one came down. The second round was a knockout. Brink went through the first collapse without a problem, but this time he thought he was going to suffocate. He held his gloves pressed over his nose and mouth, just as he did the first time, but the soot went right through his gloves, up his nose, and into his mouth.

Brink, Steinman, and Garcia tried to open their eyes but it was too painful. The bombardment of silica, dust, and smoke stung as salt in an opened wound. They could only open their eyes to a narrow slit, and what little they saw made them count their lucky stars.

When the second Tower collapsed, it finished off what the first Tower missed. The corner where Hartigan and Schwerner had picked up the woman was gone. The plaza was gone; most of the Customs House was gone, including the very spot where they had stood during the first collapse. The Plexiglas walkway that connected the plaza to Building Seven was gone. It had collapsed to the street and landed on top of fire trucks, popping one after another into flames. The only thing left standing was the escalator and a twenty-foot section of a paved pathway that led from the top of the escalator to the northwest corner of Building Five. Brink, Steinman, Garcia, and a small group of firemen were huddled against a wall on that section.

Nearby, Brink could hear desperate voices. "Help me!" they cried. But he couldn't see them. They were invisible in the smoke. He wanted to walk to them, but he was afraid if he departed from the wall, he would be lost as a drifting astronaut cut loose from a safety line. He turned on his flashlight and aimed it towards the cries for help. The only thing he could see was the light itself, shining out and flashing back, as high beams in a fog. Then a gray form moved towards him. As it got closer, he could see a man materializing out of the whiteness. It was a fire captain. He was frantic, lost. He kept saying over and over again he had to go up and get his guys.

"Cap, I don't know if there's anyone left up there," said Brink.

The fire captain ignored him. He stumbled pass the officer as a hasty apparition and vanished in the smoke. The next face Brink saw was Purtell emerging from the escalator stairs. He stood on the top step and was shocked to see Brink, Steinman, and Garcia, standing knee-deep in dust and debris. He said, "What the hell are you guys still doing here?"

What kind of a question was that? It wasn't as if they had asked to be buried up to their necks in the middle of the worst attack on American soil in history!

"Well, what the hell are you doing here?" said Brink.

"I came up to see who was here."

"Obviously, not many of us."

Hartigan and Schwerner were lying at the bottom of the escalators. The woman they had brought down with them was curled up on the ground in a complete state of shock. Not one peep was coming out of her. The two cops looked up and saw an ambulance rolling down Vesey Street. It stopped at the foot of the escalator. Through the chalky haze the bold red letters and the spinning turret lights were no more than a ghostly illumination. A medic jumped out of the ambulance, picked up the woman, and walked her towards the glow of the ambulance.

The medic put her inside the ambulance and on an orange-vinyl stretcher; he put a plastic green oxygen mask over her face, closed the double doors, and rolled away.

On the plaza, Brink strained and saw Garcia in front of him, standing by himself on the opposite corner, about twenty feet away. He called out, "Mike, how does it look over there?"

"Not too good!" Garcia shouted back. "There's a wall of fire and it's comin' straight at us!"

On that warning, Purtell, Brink, Steinman, and Garcia, came down the stairs and regrouped with Hartigan and Schwerner. So here they all were. A battered bunch. They were cut and bruised, with one busted elbow and many burnt eyes. It was time to retreat.

They forced themselves to take long strides. Stretching their legs over heaps of rubble, they held the building line. They passed Building Seven, it was on fire and covered in debris, and went north on West

Broadway, and then made a right on the first corner they came across, at Barclay Street. There were lots of cars on fire with tires beginning to pop. It sounded as M-80 fireworks going off. By this time everybody was gun shy, and they winced and recoiled at every bang. Brink was pissed nobody was putting out the fires, but then he saw the rows of crushed fire trucks, and that answered his question. It was a moment that snapped him back to reality.

Standing in the middle of the street was an Asian woman with a camera to her face. She had press credentials dangling around her neck. Purtell shouted to her, "Lady, you gotta get out for your own safety!"

"I'm doing my job," said the Asian woman as she kept on taking pictures.

Purtell grabbed her by the shoulders and said again, "It's not safe." He gave her an incentive push and she ran off and disappeared down the road.

The four remaining men of Team Five were looking for a place to take them far from the devastation—some place quiet and sane. They came across a building with big pillars and steep steps. It looked safe. Purtell peeled away from the team, but the four cops veered off to their right to see if they could get inside the building. They thought it was a bank and the doors would be locked. Brink leaned down to remove a halogen tool from his bag with the intention of breaking the lock, but Schwerner reached over his head and pulled the handle, and the door swung open. They entered through the tall, wooden doors and saw the rows of pews and a white-marbled altar surrounded by religious statues and stained-glass windows. It was not a bank; it was the Church of Saint Peter.

The air was clear inside, uncontaminated by what had happened a block away. It was possible to breathe at last. Bobby Steinman sunk down in a pew, grimacing with the pain of his injury. His elbow looked worse—it was black and blue and distorted from the swelling. The dust on their skin was starting to itch. The others went hunting around the church looking for something to clean themselves with..

Saint Peter was a good-sized church. On an important religious celebration, such as, an Easter or a Christmas morning Mass, it could probably hold four-hundred or more parishioners. It was dark inside, except for the three dimly lit chandeliers that hung from the high dome ceiling and the flicker of tiny flames burning in red-colored glass votives at the front of the church, and blue-colored glass votives at the back.

Schwerner found a water-can fire extinguisher sitting on the floor, and they poured the liquid into the palms of their hands, scrubbed the dirt from their skin, and dug out the muck impacted in their ears. Everyone took this opportunity to cough up or vomit the cement dust and other foreign particles they swallowed or inhaled.

Brink found a basin of holy water. It sat on a pedestal in a back corner of the church. He splashed the water on his face and wiped his eyes. The other men came over to wash out their eyes, too. There wasn't much water in the basin—just a cupful. Then they noticed two half-moon shaped basins jutting out from the back wall with more holy water. They scrambled to the newly discovered water, but it contained less, about two ounces, just enough to wet the finger tips and dab it on their eyes. Then Brink walked to the front of the church and he stood by the altar. He'd never been much of a church-going guy and prayer always seemed so unnecessary, but now he wanted to pray. "Thank you for getting me through this. Let my friends be okay. Give us strength to find survivors." As he stood there with his eyes closed, he could feel the others walk up and stand beside him.

Then the parish priest appeared from the back of the church and he stood there looking at these dusty men. Brink apologized for making a mess in his church. "I'm sorry, Father," he said. "Do you have anything to get this dust out of our eyes?"

The priest went to the little room behind the altar and opened the drawers. He took out the vestments and the white linens embroidered with little crosses, the same linens that are laid over the communion chalices, he soaked them under running water and handed them to the cops. The guys gave him an *are-you-sure?* look. The priest smiled and shrugged his shoulders. They wiped their faces and cleared their eyes. Brink took the wet linen and tied it around his neck. It was very comforting. It felt holy and nice and cold.

As they were washing their faces the men heard someone shouting their names from the behind the altar, "Hey, Richie! Dave! Bobby! Mike! Evan!" They turned around and saw it was one of their ESU bosses, Sergeant Carl White. He had been in the back of the church the whole time. When the South Tower collapsed White ran up Church Street and ridden out the dust cloud in the sanctuary of the church. He was excited to see five familiar faces and immediately ran over to them.

Hartigan noticed White was holding a cellphone and asked to use it. He called his wife. She had been watching the events on TV and she knew he'd be in the thick of it. The moment she saw the Towers collapse she rushed to their son's school and pulled him out of class. Hartigan made his call short and to the point and passed the phone to the other guys anxious to call home. Steinman and Schwerner tried to call their wives, and Brink and Garcia, who were unmarried, tried to call their family, or their girlfriends. But the phone didn't work for them. The wives of the officers had been frantically trying to find out where their husbands were, and somehow they had gotten the word Team Five was on the list of the missing. Hartigan's wife had been getting calls from his teammates' wives, and now she was able to reassure them they were safe and sitting in a church.

Team Five sat in the church for a long time. Time didn't matter now. They sagged down in the front pew. Every ounce of energy had been squeezed out of them. They felt as though they had just gone through a war—if not a war, at least a battle, and as men that have survived a battle together, they felt close to one another. They sat in silence. Talk was unnecessary: each knew what the other guy was thinking. They just wanted to savor this new friendship, this new blood.

The men took turns looking at Steinman's elbow, and they all agreed it looked broken, and he better not move around that much. Bobby Steinman was a tough little bastard. Here he was with a busted elbow and the whole time he never complained or asked to go to the hospital. He just pushed through the pain and evacuated all those people off the plaza. This was something Lanoce and the others admired about Steinman. They'd tell him he looked as a geek with his black rimmed glasses, his crew cut, and his roly-poly physique, but they all knew they'd go to battle with him anytime.

Once they were a bit rested, they figured it was time they left the church to return to the original Mobilization Point at Church and Vesey, but a message came over the radio ordering ESU personnel to report to the front of the Woolworth Building, on Broadway and Spruce. When they got there, new groups of men were just arriving in clean and crisp uniforms as though they had just stepped out of the locker room. They looked at the men drenched in gray dust and wondered what had happened to them.

The bosses stripped Team Five of their equipment and handed it over to the newly arrived cops. Then they tried to break up the team, but the guys protested. They were now a band of brothers and refused to be separated. Only Steinman was separated from the team so he could go to the hospital to have his elbow looked at. The rest of the team was ordered to report to Stuyvesant High School (by the afternoon, had been turned into the ESU's command post) to show Inspector Wasson they were still alive and have him remove them from the list of the "missing."

On the way to Stuyvesant High School, Brink wanted to call his family and let them know he was okay. As he was trying to find a phone, he overheard other men's stories and they were saying things as, "Yeah, a plane hit the Pentagon," and "They shot down another plane in Pennsylvania." Brink was flabbergasted and he kept asking everyone, "Are we at war? Who's doing it? The Russians?" He was thinking Old School—the Cold War.

Maybe he hadn't been keeping up with current events or his thoughts were just scrambled by the circumstances of the day but, for him, it was as stepping into the surreal. Earlier in the morning, when he first pulled up at West and Vesey, he had seen the South Tower hit by the second plane and his initial response was, "What a friggin' idiot this pilot is. Didn't he see the smoke comin' from the other Tower? Why didn't he steer away?"

Brink didn't believe the Towers were completely gone. When he looked up there was still a pillar of thick smoke suspended in the spot where they once stood. It looked as though something was still there.

He asked somebody, "How much fell?" When he was told the buildings were completely down, a devastating chill went through his body. He knew two of the guys from his command were gone, Walter Weaver and Jerome Dominguez. They had been in the South Tower with Sergeant Gillis and Brink was sure they must have been killed.

Weaver and Dominguez were his good friends. "Wally" Weaver had worked for six years at the 4-7 Precinct in the Bronx before getting assigned to Three-Truck. He was thirty years old at the time and full of energy. He had been excited to be in Emergency Service and was proud of its history and traditions. He and Brink hit it off and became fast friends. They partnered up a lot at work and hung out together off-duty. In the fall, they had a side business shrink-wrapping boats. Weaver liked his outdoor sports: fishing and game hunting. If Brink had to describe Wally in a nutshell, he'd say he was such a great guy he'd be the first to give the shirt off his back for anyone.

Dominguez was a big bear of a man, who always had a smile on his face and was always joking around. He loved his motorcycles, and he loved the outdoors, and he loved his girlfriend, Jessica, who was also a cop that worked in the Bronx. Dominguez and Brink liked to go riding together. Just this past April, he had accompanied Brink to purchase a Harley. Brink had his four-year old son with him and didn't want to put a small child on the back of the motorcycle, so Dominguez rode Brink's new bike all the way from the Harley-Davidson dealership in the Bronx to Brink's house in Suffolk County.

What was especially difficult for Brink was he was supposed to work with Dominguez today. They were assigned to go to the range together, but it had been canceled due to the mayoral primaries, so they had both been reassigned to Two-Truck in Manhattan and work patrol in Adam-Two. Brink had his whole day planned. He was all psyched to work in Harlem and then grab his meal at the Chicken Fair at 88th Street and Broadway. Earlier that morning, Weaver came in the locker room, passing out decals with the ESU insignia. He had picked them up at the Field the day before when he had attended a course in the use of the distraction devices they liked to call "flash bangs." He thought the decals would be a nice touch to stick on their helmets. As he was handing them out, Weaver asked Brink if he wanted to switch places. He said, "Hey, Dave. I'll take the fly car for you to Two-Truck. That way you can work with Mike Garcia."

Brink had fifteen years on the job and nine of those years were in ESU. That made him the senior man over Weaver, who had three years in ESU, and Dominguez, who had two years. There was an unwritten rule in the police department you always defer to the guy with seniority. Brink was in the middle of training the new guy, Garcia, and indeed, he didn't want to interrupt the momentum he had going with him.

"Okay, Wally," said Brink. "You can take the fly for me, if you want. I'll stay in Three-Truck and work with Mike and continue breaking him in."

So Brink stayed in the Bronx, and Weaver and Dominguez went to Manhattan and worked in Two-Truck for the day.

Although, Brink had resigned himself to the death of his two friends, the other guys in his unit tried to think more positively. They kept insisting they were okay. But Brink shook his head and said grimly, "No, they're gone. Nobody could survive that." It was better to think that way; hope would just drive him crazy. Nevertheless, Brink went looking for Dominguez and Weaver's truck. He walked around the perimeter and checked all the REPs until he saw the number "5593" written on the side of one of them. The glass was shattered and the windshields knocked in. He reached inside and grabbed Dominguez and Weaver's dark blue uniform baseball caps. They were full of dirt and he shook them out and put them inside his shirt for safekeeping.

The First Responders

19

TEAM THREE: Trapped!

Team Three was trapped inside the Customs House, slowly coming back to their senses after the shock of the collapse. They didn't know how long they had been in darkness. They didn't know if they were lying in their graves. One second there was an ear shattering noise and the next dead silence and nothingness. When DeMarco became aware he still had thoughts rolling around in his head, he told himself to move his fingers, and when his fingers moved, he knew he was alive. Then he told himself to take a deep breath, but he couldn't find any air. He felt himself suffocating. He struggled to put on his breathing apparatus, but the face mask was filled with so much crap the instant he threw it up to his face he sucked it all in. He could hear the others coughing in the dark, sucking in the same thick dust, but in the deadly blackness he couldn't distinguish a single shape or object. He couldn't see his own body or get a sense of anything out there. He yelled, and Beaury and McNally yelled back to him. The three of them, on their hands and knees, groped around in the dark for one another in a kind of scrambling fear they might be the only ones alive. When they found each other, they grabbed on and didn't let go for fear their buddy would slip back into a great black vacuum.

They could feel something flat and solid next to them. It was a wall. They leaned against it and used it as support as one by one they slid onto their feet. As long as they could feel that wall, they knew something was still standing. DeMarco felt for the mini-mag-light on his gun belt and was relieved to find it was still there. He clicked it on and lit up his teammates' faces. The flashlight was smaller than his hand, but those little mags and their tiny white star krypton bulbs had one hell of a kick. Whoever invented those things was a genius. Everything else he had been holding was lost. Everything not attached to his body had been knocked off: his helmet, the first-aid bag, even his eyeglasses.

Their radios had been off the entire time, but now DeMarco turned his on and put out a "10-13" distress call over Tac-g. In the smoky confusion, DeMarco couldn't remember the name of the building they were in or what the surrounding landmarks were. "Millennium Hotel" popped into his head, and he told whoever was listening at the other end they were near that structure. Of course, they were nowhere near the Millenium Hotel, but at least he got a message out three cops were in trouble. Then DeMarco thought about what he was transmitting. He felt ridiculous. *Two skyscrapers just came down with thousands of people in it, so, why should anybody worry about a bunch of cops trapped in a building?* But somebody did hear their transmission and was responding. While they waited for help, they started to inch their way to where they had last seen Curtin and D'Allara. The three men began to yell in that direction calling out their names at the top of their lungs. They weren't getting any answer so they tried to move closer.

The two bomb squad cops, Claude Richards and McNally had also lost contact with each other. McNally yelled like crazy for his partner, but he wasn't answering. The last thing he remembered was walking through the Customs House. Richards was a few steps behind him, just inside his peripheral vision. They'd been friends and partners since 1983 when they were cadets in the Academy. He had always been by his side; but now he was gone.

DeMarco remembered seeing a security door with a metal detector in the lobby. He was sure if he kept going he would find it and maybe slip into an office, locate a door or a staircase and get out of the building. He put his hand on the wall and glided it over the smooth marble to lead everyone in that direction. Behind him, he felt someone tugging on his air tank. From the impression of his height and the pitch of his hollow breathing inside the plastic of his mask, he knew it was McNally.

All at once, DeMarco felt his foot stepping on air and then a sudden sensation of gravity. He stopped short, and something slapped the face of his Scott mask. He felt it punch the plastic and bounce off. He searched for the object with his light while his left hand slipped around the edge of the wall. When he found it, he saw a bundle of blue electrical cables hanging in midair as a twisted jungle vine, as though they'd been ripped violently out of the wall. Then he pointed his mag light down to his foot. His boot was barely visible floating in the foggy blackness. There was no floor in front of him, just a gaping hole. DeMarco caught himself and stumbled back. He had a horrible feeling it was an elevator shaft. He was thinking, *how did I miscalculate that?*

"Turn around! Turn around!" shouted DeMarco. "We can't go any further!"

They did an about face and started moving along the wall in the opposite direction towards where Beaury remembered seeing the big revolving glass doors. Maybe they could get to them and go out that way. They stumbled around as blind men without canes and followed DeMarco's small circle of light.

DeMarco aimed his light into the pitch black. They began bumping into other people lost in the dark. First there would be the murmur of a disembodied voice and then hands reaching out to grab an arm or a shoulder. They found Ned Beatty and Sergeant Francis. A moment later another human form moved towards them—a black mass with a broad chest and thick arms wearing a suit and tie. They couldn't see his face, but from what little of him they could see, they knew he wasn't a cop. He was a security guard who worked for the Customs House. The security at Building Six didn't wear uniforms, but a dark blue suit with an identification tag attached to the lapel. Why he was still inside, where he came from, or what his name was, nobody asked.

Shoulder to shoulder, they were now six men hanging together against the security of the wall, heaving their breath inside their masks. They began to yell out in the dark, hoping somebody would hear and dig them out.

Here and there, small patches of fire began to ignite, with flames creeping up between the gaps of the broken floor. There was an eerie, orange glow in the blackness, while the flames made everything hotter and hotter. Suddenly Beaury became excited and called out he could see daylight overhead, but DeMarco was less optimistic and told him, "No, you're seeing firelight."

There was a huge hole in the side of the building where the windows were blown out. Ordinarily that whole area would have been lit up by daylight, but now it was blackened by the thick smoke and dust. Slowly the dust was settling. As the dust particles fell to earth, layers of smoke peeled away and sunlight began to filter through.

"I found a way out!" exclaimed Beaury. This time he was sure of what he was seeing.

Now the other men saw the light too, and somebody yelled to Beaury, "Put your hand on the wall and follow it out!" He touched the wall and, as his hand slid across the stone, he took the lead and started bringing them up through the building.

The light wasn't strong enough for Beaury to see where he was going, and he tripped on something sticking up in the rubble and fell on his face. It was a bad fall. The pain shot through his skull and there was a flash of light behind his eyes as neuron after neuron short-circuited and then reconnected. Nothing, thankfully, shut down. He was still conscious and nobody behind him knew he had fallen. Everyone was banged up at this point, sliced and bruised by sharp things in the dark. Beaury quickly got back on his feet and was moving again towards the sieve of sunlight. Now they were climbing over a mound of beams and chunks of cement, these led them up to a third floor platform, and they found themselves standing outside.

One whole side of the building was gone, and the only thing standing was this platform and the parapet wall. Beaury saw a ladder twisted over on its side and he went to get it. They all grabbed the ladder, held it upright, and lowered it over the side of the building. There was a scaffold hanging just beneath the portion of the building where they were standing and the ladder was long enough to reach it, but it was three stories down to the street from the scaffold, and was too long a jump for any man, no matter how badly he wanted to get down.

DeMarco looked out across the city scape and saw an unrecognizable world. It was a place so far away, so unreal, that it might as well have been a another planet. It was as though an earthquake or a war had destroyed some place you never heard of or cared about, and you were watching it on the evening news. And yet, here he was in the middle of it as the last man on earth or a shipwrecked survivor on a deserted island. Manhattan Island. A ghost town.

Everything was covered in a blanket of gray powder. It reminded DeMarco of the aftermath of Mount St. Helens when its volcano erupted and spewed burning ash on every building, car, and street. He looked at the others and saw they were caked in dirt and sweat, and then he looked at his own arms and uniform and saw they were in the same condition. He tried to make out where he was and realized he had given the wrong location over the radio. The North Bridge that connected the plaza to the Winter Garden was destroyed and lying in the street. Beneath its rubble were the twisted remains of fire trucks, and, as far as the eye could see, there were no people in the streets. Finally he recognized a landmark in the distance. It was the arched-bridge near the intermediate school that crosses over West Street at Chambers.

At this precise moment, DeMarco and Beaury saw two men—ghost white and almost invisible, standing in the fog and the rubble. It was two of their own guys running towards them over the mounds of debris—Winwood and Stefanakos. DeMarco and Beaury hollered until they thought their lungs would burst.

For the past thirty minutes, Stefanakos and Winwood had been climbing over the rubble. They were outside observers of the collapse and the radio was their only link to the guys in the Towers. After the first Tower fell, they ran to the Trade Center to try and help their friends, but the magnitude of the destruction stopped them. All they could do was stand at the corner of West and Vesey and look on in horror.

Then the rumbling started again, and they knew exactly what it was—the same crashing sound, as a distant echo returning from the first collapse. It was Armageddon all over again as the North Tower dominoed to the ground. Stefanakos and Winwood swung around and ran with everything they had.

Somewhere along the way Peter Appice hooked up with them and, as they all ran, he was pulling up in the lead. Appice was a tall, heavy-set guy, and he was flying. Winwood, the thinnest and smallest of the three, was lagging behind. He had a ton of equipment on his back, and the world through his Scott mask was distorted, as looking through a fish bowl. So he just zeroed in on Stefanakos and Appice. All he saw was their rear ends turning towards two large, metal doors. The dust cloud was over taking them, and they crashed through the doors and inside the safety of Stuyvesant High School, on the banks of the Hudson River, four blocks north of the Trade Center. Then shouting came over the radio. It's gone! Everything is gone!

Say that again, officer. What's gone?

You don't understand. Everything is gone!

The hysteria quickly turned to frantic calls for help. Stefanakos and Winwood heard Beaury and DeMarco putting over the Tac-g frequency they were trapped in a building. DeMarco said he didn't know exactly where they were. He was struggling with his words, trying to figure out his location, and then finally he said he thought that he and Beaury were near the Millennium Hotel.

"Let's get the fuck outta here!" exclaimed Winwood. They ran out of the school and headed back to what was left of the Trade Center.

Stefanakos knew the Millennium Hotel was at the base of the South Tower, and he also knew Beaury and DeMarco had gone to the North Tower with Sergeant Curtin, so, how could they be over there? But he wasn't going to argue with them. He figured, maybe something had happened so they ended up near the hotel, or maybe DeMarco and Beaury were in such a state of panic they became confused, as was the case.

As Stefanakos and Winwood approached the collapse, they started seeing people staggering up West Street towards them. They were completely white. From head to toe, their clothes, their faces were covered with chalky gray powder. They looked as walking statues. Stefanakos was trying to find other cops, but even though they wore dark blue uniforms, he couldn't distinguish them from anybody else. They started grabbing people and trying to identify them. It wasn't until they heard their voices they knew who they were talking to. Stefanakos grabbed the first guy and asked, "You okay?"

"Yeah," he said. It turned out to be Sergeant Amendolare.

"Keep goin' up," said Stefanakos. "Stuyvesantt High School is to the left."

Then they grabbed the next guy as he passed. "You okay?"

"Yeah," answered Cliff Allen.

Next, there was Dave Norman and Roger Mack. He knew they had been the first team into the North Tower and here they were, walking out alive. The feeling was intense. Stefanakos was thinking *these were our guys and they're okay. So, everybody has to be okay.*

They continued directing everyone over towards the high school, and then Stefanakos and Winwood made their way back down to the Trade Center. The first thing they saw was the Customs House. Part of it was still standing. The eight-story structure had been severely damaged by the debris cascading from the collapsing Tower. All the windows were shattered, and falling steel beams had punctured through the center of the roof.

The two men began to climb the rubble. In between the chunks of cement and steel trusses were pieces of human flesh, here a detached arm, there a leg tangled in a mess of metal. They climbed until they were so exhausted they couldn't climb anymore. As they looked down, they saw a dazed fireman stumbling over the ruins as a boxer picking himself up from a knockout in the twelfth round. It was at that moment the magnitude of everything finally registered for them.

Winwood said, "O, my God. What're we goin' to do?"

Stefanakos turned around to speak, when suddenly, by the grace of God, something made him look up to his left and see two men hanging over the third floor railing of the Customs House. All he saw was the top of their heads, but it was enough to recognize Beaury and DeMarco. Beaury was screaming over and over again, "You gotta get me outta here!"

What the hell are you guys doing there? Stefanakos was thinking. They were not at all where they said they were. *You're not supposed to be here; you're supposed to be over there!*

They ran back down the rubble and over to the twisted remains of an over-turned fire truck that said "Ladder Five" and pulled off its thirty-five-foot extension ladder. They propped it against the building and extended it to the parapet wall where the two men were standing, but the second they had the ladder fully raised the top portion slid back in and left a gap of ten-feet below the scaffold hanging half way up the side of the building. Stefanakos and Winwood tried a second and a third time to extend the ladder, but the top portion kept slipping down.

Beaury was watching this and was becoming frustrated. He wanted to get the hell out of there and that ladder wasn't cooperating.

Frantically, Beaury yelled down instructions, "You have to pull the outside switch!"

No matter what they did the ladder refused to extend to its full length. They had no other choice but to leave it ten-feet short of the scaffold. It was the best they could do.

Winwood called up to Beaury, "Billy, just get on the damn ladder! Hang off! Jump! Do whatever it takes to climb down the ladder."

But Beaury didn't come down. He had spent his entire career dangling off roofs and bridges, but his fear of heights had him thinking twice about the sturdiness of the whole set up. He'd have to climb down one ladder to the scaffold and then suspend from the scaffold to the extension ladder. He was a little shorter than average height and didn't have the longest legs and, as desperate as he was to get off the platform, he wasn't looking forward to hanging in midair and swinging his foot around to feel for the damn ladder. He stepped out of the way and let McNally go first.

Now this was a surprise to Stefanakos. He didn't even know McNally was up there. He had only seen two guys behind the parapet wall and now here comes McNally climbing down and jumping off the ladder.

"My partner's right behind me!" said McNally, excitedly. He was pointing to the rear of the Customs House. But his partner, Claude Richards, had somehow disappeared—plucked off the face of the earth "I gotta go find my partner!" McNally kept saying. He wore a panicked expression and his voice was cracking. "There's a big hole!"

After McNally, next to come down the ladder was the security guard. He was a big man, and the ladder shook as he climbed down. Right after the guard was Ned Beatty, and he was flying down the ladder as a speeding bullet, tripping over his own feet as he tried to get from one tier to the next. Stefanakos was beginning to wonder how many people were up on the platform. As he watched Beatty fly past he was thinking, *where did you come from?* He was expecting to see only his own guys, and so far it was a civilian, a Bomb Squad detective, and a Port Authority cop. When he got to the bottom, Beatty took a stance off to the side without acknowledging anyone. His face was pale and distant. He had the look of a pilot who had just walked away from a crash-and-burn landing and couldn't believe he was standing there in one piece.

Finally, Beaury took a deep breath and got ready. Everybody was waiting for him down below. Stefanakos was beginning to think somebody was hurt up there, and he started up the ladder. But before Stefanakos got very far, Beaury threw his legs over the wall and started climbing down to the scaffold. He was moving fast and couldn't wait another second to touch the ground. Fear of heights or no fear of heights, a wobbly ladder and thirty feet wasn't going to stand in his way of getting out of this hell hole.

"Get off! Get off!" Beaury yelled to Stefanakos.

Stefanakos quickly backed down the ladder to get out of his way. It was either that or get a heel kicked in the chin.

DeMarco looked over at the Port Authority sergeant and waited for him to get on the ladder, but Sergeant Francis was stalling. He gestured for DeMarco to go first, and then he stepped back. DeMarco figured the sergeant wanted to be the last man out—that he was making a statement, even if it was only to himself. These were his buildings; this was where he worked. He nearly lost his life here.

After DeMarco and Sergeant Francis finally climbed down, Stefanakos still looked up at the 3rd floor platform and waited a few seconds to see if anyone else was coming down. But there was nobody else.

Beaury was upset and, in broken, disconnected speech, he tried to explain what had just happened. Stefanakos didn't like what he found himself thinking. Less than a third of Team Three had climbed down the ladder. There were supposed to be seven men, but only two came out. The sick sinking feeling that the unthinkable could be true came over the officers as they tried not to imagine the fate of their friends.

They were glad to see those that *had* made it out, however. They embraced each other in an emotional reunion. Beaury was ecstatic. He could hardly believe he was alive. A skyscraper had missed his head by a few feet. It made him feel wildly, impossibly lucky. It was as if he absent-mindedly stepped off a curb in front of a fast moving truck, but at the very last spilt second somebody had grabbed him from behind and pulled him out of the way. He could barely restrain his emotions. To him, Stefanakos and Winwood were his guardian angels, the invisible hands that had pulled him out of the way.

Everybody began to wind down from the scare of their lives. They composed themselves and started to split up. McNally mumbled something about getting back to his command and started heading north up West Street. The security guard was nowhere to be found. He must have walked off when nobody was looking. Stefanakos glanced over at the two Port Authority cops who stood off to the side. They were motionless. Their faces had the look of shattered glass not yet fallen from the frame.

"You guys okay?" Stefanakos asked them.

They answered they were okay, and then just turned and walked away. They didn't look okay, thought Stefanakos. It was eerie, the way they just walked off like that.

As Stefanakos, Winwood, DeMarco, and Beaury turned to leave, Winwood heard some voices above his head. It sounded as though it was coming from the Customs House. He took a few steps back into the street and looked up. Standing in the blown out windows on the upper floors were a handful of civilians. They were leaning out and waving.

"We're up here!" they called down.

The Customs House had been evacuated immediately after the first plane crashed into North Tower, but it was possible a few employees remained behind for one reason or another. One reason, it turned out, was the Head Customs Agent had returned to his office to use the fax machine. He wanted to get everybody's names to Washington DC to account for all his employees. Now they were stranded in half a building that no longer had a roof or any exits.

"How you guys doin'?" Winwood called back up.

"We're okay," they answered.

The First Responders

AFTER THE COLLAPSE

Seven minutes after the second Tower collapsed, Morley climbed out from under the fire truck and pulled his prisoner to his feet. He still had him; he hadn't blown away with the dust. Mr. X looked armless with his hands bound behind his back. The dust irritated his eyes and he was blinking back stinging tears and the smug look he'd been wearing since the 21st floor had finally been wiped off his face.

Morley looked for signs of life. The streets were empty except for a few firemen emerging from the shelter of doorways, or under fire rigs. Then he saw Hollifield in the middle of the road. He was wobbling around on shaky legs and clasping his chest. It looked as though he was having a heart attack. Morley tried to grab him but the lieutenant resisted. He didn't want help.

"I'm okay. I'm okay," said Hollifield, hacking and gasping for air.

"Fuck you, you're 'okay.' You're *not* 'okay'," insisted Morley.

During the dust cloud Hollifield had dived under a fire truck. Debris had fallen on the truck and the undercarriage came down on top of him and pressed hard against his chest. He had been able to squeeze out but many of his ribs were hurting.

Morley wanted to get out of the area, but everywhere he looked there was a wall of white dust. Suddenly he spied clear air towards the water. He decided to go that way, dragging his prisoner with one hand and holding the lieutenant with the other. He was now on West Street, walking north, looking around for a medic. Four blocks up on Murray Street was Saint John's Hospital.

The front of the hospital looked as a TV episode of *M.A.S.H.* All the nurses and the doctors were standing around in the street with their hands plunged deep in the pockets of their white lab coats. They all had the look of anxious waiting, as if, any second now, helicopters and ambulances would be arriving with the casualties of war.

Morley was coming up the hospital's driveway. He was walking lopsided, trying to support the weight of the two men. He pulled the prisoner behind him and pushed Hollifield in front of him, and shouted, "Medic! Medic! I think he's havin' a heart attack!"

Immediately, two EMTs rolled out a stretcher from the triage. They ran over and grabbed Hollifield, put him down on the stretcher, wheeled him up the driveway and to the emergency room. As he was being carted away, the lieutenant lifted his head and motioned towards Morley's prisoner, and yelled, "Whatever you do, don't loose that guy!"

Morley figured since he was already at the hospital he'd go inside and get his eyes rinsed. The dust irritated his skin and his lungs hurt. He walked his prisoner to the triage. The only patients he saw were cops and firemen. They were sitting in pairs and helping each other pour water over their faces to rinse the dust out of their eyes. It was as a buddy system where each person was helping another. There weren't any medical personnel except for one doctor, but he wasn't helping anyone. He was too busy walking around in his green scrubs with a video camera stuck to his face, videotaping the patients. He'd walk slowly through the room and let his camera pan slowly from one dirty face to the next. Morley was annoyed the doctor wasn't helping anyone. When he pointed his camera at him, Morley smirked and then made sure the doctor could get a shot of him pouring some water on his prisoner's face. *Look. I'm taking care of my prisoner. Now, go away.*

A dusty man in a business suit walked over to Morley. He had a big smile on his face and was holding two plastic bottles of sterilized hospital water. He offered one to Morley and said, "Hey, Timmy! How yer doin'?"

Morley had no idea who he was, but he took the bottled water anyway.

"Who are you?" asked Morley.

"You don't remember me? I'm Greg's friend," said the man. "I work for the Secret Service."

Greg was an old college buddy from Saint John's College whom Morley had run with on the school's running team. They had gone to each other's weddings and the christenings of their children. Morley went on to join the NYPD and Greg joined the Secret Service. The man he was talking to was Greg's partner. Somewhere along the way they must have met at a social event, but for the life of him, Morley couldn't say he knew him or remembered his name. Even after he washed his face he still didn't recognize him. They shook hands and said how they couldn't believe they'd run into each other, and then they went their separate ways.

When Morley left the hospital, he started to wander over to West Street again. He was still hanging onto the prisoner, and it was about time he did something with him, but the streets were deserted and he couldn't find anybody to turn him over to. Hollifield was in the hospital, and the guys from Team One had disappeared. Then Morley thought he saw an ESU cop walking towards him. When he came closer, he realized he had a Bomb Squad patch on his sleeve. It was Detective McNally.

He stopped McNally and said, urgently, "We gotta set up a perimeter! We gotta keep people back!"

Morley was thinking about secondary explosions and more bombs. He thought a "frozen zone" should be set up to keep people away from the Trade Center, but McNally was too numb to care. He glanced briefly over at Morley, and said, "My partner's dead."

Morley didn't know what to say except, "I'm sorry." He stepped back and let McNally pass. Then he gave his prisoner a tug and kept on walking.

Suddenly, Chief Hale side-flanked him. Hale had his hands up in the air and a bewildered look on his face, which was understandable considering everything that had just happened, what with two Towers collapsing, and all, but that was not what he was in shock about. He couldn't believe Morley was still walking around with the prisoner. He said, "Holy shit! You still have that fucking guy?"

Hale's sudden burst of expletives took Morley aback. It wasn't something he expected to hear from a four-star chief.

"Don't move," Hale insisted. "Don't go anywhere."

The Chief disappeared around a corner and a minute later drove up in a dark blue van. Morley slid open the side door, shoved Mr. X in the back seat, and jumped aboard. They drove over to Stuyvesant High School.

The school's auditorium had been turned into a refuge. Firemen and cops were standing around as zombies. Morley looked at their faces to see if he recognized any of them. He was looking for the firefighters from the 31st floor and he was looking for the guys from Team One. He feared they were all dead.

Then he saw some ESU cops standing against a wall and yelled to them, "Anyone here seen One-Truck?"

Nobody answered. He asked again, but they still didn't answer. Morley was pissed he was being ignored. Then he realized they had seen the Towers come down. They were all in a state of shock.

Soon, the FBI showed up to debrief the prisoner. They took him to an office in the back of the school. They asked Morley to write out everything that had happened, but he was too pumped, too excited. His hand was too shaky to hold a pen.

After some time passed, the Feds wanted to take Mr. X to the temporary police headquarters at the Police Academy. Once again, Hale, Morley, and the prisoner piled into the blue van and drove uptown to 20th Street and Second Avenue.

At the Academy, they went to the second floor where the offices were located. There was a lot of activity going on. Morley stood by the door and watched the room. The Mayor and the Police Commissioner were there, and the office was packed with important people. Chief Hale walked over to Giuliani and spoke to him. Morley didn't know what Hale said to him, but he must have told him about Mr. X, because Giuliani looked over at Morley and made a beeline through all the people in the room and walked towards him with his hand extended. Morley stood there sweaty and white as a snowman, but the Mayor didn't mind he was a filthy mess. He shook Morley's hand, and said, "Good job."

Mr. X was taken away to be debriefed by HIDTA, a Criminal Intelligence Division of the NYPD. The initials stood for "High Intensity Drug Trafficking Agency." It has been around in the Department since the year dot. It was created to keep tabs on drug dealers, but in recent years, they started to include gang members, career criminals, and now terrorists. In spite of their new list of inductees, the Intel people never got around to updating the acronym.

After the Mayor walked away, a police inspector standing nearby in the hallway, approached Morley and asked what the handshake was all about. Morley was still reeling from his escape in the collapse and he was hyper and tense and was more than happy to tell the inspector, and anyone else who'd listen about the strange man he arrested in the North Tower. But before he could finish his story a man in a dark suit—who was standing across from him and eavesdropping on the conversation—stepped forward and interrupted. "If you know what's good for you," said the man. "I wouldn't repeat that story."

Morley was stunned. He gave him a hard look and said, "Who're you?"

"Never mind who I am."

That answer infuriated Morley. He said, "Oh, yeah? Fuck you."

Morley didn't like being intimidated, and to prove how much he didn't like it, he thought he'd repeat his story to the police commissioner. He entered the room full of people and saw Kerik sitting behind a mahogany desk. He was busy talking on his cellphone. His assistants sat compliantly to his left side and to his right side, shuffling papers, writing notes, and taking messages from the revolving parade of men with ID badges that walked up to the desk every two seconds with some kind of news they wanted passed to the Commissioner. Morley stood in front of Kerik and waited to get his attention. But the Commissioner never looked up to acknowledge him, and Morley felt annoyed. He thought to himself *You have any idea what I just went through?* The dust on his skin started to itch. It was all he could think about. He wanted to scratch his head. Morley wore his hair in a flat-top crew cut, and a thin layer of dust sat on his head as snow on a roof. He brushed his hand across the short bristle of hair as running a fingernail down a row of teeth on a plastic comb. This caused the dust to fly off his head in a puff of smoke and land on the desk. It fell directly in front of Kerik and immediately caught his attention. He and his assistants shot back two feet from the desk in order to avoid getting covered in the stuff. Then they swung around on the wheels of their swivel chairs, and examined their trousers and suit jackets for the inconvenient and messy gray smear of World Trade Center dust.

Morley gave up on talking to the Commissioner. He turned and walked out through the packed room. Morley noticed Hale standing alone in the middle of the crowd. He saw his hands were shaking. All the emotions and all the exertions of the day were overcoming him. He thought Hale was going to collapse, and he rushed over to his side. "Come on, keep it together," said Morley, and he grabbed the chief's arm.

He ushered Hale out of the room and down the hall and took him inside an empty office. He found him a chair and got him a glass of water, but the chief couldn't hold it without spilling it, and Morley had to help him drink it down.

Hale rested for a minute. Then he pulled himself together and stood up. He brushed his hand down the front of his jacket and gave the hem a little tug. He said he was going to shower and change into a clean uniform and go back down to the Trade Center. Morley wanted to go with him, but Hale motioned with his hand and told him to stay at the Academy and relax.

Morley didn't want to stay at the Police Academy and relax. There was nothing to do but sit around. He saw a lieutenant he knew from the police running team and he gave Morley soap and a towel to wash up. Morley was hacking up black smoke, and he was worried his days as a runner would be numbered, so he went to Cabrini Hospital, across the street from the Police Academy, and got checked out. The nurses took his clothes and shoes, contaminated with the dust of pulverized glass and cement, and dumped them into a plastic bag with a tie string. He even had to remove his Nicole Miller tie and throw it in the bag. Then the nurses gave him clean but used clothing from the charity bin, but they didn't have any shoes that fit, so Morley left the hospital in his bare feet to wander around and look for something to put on them.

Lexington Avenue was one block west of the Academy. There are restaurants and stores there, and Morley walked up and down the block a couple of times before he could find a shoe shop. He bought a junky pair of Reebok jocks for thirty-six bucks and went back to the Police Academy. At midnight, somebody from the Academy drove him home. His lungs and feet were killing him. His mind was busy, rehashing every single thing said and done that day. He thought *Did I do all that I could?*

During the drive home to Nassau County, Morley stared out the car window at the blackness. The highways, and its constant traffic in a city of 8.1 million people, were now empty and quiet. They were on the Grand Central Parkway, going east. They passed LaGuardia Airport. The airspace surrounding New York City had been closed down since this morning. The runways sat dormant and dark. Next, they drove by Shea Stadium. The giant multi-colored neon sign of a baseball player swinging a bat that lights up the Stadium's façade was shut off. On the Van Wyck Expressway—at the very point where it merges with the GCP—there was a lone car with a spinning red light on the dashboard, silently racing in the opposite direction.

When Morley was dropped off in the front of his house, it was dark and all the blinds were drawn. A dim light inside the front room shined between the aluminum slates as a paper lantern. He knew his wife was waiting up for him and he knew his two small children were probably sound asleep in their beds. For a brief moment, he couldn't help but feel an unbearable pain of loneliness.

21
THE SURVIVORS

Immediately, after their rescue from the Customs House, DeMarco and Beaury walked aimlessly up West Street. They were going north, looking for where the devastation ended and civilization picked up again. They hadn't walked more than ten paces passed Vesey Street when two cops from their unit, Tony Conte and Appice, grabbed them and pulled them over to where a paramedic was using a fire hose to wash down an ambulance. Conte borrowed the hose and turned it on DeMarco and Beaury. The water hit them in the face, washed the dust out of their eyes, and cooled them off.

As DeMarco bent down under the stream of cold water to rinse the dirt out of his hair, he looked up and saw a van racing down West Street. It was the only vehicle going anywhere and it looked out of place on the deserted street. All he could see was dust kicking up from the tires, as a boat cutting through the waves. Then it came to a screeching halt in front of him, and a man whom he knew as John, the guy who owned the gas station on the Bowery at Third Street and who fixed all the cops' personal cars, jumped out and threw his arms around him. Then he hugged everybody else he saw standing there. He jumped from DeMarco, to Conte, to Beaury, to DeMarco again, hugging and squeezing as long, lost kinfolk. That was the last person DeMarco ever expected to see in a situation as this—his auto repairman.

"I knew you guys wud be down here and I hadda see wut happen'd," said John the mechanic. "Where can I take yous?"

He offered DeMarco a ride in his beaten up van that looked as a refurbished ambulette, but DeMarco declined. He said he had to try and look for a supervisor and find out what the hell was going on.

As DeMarco and Beaury continued up West Street, an ambulance pulled up alongside of them and the driver rolled down his window, looked at the two cops, and said, "Hey! You guys all right?" That was some question! After what they had just been through, they didn't know whether to laugh or cry, it seemed so ridiculous. Beaury waved them on and said, "Keep on goin'. Some of our guys are trapped down there." Two seconds later another ambulance stopped, the medic rolled down his window, and said, "Here, take some oxygen." And then a third ambulance stopped, "You wanna go to the hospital?" Every time Beaury gave them the same answer and waved them on. He was starting to get a complex. He had no idea what he looked like, but he figured, *If I look anything like how I feel, I must really look like shit.*

Chambers and West Street seemed to be the corner that everybody—firemen, police, everybody—was pulling back to. It was the line in the dirt, the point of no return, the "do not enter" sign in the road. It was a clearing, where the sun was out and the air was somewhat breathable. One block south there was a wall of smoke that reached up twenty stories or so, and from the edge of it, waves of dust-covered firemen were materializing as the ghosts of lost souls. DeMarco and Beaury walked to Chambers Street and lingered there for a while, trying to get their bearings and trying to see if anybody was around to whom they could ask, "What's next?" There were other cops and firemen drifting by, but they all had a dazed look in their eyes and were probably just as out-of-it as DeMarco and Beaury. Then DeMarco noticed Blihar standing across the street, and it suddenly dawned on him he hadn't seen him since the stairwell. He thought he was dead. DeMarco wondered what his story was and crossed the street to ask him. Blihar in turn had thought DeMarco was dead. Blihar briefly explained his turn-around on the stairs, and then walked away. It was strange, to see someone alive you thought was dead, and the only reaction is a nod and a few words.

DeMarco was still wearing his Scott-pack and wanted to get rid of it. He decided he'd go east and unload his equipment on his truck. The last thing he saw as he was departing, was Appice trying to put Beaury into the back of an ambulance, but Beaury was fussing and fending off the medics with all his Irish tenacity, because he didn't want to go to the hospital and, in his own words, "lay in some nice clean bed with nurses taking care of him while his friends were down here buried under smoke and rubble." Everybody was saying they understood but you have to take care of yourself first. They put him into the ambulance and eventually he quieted down long enough for everyone to feel it was safe to leave him alone; but as soon as the medic jumped out of the back of the ambulance and went around the front and climbed into the driver's seat, and Appice had walked away, Beaury pushed open the back doors and slipped out.

Beaury saw a small band of ESU officers gathered on a street corner and walked over to them. He stayed with them and followed wherever they went until he found himself standing in a park on the water.

I was shot, said Beaury. He was dissociated. He felt as though he had left his body and gone somewhere else. He started to think about the Towers and everything he had been through. Images of it came to him one after another, as in a slide show, flashing on the screen and fading away. Falling bodies, flames, smoke, piles of rubble, the dark. He couldn't break the chain of silent images, and when he snapped out of it, he suddenly became aware he was on Canal Street near the Holland Tunnel, a good half mile from where he had escaped the ambulance. How he had gotten all the way up there, he had no idea. But he remembered seeing a large silver coach bus—the kind that takes your blue-haired granny to Atlantic City—pulling up and letting off a group of iron workers who had faces as tough as squint-eyed bulldogs with chains as thick as bricks wrapped around their necks.

"Wha' happened? The World Trade Center fell?" asked a huge man with the chains.

"Uh huh," said Beaury.

"We're here to pick it up." The man of steel flexed his muscles as a circus strong man.

Yeah, okay, thought Beaury, *you probably could.*

And then, as though it was as easy as tapping his heels together, he found himself at the North Cove Marina standing in front of the granite wall of the Police Memorial. It was a serene park with a pool and a waterfall and it sat at the very end of Liberty Street, by the water's edge.

While Beaury was trying to find his way back to reality, ESU had turned the park into a parking lot. The benches were pushed back and the small trees were cut down to make room for the assembly of trucks and men. All of the Emergency Service Units had been ordered to muster at the park. It was time to do a head count and assess the damage.

The First Responders

After the North Tower collapsed, the ESU cops wandered the streets, wide-eyed at the devastation, not sure where they were. Street signs and landmarks were destroyed or twisted backwards and everything once recognizable was hidden under the snowstorm of dust. They were trying to find somebody they knew, and when they did, it was easy to get separated again. One minute they were there and then the next they were gone, vanished in the dust cloud or lost in the stampede of people running for their lives.

There was a new fear a main gas line running under the Millennium Hotel was going to blow. Everyone started running away from the Trade Center one more time. Suddenly, shouts of "Shots fired! Shots fired!" came over the radio. The radio went crazy. Everybody ducked and looked around. They thought the terrorists were in the streets shooting at everyone. It turned out to be friendly fire. It was cops shooting their way out of lobbies and foyers in buildings near the collapse. For instance, a young rookie officer walked up to his sergeant and nervously told him he fired his gun through a glass plate window. He'd been trapped inside a building, a pile up of rubble sealed the door, and the window was his only way out. The rookie thought he'd have to fill out paperwork and follow the Department's "firearm discharge" guidelines! The sergeant gave a stifled grin and then pretended he never heard him, as if to say, of all the times to worry about it, kid, this wasn't it. God will forgive you; maybe, even the Department will forgive you. On the radio, Central was calling 10-13s and throwing out street names faster than a hog auctioneer at a county fair. It was such confusion. No bosses were taking charge. Cops were cops and *they* were taking charge. Otherwise, it was every man for himself!

Frank DeMasi walked the streets for an hour and a half after the North Tower fell, trying to find another Emergency cop. The last thing he remembered after the collapse of the South Tower, he was pouring water over Garvey's head—after he had passed out—trying to cool him off, when suddenly somebody started screaming the North Tower was coming down. Cooling off Garvey must have taken longer than he thought, because there was a half-hour interval between the collapse of the two Towers. He thought he'd been helping Curtis for about a minute. That's how chaotic it was. That half-hour felt as a minute. Now, at this point, all he knew was he didn't want to get caught in the debris cloud again. He remembered pulling Garvey to his feet and pushing him up the block. They were going west towards the river, and there were thousands of people running with them. DeMasi lost Garvey. He fell away from his hands and disappeared in the stampede. DeMasi ducked inside the lobby of an office building and waited for the storm to pass. When it was all quiet, he got on Tac-g and tried to locate his unit, but the radio was silent. Nobody was answering.

When somebody eventually did answer, DeMasi was told the new mobilization point was somewhere near City Hall. DeMasi thought that was a long way to walk, but when he was half way there, somebody on the radio changed the location. He had to turn around and walk back and, before he reached the new location, they changed it again. It was frustrating. Then, somewhere on Church Street, he ran into Mario Zoavic, from the A-Team (Apprehension Team). Mario was the first ESU cop he'd seen in nearly two hours. It was an incredible feeling to see him. Zoavic was driving the CARV-Truck (Construction Accident Response Vehicle), and he said, "Come on, Frank. Jump in the truck with me."

They drove through the financial district, down the streets that were still passable. Then they heard the voice of Sergeant John Lambkin of One-Truck on the radio ordering all ESU personnel and equipment to muster at the North Cove Marina.

THE SECOND RESPONDERS

Sergeant Lambkin lived upstate, in a suburbia neighborhood somewhere in Rockland County. He was part of the wave of second responders. They were the guys who were off-duty and at home, enjoying the day off, sleeping late. Lambkin was scheduled to do a "4 to 12" that day, but September 11th was his son's birthday, plus he was in the middle of painting two rooms in his house, so he took the day off to be with his son and finish his chores.

The First Responders

Lambkin woke up early and put his son on the school bus, came home, sat down in front of the TV sipping his coffee, and just as so many others in America, he put on the news. The first Tower had already been struck and it was burning as a bon fire. Wow, he thought, the Fire Department really has their hands full today. Then a second plane hit the second Tower. He put down his coffee cup, wrote a little note to his wife, and called Mike Hanson and Charlie Deluchio, two of his buddies who lived near him in Rockland and who were also off that day. Mike and Charlie, it turned out, didn't have the TV on and didn't know about the two plane crashes. Lambkin said, "There's been an attack at the World Trade Center. Grab your gear; we're goin' to work."

The three men jumped in a car and raced down Palisades Parkway to the George Washington Bridge, closed to traffic. They flashed their shields, and the cop on the bridge let them through the barricades. On the upper ramp they looked down and saw the massive, black smoke over the tip of Manhattan. They exited from the bridge into Manhattan and connected to the FDR Drive, also closed to traffic—all lanes empty, except for emergency vehicles and off duty cops and firemen trying to get to work. From the FDR they went cross town and pulled up the block on 21st Street, to the 13th Precinct and One-Truck's quarters. The precinct cops had cleared the street for ESU because they knew this was what ESU does: rescue people and handle big jobs.

Lambkin, Hanson, and Deluchio ran inside and grabbed what they thought they'd need: uniforms, hard hats, harnesses, and safety equipment. They left the big equipment behind. They figured at this stage of the game it would be search and rescue and the recovery of major body parts.

The precinct cops brought vans up to the door, all gassed up and ready to go, and Lambkin, Hanson, Delucchio together with a few other guys who had just shown up at quarters, jumped on board and drove the vans downtown. As they got closer and closer to the Trade Center, everything hit them smack in the face: the debris, the smoke, the mass exodus from Lower Manhattan. They pulled the van to the curb and parked it somewhere on the Westside. They were fifteen blocks from the impact area and even that far away they still had to tread through six to ten inches of cement dust.

When the three men reached West and Chambers Street, they met up with Amendolare, Allen, Norman, Mack, and DeMarco, who were covered from head to toe in dust. Lambkin hadn't seen the devastation of the Trade Center yet, and DeMarco warned, "John, its bad. Real bad." DeMarco looked shaken up, and the tone in his voice made Lambkin go cold inside. He had always considered DeMarco one of the calmest and most laid-back guy he knew. There could be bullets flying passed his head and he'd just shrug and say matter-of-factly, "Oh. They're shootin' at us." But now, he knew for DeMarco to be upset they had to be in for some long, long days.

Lambkin kept walking south. Somewhere near the North Cove Mariner, Inspector Wasson grabbed him. Since Lambkin was one of the fresher bodies, he said, "John, I'm putting you in charge of the recall. We need an account. We're missing alotta people."

Missing a lot of people? His heart sank and his mind got stuck wondering who was missing and where they might be. But he didn't want to be thinking like that, so he got busy on the radio and called everyone in. "All ESU units muster at the Police Memorial, Liberty Street, North Cove Mariner, by the water. Forthwith."

Slowly, the men started dragging their bodies into the park as if they were pulling balls and chains. DeMasi arrived and jumped out of the truck. It was a wild feeling for him to see all the Emergency cops there. He saw his partner, Nessenthaler, whom he hadn't seen since the first Tower went down. Then there was Garvey in his white T-shirt, looking a little shaky and sitting on the edge of the three-foot high stone wall with water pouring over it into a pool.

When Stefanakos walked into the park, a group of guys leaning against the wall suddenly straightened up in amazement and exclaimed "Holy shit, you're alive!"

Stefanakos was shocked anyone would think he was dead. "Of course, I'm alive,"

When anybody walked into the park and saw their friends and colleagues, it felt as one big homecoming. Everybody was in a state of shock, and they hugged everyone they came across. Stefanakos looked around and saw that Tommy Langone and Paul Talty had never made it to the Police Memorial, but it never occurred to him they were really gone. He only knew they weren't *here*, yet.

When it looked as though everybody who was going to show up had shown up, Lambkin had the men fall into formation against the granite wall in numerical order according to their command: One-Truck, Two-Truck, all the way up to Ten-Truck. The bosses went up and down the line, counting heads and writing names, and then they brought the rosters to Wasson and Lambkin.

Roll call was eerie. The men stood in gloomy silence and listened to the names of the missing being called over the radio.

"Sergeant Gillis on the air?" No answer.

"Ronnie Kloepfer on the air?"

Oh, no. Don't tell me Ronnie's gone, sighed DeMasi.

The command post at Church and Vesey was now abandoned. When the first Tower fell, it spilled tons of paper into the streets. When the second Tower fell, the fire in the building fell with it and ignited all the paper. Trucks were going up in flames and Winkler, Lutz, and few of the other guys were running around with fire extinguishers trying to save what vehicles they could.

Winkler didn't go to the North Cove Mariner. He couldn't be bothered with all this moving around. There were times Winkler wished he had taken the sergeant exam and ascended through the ranks to captain or inspector. Then he'd have some clout in a situation as this. He certainly wouldn't be keeping forty guys around for a roll call. As soon as he had seven or eight men, he'd put them on a team and send them back in for search and rescue. As soon as the next seven or eight guys showed, he'd put them on another team and send them back in, and so on.

Of course it wasn't that Winkler didn't want to know who was missing. He was constantly calling a roll call over the radio. He knew some guys would never answer, but he kept calling them anyway. Sometimes a guy would be called and five minutes would go by and suddenly he'd be there, "Yeah, yeah. I'm here."

"What about these guys?" and he'd mention names of those who hadn't responded.

"I don't know."

Then they'd come back on the radio, "Yeah, I got [so and so] over here."

And this went on all day.

By the time the roll call was finished at the Police Memorial they now had a rough idea who was missing. "Okay, guys. We're going to divide into teams and go back to the Towers," said the bosses. It was time to go find these guys.

Lambkin sent a few teams out to retrieve tools and weapons from the trucks parked around the perimeter of the Trade Center but were so severely damaged they couldn't be driven to the park. They brought the tools and handed them out to the men and secured the weapons in other undamaged trucks.

Now the guys were broken down into teams consisting of one boss and eight cops. Stefanakos and Winwood were put on a team with a boss who was new to the unit. He marched his men out of the park, east on Liberty Street.

All morning since the radio transmission of the first plane crash, Stefanakos had been walking around in a dream. Now he felt awake. Ordinary reality was returning in bits and pieces. First, the sounds came back. Nothing specific; nothing he could put his finger on. Radio chatter, somebody talking behind him, a pebble kicked up under his boot. There were sounds that weren't there anymore, like traffic. No honking horns, no engines revving and then stopping at a red light. Then the smells came back—of something burning. It smelled metallic and phosphorus, and it settled in the back of his throat as puke, except he couldn't bring it up.

Then just as he was making a left turn at Greenwich Street on Liberty, the Trade Center came into view and his stomach turned over. All he saw was a massive pile of what was once the Towers and the standing piers sprouting from the ground as a bombed out cathedral. It reminded him of the last scene in *Planet of the Apes* when Charlton

The First Responders

Heston turned a jagged corner of a sea cliff wall and saw the Statue of Liberty broken in half on the beach.

The teams continued down Greenwich and then came to a halt at the perimeter of the Trade Center. They gazed at the pile as if to pay homage in front of a funeral pyre. It was a massive rat's nest of steel—twisted metal on top of twisted metal. The heat was unbearable, and it hit them in the face as a blast from a furnace. Worried looks spread over the sergeants' faces as they surveyed the terrain. What could they do? They realized that, given their hand tools and the state of the collapse, there was *nothing* they could do until the arrival of heavy equipment. The teams withdrew and then dispersed, awaiting further orders.

Lambkin didn't want to disperse, so he went looking for Winkler. Perhaps they could put their heads together and figure something out. He found him by the Woolworth Building on Broadway and Spruce. After some of the paper fires were put out, Winkler and Lieutenant Reardon set up a temporary headquarters there. Lambkin asked Winkler, "Kenny, is there anything you learned at Oklahoma City that can help us here?"

Winkler had been part of the FEMA Urban Search and Rescue (US&R) New York Task Force One and he had spent a month in Oklahoma City going through the rubble of the Murrah Federal Building after it had been car-bombed by two members of a white supremacist militia group. There are 28 teams in the US&R program. New York City is NY-TF 1, comprised of FDNY firefighters and NYPD-ESU cops. Every month the names rotate, waiting to respond to a disaster.

"The first thing is everyone has to work in a one-to-one buddy system," said Winkler. "Nobody goes anywhere without anyone else knowing." That was crucial information, because the pile was so dangerous and unstable it would have been easy for someone to slip and fall down a void and never be seen again.

At this point, the commanding officer of ESU decided to move the temporary headquarters to two different locations, one to the north of the Trade Center and one to the south. Lambkin and Winkler tried to set up a temporary headquarters on the south side. They went up and down Vesey and Liberty Street looking for a building to use, but every time they found what they thought would be a likely spot, somebody would say it was unsafe and it was going to collapse. They headed south on Church Street, one block past of what was left of the South Tower, and then another block south of the Burger King on the corner of Liberty Street. Then they went west down a little road and took over one of the two American Stock Exchange buildings on Broad Street.

The hardest part was when Lambkin and his team started climbing onto the pile. They went looking for voids—"pockets" or "honeycombs" inside a collapsed area where somebody could have slipped, fallen inside, and still be alive; but every time his team started to work their way into a location that looked likely, somebody would start screaming over the radio, "Come down here! We may have a possible!" And Lambkin would pull out and troop down and across and up and around just to get to the other side of the pile only to find out it was a false alarm.

Beaury wanted to go back to the ruins to look for Sergeant Curtin and D'Allara. He led two cops, Richard Miller and Sergeant Clay White back over to the Customs House and told them his story. He showed them the ladder he had climbed down and he pointed to what was left of the building that, by this time, was completely engulfed in flames.

The guys who had been directly in the vicinity of the collapse started to feel their aches and pains. Amendolare's heart was racing, Norman still had something in his left eye, and DeMarco had a pretty bad cut on his leg. They went to Saint Vincent's Hospital, but when they arrived, the nurses wouldn't let them come into the ER until they were decontaminated. They made them stand in a small cubbyhole that was practically out on the street. They had to remove their clothes and gun belts and put them in a bag and then wrap themselves in a sheet.

When they finally went inside they were stunned to see the emergency room was empty. There weren't any injured people. You'd think this was a good sign, but it wasn't. Maybe there were a few rescue workers here and there getting their eyes washed out, but as the nurse glumly said, "Not too many coming in."

Norman's cornea was scratched and his eyes were irritated and half-closed. The only advice the doctor could give him was to stay out of "smoky environments." Norman looked out the window of the examination room and all he could see were smoking buildings. He said, "Where do you think I'm goin' after this?"

The doctor caught himself, as if he had forgotten the obvious (which he had!) and said, "Oh, yeah. That's right."

When Norman was ready to leave the hospital, the nurses gave him an old sweater and a funny colored pair of flood pants from their pile of donated homeless clothes, and then he went down to the front desk to get his gun. The lieutenant who was handling the signs-in and the signs-out gave him a hard time about getting any of his stuff back.

"It has to be decontaminated," said the lieutenant.

"Well, what's ever on that gun," said Norman. "I ate it."

Then the lieutenant went on about how Norman couldn't be allowed to leave the hospital until a psychiatrist had debriefed him. Norman was thinking, *There's too much work to be done to waste time talking to a shrink.*

Norman ignored the lieutenant's warning and walked out of the hospital. He felt as a vagabond in the mismatched clothes, his pants too short and his gun belt slung around his hips, but he couldn't give a damn what he looked like. He flagged down a taxi and went back to his command at One-Truck, changed into a clean uniform, and returned to the Trade Center.

The hospitals in general had the idea they had to psychiatrically debrief every cop who walked through the door. That was the last thing on anybody's mind. One of the officers, Bob Brady from Nine-Truck, had a bad dose of dust inhalation. He was taken uptown by ambulance to Saint Luke's Hospital, two blocks east of the Henry Hudson Parkway on a six city-block radius from 114th to 120th Street, with Amsterdam Avenue on its east side, Broadway on its west side. The nurses took him to a room and told him not to move because they were sending for a psychiatrist to talk to him. In his mind, he thought *Patch me up and get me out of here so I can go back down to the Trade Center.* In walked a psychiatrist who looked as though she was barely twenty years old. She didn't know what to ask, and the whole time she was fumbling with her text book questionnaire, Brady had his eye on the door trying to calculate the shortest escape route. As a diversion, he asked, "While I'm here, can I give blood?"

"I'll go find out," said the psychiatrist. The minute she left the room, Brady ran out the door and into the hospital parking lot at 114th Street and Amsterdam Avenue. What he saw outside looked as the end of the world. There were people running in all directions as bees fleeing a kicked over beehive. In the midst of all this mayhem was a panic-stricken police captain.

"They're bombing the emergency rooms!" shouted the captain. "They're bombing the emergency rooms! We gotta get outta here!"

Brady didn't know where the captain got the idea there were bombs in the emergency rooms, but just in case he was right, he thought it might be a good idea to take some kind of defensive measure. The captain, however, was too shaken up to make a decision, so Brady took charge.

"Okay, we'll get through this," said Brady, in a reassuring tone.

"We gotta get outta here!" screamed the captain.

"Captain, let me have your radio."

Brady didn't have his gun belt, because when he had boarded the ambulance to go up town to St. Luke's, he had given his gun and radio to his partner, Tommy Gilliam, for safekeeping. The captain handed his radio to Brady.

"Central, give me two sanders on the corner of 114th and Amsterdam," said Brady to the dispatcher.

Within minutes, two sanitation trucks showed up. They must have been around the corner the whole time. Brady told the captain to put a sander on each side of the street and assign a cop to the corner; that way the street would be blocked. This was the best Brady could do for him, but the captain was so out of it he didn't even notice when Brady put the radio back in his hand.

Brady took off on foot to get back to the Trade Center. He was all the way uptown (St. Luke's is at least six miles north), but he managed to hitch a ride on an ambulance half way there. From the random radio transmissions he heard around him, he pieced together that ESU had been sent to Stuyvesant High School, and he headed over there. The minute he walked through the school doors he saw everyone standing around with long, gloomy faces and knew something else was wrong. He was afraid to ask. He didn't want to know if there was something worse than two buildings coming down. Then, one of the guys from his command, Davey Adams, walked up to him and said, "We're missing alotta guys."

Brady said, "Wha'd'ya mean 'missing'?"

"They're not answering their radios," said Adams, dismally.

Brady's heart sunk. Strangely, the first thing he thought about were all the fire trucks in front of the building. He had a sickening feeling all those fire trucks had been crushed and all the firemen had been killed in them. Then he thought about how earlier that morning, when he was first coming into the City, he had gotten stuck in the Brooklyn-Battery Tunnel for ten or fifteen minutes until he could pull a lane. He remembered as he was coming out of the tunnel, a traffic agent who was trying to get him through traffic kept yelling, "We need a blanket for the body parts!" Legs, arms, and organs were falling from the Towers and landing all over the place. Brady looked at him wide-eyed and shrugged, not as a brush off, but as if to say there wasn't anything he could do. Now, he was thinking the traffic agent must be dead, buried under the collapse of the two Towers. Brady felt bad, and he was sorry he hadn't had a blanket.

Slowly but surely, the guys trickled into the school and gathered in the auditorium. Others were standing along the wall and huddling near the door to watch who would walk in next. Occasionally, someone would begin weeping and exit the auditorium and go to the street to stare out at the smoky skyline and listen to the windows popping from the fires in the buildings.

When Stefanakos entered the auditorium he looked to the back wall and the first person he saw was Mike O'Brien. O'Brien worked the Second Squad and had been at home, but as many off duty cops that day, he rushed to the Trade Center. He grabbed Stefanakos in a hug and both men cried. O'Brien said, "They had you as dead."

Twice in one day somebody had Stefanakos dead. But that was what it was like: rumors and more rumors. Stories were floating around this guy was gone and that guy was gone.

"Paul and Tommy are missing," said Stefanakos.

"Paul just had a baby," O'Brien answered with disbelief.

"Mike, I don't know what's going on,"

Stefanakos realized he was still wearing all his gear. He had on the Scott-pack, rappel equipment, and the Roco harness he'd been wearing since nine o'clock that morning. It was four o'clock in the afternoon and he didn't even know it was on. Usually when he'd remove his gear, it was as "Thank God, it's off." But when he dropped his gear to the floor, this time there was no feeling of relief.

When Beaury walked into the high school, everybody turned around to look at him. They knew what he had been through; still, the immediate reaction was shock. Beaury strode off to be by himself and sat down in the back row of the auditorium. He felt an overwhelming sadness, and as much as he tried to hold his emotions back, he could not. His best friend, Kloepfer was missing, and so was his partner, Valentin. Beaury's eyes were red and swollen, and his face was drained of color. Everybody kept walking up to him and saying, "You gotta go to the hospital." But Beaury refused to go. As far as he was concerned, he felt fine. Finally, just to shut everyone up, Beaury gave in and went to Beekman Hospital.

Earlier in the day, Beaury had hitched a ride to One-Truck and used their showers to wash up. When he removed his clothes, he noticed he had burns on his back, buttocks, and down the back of his legs. They were red and blistered and looked really bad. The only part of his back that wasn't burnt was in the middle where his air tank had pressed against his skin. Beaury ignored his burns and put the same dirty uniform back on. The mere touch of the stiff dark blue fabric stung his wounds as jabs of razor blades.

At the hospital, he didn't tell the nurses about his burns. He was afraid if anyone saw them they'd make him stay in the hospital. He'd have to grin and bear it. He let the nurses scrub out his eyes and place him on oxygen for two hours, and then, when nobody was looking,

The First Responders

he slipped out the door and made his way back to Styuvesant High School.

By late afternoon, in the auditorium of Styuvesant High School, the list of the missing was more or less completed. They weren't answering their radios and hadn't been seen by anyone or been treated at a hospital seemed to seal their fate. Mike Curtin, John D'Allara, Walter Weaver, Joe Vigiano, Vinny Danz, Rodney Gillis, Ronnie Kloepfer, Brian McDonnell, Steve Driscoll, Jerome Dominguez, John Coughlin, Santos Valetin, Paul Talty, and Tommy Langone were all missing.

Stefanakos was in total disbelief. These were guys he knew for years and saw every day on jobs. They were his ESU idols. He had known Vinny Danz since 1991, when they both worked together as Housing cops in the Bike Unit at PSA 9 in Queens, and then later, at Housing's Emergency Rescue Service, and then ESU's Three-Truck in the Bronx. And he had known Coughlin since 1993 when he was his supervisor in Housing's ERS. This morning, Stefanakos was just on the phone with him. They liked to talk politics and sports, and reminisce the same old, funny stories.

Stefanakos had also been on the phone this morning with Ronnie Kloepfer. It was a beginning-of-tour ritual for him to call around to the other trucks but for no other reason than to bust chops and say hello. They were trying to guess what antics Ronnie's partner, Santos Valentin, who was the unit's in-house comedian, would get himself into today. Stefanakos asked, "What's Santos up to?"

"He's in full form," said Kloepfer. "He's dressin' up in his tutu today."

Rumors were flying around 123 cops were gone and 700 firemen and 12,000 civilians were also missing. There was even a rumor the entire personnel of the 1st Precinct had been sucked into the abyss. At ESU, what they knew for a fact, though not quite *that* dire, was bad enough: fourteen guys were gone. At one point Stefanakos saw Inspector Wasson. He knew the Inspector and Paul Talty were childhood friends and he wanted to break the news to him. Wasson didn't know Paul was missing. When he heard the news he turned away and cried.

The Untold Story of the New York City Police Department & 9/11

The Bell 412 helicopter sat for hours on the pier in New Jersey waiting to transport injured people, but nobody called for a med-vac. At approximately five o'clock PM, Aviation was ordered to return to Floyd Bennett Field.

Sergeant Kennedy and Officer LaSala didn't want to go back to Brooklyn. They had just been standing by listening to the radio while their friends were going through hell. They heard Sergeant Hargrove on the radio trying to locate an officer from the Field who had chest pains, but nobody knew what hospital he had been taken to, so Kennedy volunteered to go look for him. He hitched a ride with some New Jersey State troopers who had been standing by at the pier, and LaSala asked the helicopter pilot to drop him off in Manhattan, in the chopper's return to Floyd Bennett. The FBI had control of Pier 34, at 34th Street and the West Side Highway, and they gave the police helicopter permission to land. LaSala jumped off here, slung his camera bag over his shoulder, ran to West Street and flagged down a passing patrol car from the 1st Precinct. They dropped him off somewhere around West Broadway and Chambers. As he was making his way over to Stuyvesant High School he heard a repetition of popping sounds that started off slow and then picked up speed as a string of firecrackers *Pop! Pop! Pop! Pop! Pop!*—and then a rumbling. He looked down West Broadway and saw Building Seven imploding to the ground. LaSala scrambled for his video camera, but by the time he put the viewfinder up to his eye, he only caught the tail end of the collapse and a cloud of dust.

At Floyd Bennett Field, a second Bell 412 helicopter had been prepped for air rescue, but it never got off the ground. Shortly after ten o'clock this morning, police officers John Busching, Tommy Kirklava, Tony Conte, and Daryl Summers were getting the ropes fastened and looped on the helicopter. Before they could finish the rig, the Commanding Officer of Aviation, Inspector Joseph Gallucci, ran across the airfield and told them the South Tower had collapsed and air rescue was canceled. He said the helicopter would now move to a med-vac platform. Since two of the four cops were paramedics and the other two were Emergency Medical Technicians (EMT), Gallucci divided them into two teams and told them to stand by until they were needed to airlift the injured. For the next God knows how many hours, Busching and the others paced back and forth on the tarmac listening to the radio and watching the smoke above Lower Manhattan drift over to Brooklyn.

Nobody called for a med-vac; and by late afternoon, they were getting antsy. When the helicopters returned to base, Busching, Conte, Kirklava, and Summers, met the pilots to hear their eyewitness report. The news was bleak, and they knew a lot of their guys were missing. They asked Gallucci to let them go so they could get down to Lower Manhattan, but Gallucci said it wasn't up to him: the only person who could change their assignment was the Commanding Officer of ESU, Inspector Wasson. The only way they were going to find him was to fly into Manhattan and look for him, and that was what they did. The helicopter landed on the grassy area by the river next to Stuyvesant High School. As luck would have it, standing in front of the school was Wasson. The guys ran over and asked him if he needed their help, and Wasson, said, "Absolutely. I need more people." Since two of the four cops were paramedics and the other two were EMTs, he spilt them into two teams, one paramedic and one EMT on each team, and sent them out to do search and rescue.

By the afternoon, the FEMA equipment arrived at the Trade Center. FEMA personnel had already been in New York City since Monday, September 10th. They had been setting up their equipment at Pier 92 for a scheduled September 12th bio-terrorist war game exercise. Immediately, the equipment was packed up and moved to Stuyvesantt High School.

At approximately, 5:00 PM, Sergeant Hargrove and his men from Ten-Truck were ordered by the ESU Command Center to take the FEMA equipment from the school and bring it down to the Trade Center and unload it somewhere near a playground that had racket courts. This was about the only way to describe where things were. The street signs were twisted back as pretzels, the area was unrecognizable, and landmarks were the only points of reference.

When they found the playground, Stefanakos saw a payphone on a corner and he made a third call home. He spoke to his brother, Jim, and he wanted to let him know he was all right But before he could get a word out he heard behind him the sound of glass popping and saw people running in the street. Building Seven was coming down! Stefanakos said a quick "talk to you later" to his brother, hung up the phone and ran.

The collapse of Building Seven forced the police to retreat again. They returned to the high school, and for the next two hours, they sat in the auditorium and waited for instructions. By nightfall, ESU made a third attempt to get into the site. This time, instead of the men walking the six blocks to the Trade Center, they boarded MTA buses and drove down. There were no streetlights or lights coming from storefronts or windows of office buildings. There was no electricity in Lower Manhattan at all, and every street was pitch black. Nobody could see where they were going and everybody had to use hand-held porta lights to get around.

Sergeant Hargrove, Stefanakos, and Winwood were teamed up with Sergeant Mike McGinnis and officer Eddie Torres from Two-Truck. Their orders were to go back to the playground—where they had left the FEMA equipment—and now move the equipment over to Financial Center One, the forty-story office building on the corner of West Street and Liberty. The building had structural damage, with blown-out windows, cracked walls, black soot covering every inch of every floor and ceiling. They brought the equipment into the lobby, unloaded it, grabbed whatever tools they could carry, and walked down Liberty to Greenwich Street. They went up and down the edge of the debris pile, poking and probing but without finding a good spot to dig in.

All day Stefanakos kept his head down. In his peripheral vision he noticed an orange light. Then for the first time since this morning Stefanakos looked up and saw the horizon. Everything was on fire—he never noticed it before. All the buildings on the perimeter of the Trade Center were devastated. The Verizon Building on Vesey Street was roaring in flames, and next to it was the German Bank; its center had caved in and the steel columns were still inlaid. One Liberty Plaza on

The First Responders

Church Street was on fire, Bankers Trust and the Greek Church, Saint Nicholas, on Liberty Street, were also on fire.

At two o'clock in the morning, everybody was dismissed for a four-hour break. The NYPD would be spilt into two squads: a day squad and a night squad. ESU would start a morning shift at 6:00 AM and an evening shift at 6:00 PM. Precinct and other police personnel would start two hours earlier and leave two hours later. It would be, at a minimum, twelve-hour tours, and no days off, indefinitely.

As Sergeant Hargrove was leaving, he received word the families of the missing police officers had arrived at One Police Plaza. Facing the families was going to be tough. He went to headquarters and found Paul Talty's father, John Sr., and his four brothers, Kevin, John, Mark, and Steven, waiting on the second floor. They hadn't heard from him all day and they wanted to know where he was. His wife, Barbara, was not told he was missing. She was home with a two-week old baby.

His father sat there, shaking his head in a slow swing of disbelief, and he said, "Why would he go into a building like that?"

His family didn't know the type of work he did. Talty was very quiet about his job; he left work at work. They knew he was a cop, but they didn't seem to know he was an Emergency cop, and even if they did know, they didn't understand what he did. Talty was a carpenter before he joined the police department. With his dark curly hair and gentle demeanor, he was better suited for a job with a slower pace. The only reason he became a cop was because the carpentry union and the trades weren't doing that well. He wanted steady work, security and benefits for his family. His cousin was Sergeant John English who worked at Six-Truck in Brooklyn, and that put the bug in his ear to become a cop. And Wasson was a long time friend and he helped get Talty in the unit.

Talty was a fairly new guy in ESU. He had only been in the unit for a year and a half and had switched squads midway from the "First" to the "Third." Everybody at Ten-Truck were still just getting to know him. They knew he was a big family man with a new baby at home. They knew he loved the ocean. They knew he was an expert carpenter and had a side business with his brother, Kevin, who was a contractor.

Hargrove tried to explain to Talty's father that his son wanted to be there. "I saw no fear in his eyes," he said. "The officer he was with, Tommy Langone, was probably one of the most experienced Emergency Service officers you'd ever wanna deal with. They had two-hundred feet of lifeline. They could've rappelled twenty stories out of that building if they had the opportunity to get out."

As Ten-Truck was packing up to leave for the night, Stefanakos suddenly remembered something that happened on Monday morning. It popped into his mind with such force he gave out a gasp.

On the morning of September 10th, Langone was standing in front of the bathroom sink at work. He had his shirt off and was shaving. Langone was only thirty-seven years old but he had silver white hair. As a matter of fact, he'd had silver white hair practically since high school. His revved up metabolism had turned every hair on his body white. Even the hair on his back was white.

Langone's easy going personality and Speedy Gonzales idiosyncrasies made him an easy target for teasing, and the guys would jump at any opportunity to do so. That morning in the bathroom, Stefanakos snuck up behind him with an electric shaver and started carving "E-10" (short for Emergency Truck-10) into Langone's back, but he was doing a lousy job—he kept nicking him and Langone kept jumping, and yelling, "Ah, stop! Cut it out!" By the time Stefanakos was finished, the red from the shaving had raised "E-10" through the white hair.

Stefanakos took Langone from the bathroom and paraded him around quarters to show the other guys. Everyone had a good laugh, and Langone felt as a branded man. "That's just great, fellas," he said, sheepishly. "Now, if I ever get lost you can find me."

Now, here it was, twenty-four hours later, and they were standing in a bleak, official-looking room on the second floor of One Police Plaza breaking the news to his wife, Joann, her husband was missing. Stefanakos turned to his partner, Winwood, shook his head, and said, "I can't believe he said that."

The First Responders

Maggie McDonnell had gotten word her husband, Brian, from One-Truck, was in a hospital in New Jersey. He had been in the South Tower with Sergeant Gillis and was on the list of the missing. She was relieved and grateful her husband had been found, but then the members of her support group came back, and said, "No, it wasn't him." They had made a mistake. There had been some confusion with a Port Authority police officer that had the same name as her husband. Maggie was on an emotional roller coaster ride that night.

Billy Beaury went back to his command, Seven-Truck in Brooklyn. He took another shower and tried to get some sleep. It wasn't the comforts of home, but at least he had clean clothes to put on. In the morning, his sergeant ordered him to go home, but Beaury was stubborn, and the guys at the truck knew he would be, so they figured they'd have to trick him to get him to go. Tony Romano, one of the men who lived near Beaury all the way out in Suffolk County, said, "Yeah, I'm gonna drive you home and I'll pick you up when I come back in tonight."

Beaury said, "Okay, all right." So, he went home.

That evening he waited for Romano to show up at his house—he expected him to come around five or five-thirty—but, of course, he never showed. Well, Beaury guessed, that was part of the plan. He knew they didn't want him to go back until he saw a doctor. And he knew he really needed the time off, but he didn't want to take it.

The next morning, Beaury—who always had some of the finest rides you ever saw in your life and who always had an extra one in some various stage of repair because they were always breaking down—hopped into one of his jalopies and drove back down to the Trade Center.

What was he going to do? A lot of the missing guys were his friends, and nobody was going to keep him away. Because of his emotional state, Beaury spent the next nine months of the recovery sitting it out by the tents on West Street. He couldn't bear to be at Ground Zero, but he couldn't bear to stay away.

Above - Lt. John Murphy (left), injured by falling debris, and P.O. Steven Lanoce (right). Photo by Allan Tannenbaum.

Below - One of many police vehicles "RMP" crushed by falling debris from the Twin Towers.

The First Responders

Above - ESU police officers and K-9 working in the pile at Ground Zero. The sign with arrows reads: "Air Craft Parts. Plane Parts".

Below - ESU officers board a truck from Stuyvesant High School for the ride down to Ground Zero.

The Closing Ceremony: May 30th 2002, the last beam of the Twin Towers is removed from Ground Zero. It was covered in purple bunting and began a three-mile journey through the streets of Manhattan before being driven to Kennedy Airport. There it would be kept in a hangar, maybe one day to be used in the construction of a monument

The First Responders

Right - May 30th, 2002. An elderly fireman and the "horse with no rider." Photo: David Margules.

Below Left - October 1996. PO Richard Winwood, PO Steven Stefanakos (standing, l-r) and PO John D'Allara (kneeling) at Camp Smith Specialized Training School, preparing for helicopter rappel.

Below Right - PO Richard Winwood (left) and PO Steven Stefanakos (right), ESU Ten-Truck, at Ground Zero.

The Untold Story of the New York City Police Department & 9/11

Above - After the collapse of the South Tower, NYPD helicopter lands on a New Jersey pier to save fuel for med-vac.

Below - Police Officer Jerome Dominguez, ESU Three-Truck.

The First Responders

Above - Police Officers Steven Stefanakos (left) Tommy Langone (right), ESU Ten-Truck, at a job in the Bronx.

Below - Medal Day: Team Five receive the Medal for Valor on January 18th, 2003 (front row-l to r) Bobby Steinman, Richard Hartigan, Mike Garcia, Steven Lanoce, Lt. John Murphy (back row-l to r) Evan Schwerner, Chief Thomas Purtell, and David Brink. (photo credit: Dean Steinman).

Above - October 1999. Police Officer Paul Talty (left) and Inspector Ronald Wasson (right) at the ESU graduation ceremony at Floyd Bennett Field.

Below - Promotion Party for Sgt. McKenna, August 2001: (Rear row, l-r) Paul Talty, Tom Langone, Randy Miller, Sgt. Mike McKenna, Tony Sperd, Rich Winwood, Sgt. Paul Hargrove. (Front row, l-r) Robert Grogan, Steven Stefanakos, and Stephen Blihar.

The First Responders

Above - John Vigiano Sr. lifts his grandson during a street-sign dedication for Det. Joseph Vigiano, ESU Two-Truck. Photo: David Margules.

Below - Police Officer Walter "Wally" Weaver, ESU Three-Truck.

Above - Sergeant Timothy Farrell (left) and Police Officer Kenny Winkler (right) take a break by the ESU tents on West Street. *Below* - Near the end of the clean-up. Engineers clear the pit at Ground Zero. Notice the slurry-wall in the background.

The First Responders

22
HOAXES AND BOMB SCARES

On September 11th, at 5:28 in the afternoon, Building Seven collapsed. It was only the second building in history that completely collapsed due to a fire. The first was a building in Pennsylvania that burned for sixteen hours. Building Seven caught on fire from debris falling from the Towers and burned for only seven hours before tumbling down.

The water lines in and around the World Trade Center had been damaged by the collapse of the Twin Towers. At the heart of the largest city in the world there now was a fire raging out of control. Building Seven stood in close proximity to other high rise buildings: the Federal Building was to the right, Verizon to the left, and 30 West Broadway was behind—and there was no water to put the fire out.

There are two types of an "attack" the fire department uses to extinguish a building fire: interior and exterior. In an interior attack, hose lines and manpower are inside the building. And for an exterior attack, the firemen do what is called "surround and drown": there are no firemen inside the building, but instead, they employ a "steady-mass-upstream" operation, spraying water into the building using a large dam and a hose with multi-versal nozzles, deck guns, or power otters.

The Fire Department, however, did not make either an interior or an exterior attack on Building Seven because there was two things they didn't have that day: unlimited access to the building and water to put out the fire. There was nothing to do but pull out the manpower and let it burn.

The collapse of Building Seven chased away whatever scattered search teams were on the pile. If it was dangerous before, it was beyond being a death trap now. The whole area bounded by Liberty Street to Chambers and the West Side Highway to Broadway were deemed unsafe, and the fear of more buildings coming down kept most people back and everyone discouraged. All around the perimeter were thousands of uniforms that couldn't go anywhere. If there was anybody searching on the pile—and, there were a few stray souls—they were doing it at their own risk and without the knowledge of their colleagues or bosses.

Hoax calls had been coming in all day. Most of them were from people saying they were receiving cellphone calls from loved ones trapped inside the collapse. Technicians from Verizon came down to the Trade Center and tried to triangulate the calls but they were getting nothing.

Some of the hoaxes were bomb scares. Six blocks away from the Trade Center there was a commercial truck parked on a street. It had the skyline of Lower Manhattan decaled on the side, and somebody had taken a black magic-marker and drawn a plane exploding into the Twin Towers. The residents were frightened and thought the truck was a bomb and the whole block had to be evacuated. On 9/11, more than a hundred bomb scares had been reported, including one at the Empire State Building

An anonymous caller stated they had received a cellphone call from somebody trapped inside one of the floors of Building Four. The fire chief in charge of the area picked two police officers, Richard Miller and Franco Berarducci, and a fireman, named Mike Brady, to go inside and investigate. There wasn't much left of the building. The interior was brittle and scorching hot. They were able to climb as high as the third floor. Miller stopped and said, "Who could survive this?" Not even the fireboxes were intact. "We're goin' to get killed for nothing."

Brady didn't want to stop and he was angry. He grabbed Miller and said, "I'm lookin' for my best friend, John Vigiano."

Miller answered back with the same fervor, "And I'm looking for Joe and everybody else."

Miller and the fireman were talking about the Vigiano brothers. John was a firefighter at Engine132 in Bedford-Stuyvesant, Brooklyn, last seen in the South Tower. Joe was a cop on Sergeant Curtin's team.

The fireman relaxed and released his grip. He knew Miller was right. The building was a deathtrap. They started the walk back down. Everything they touched collapsed and broke apart. After balancing on broken staircases and tiptoeing through burning floors, they managed to exit safely. The fire chief was waiting outside for them, but they didn't have any good news to tell him. This was just an example of one of the many bogus calls that unnecessarily risked the lives of rescue workers.

Then there was a twenty-four-year old woman who ran to her local precinct and said her husband was a Port Authority police officer and had just called her over his cellphone to say he was trapped in the middle of the pile somewhere near the globe. The rescue workers scrambled to find her husband, but it turned out to be another hoax. The name she gave for the trapped officer didn't match with anyone on the roster of members of the department. Under intense questioning, the woman finally broke down and admitted she was making it up. The woman was arrested and charged with reckless endangerment, obstructing fire operations, and filing a false police report.

Around eight o'clock in the evening another transmission came over the radio saying two Port Authority police officers were indeed trapped under the rubble of the South Tower. This one was for real.

8:00 PM: TRAPPED UNDER THE SOUTH TOWER

Chuck Sereika, a paramedic, never heard the radio call about the two buried cops. He didn't have a radio. He was out on the pile empty-handed except for his medical bag and a flashlight, picking his way through the rubble around the skeletal arches of what was left of the South Tower, when he heard someone calling for help. He followed the voice and, when he reached the spot where the yelling was coming from, he found a man in Marine camouflage fatigues standing on top of a knoll of smoldering debris. His name was Staff Sergeant David Karnes.

Karnes was five-foot-ten with a lean build. His face looked as though it was chiseled out of white marble. His skin was ghostly pale and his light-colored hair was shaved in a boot camp buzz cut. Above his angular high cheekbones were deep-set, piercing eyes, and he was looking at his wrist-watch as though he was making a mental note of how long it took the medic to climb up to him. The way Karnes looked was the way he was: precise and orderly.

Sereika asked Karnes what he was shouting about, and Karnes said,

"There's a couple of people down in a hole."

"All right."

"Come on," said Karnes. He moved fearlessly and effortlessly across the steel beams as a bird on a wire.

He led Sereika to the hole where they'd have to climb down. It was a six-foot drop to a narrow landing about three by three. Inside this hole was a small opening that led into a dark tunnel that sloped down into an oblivion of smoke. Karnes crouched, aimed his flashlight down the tunnel, and said, "Over there! Over there! Look at his hand!"

Sereika looked down the tunnel and he could hear one of the buried men talking. His name was Will Jimeno, but he couldn't be seen. It was as trying to find Waldo in a puzzle. He searched the dark with his flashlight for a good two minutes before he finally could make out the hand Karnes was talking about, hidden in the dark and dust.

When Sereika first saw Karnes he was shocked he was alone. He couldn't understand why there weren't dozens of men with shovels and picks digging these guys out. Instead, it was just this Marine who wasn't a Marine, anymore. He was an accountant from Connecticut who had taken his old platoon-sergeant uniform out of mothballs and driven to New York City to walk across the smoldering pile to this very spot.

Karnes' story is he arrived in Lower Manhattan in his little, red Porsche and parked it by Pace University across from City Hall and walked the three blocks to the Trade Center. He was confident no one would stop and question him in his military uniform. He'd stand up straight and look official, and that way he could walk freely through the scattered formations of firemen, the smoke and confusion.

At Church and Vesey Street he saw a group of six or seven military guys in camouflage fatigues. Karnes introduced himself to them and said, "I just got down here. Brief me on what's going on."

The military men said, "Well, Staff Sergeant, Building Seven came down and everybody has fallen back." They told him they had spent the day pulling bodies from the fringes of the pile but had avoided searches deep inside the epicenter due to continuous building collapses and fires.

The First Responders

That answer wasn't good enough for Karnes. He thought it was a good thing he was here. He knew the police would err on the side of safety. If nobody had the balls, then he'd walk to the center and do a search himself. He went up to a Marine sergeant who was standing with these military guys and said, "Take a walk with me."

Karnes wanted to walk to the Millennium Hotel. The Marine, whom Karnes identifies as Sergeant Thomas, first name unknown, didn't think this was a good idea. There were rumors the hotel was going to collapse. Reluctantly, he followed the Staff Sergeant.

The hotel was sitting as a lopsided birthday cake. Its windows were blown out and the bottom half of the building was singed black from a fireball that had hit it during the collapse. Fires were cooking and smoke was bellowing, and directly across the street from the hotel was the courtyard to the Trade Center.

Thomas was getting nervous, and he was whining about how the building was leaning and how they shouldn't be standing there. He wanted to leave at once. Karnes ignored him. He was in the middle of an epiphany. He was looking at the courtyard and he was watching the smoke open up from the center as a blossoming flower. To him, it was a God-thing. He could see the sun going down on the New Jersey side of the river. It was bright orange, and the silhouette of the buildings that made up the World Financial Center looked as a black paper cut-out pressed against the sky.

Karnes said to Thomas, "Hey, devil dog. I'm goin' in there and I want you to go with me."

Karnes walked across the street as a man on a mission. Thomas didn't want him to go in there alone, so he followed at his heels as an unwilling, but faithful puppy. Behind them was a platoon-size formation of firemen lined up and down Church Street. They were hooting and hollering at the two Marines to come back. Karnes, of course, ignored them. He kept walking straight, and soon the two men disappeared inside the cloud of smoke. From their vantage, however, the collapse site opened and they could see everything.

Karnes had been a platoon sergeant for sixteen years. He plotted a hasty patrol route in his mind. They'd start over by the North Tower and go along the Customs House and then work their way to the South Tower. As they walked, Karnes repeatedly cupped his hands around his mouth and yelled out at the top of lungs, "United States Marines, is anyone here? If you can hear us, yell or tap!" Then he'd stop and listen for something unnatural—a voice or a banging in codes—anything other than the crackling and popping of collapsing metal.

The two men moved along the North Tower depression and along the ramp. They passed the globe, dented as a bashed-in soccer ball, and Thomas took out his two-dollar disposable camera from his shirt pocket and took a picture.

It was getting dark, and Thomas wanted to leave. He said, "We're gonna die in here."

"Don't worry, Sergeant Thomas," said Karnes. "I have my Marine Corp Field flashlight right here with two D-cells." He patted the little flashlight with its ninety-degree elbow hanging out of his pocket.

Karnes turned his attention back to his mission to find a survivor. He put his hand around his mouth as a megahorn and called out again and again. Finally there was an answer. It was faint and muffled, but it was definitely a voice.

Karnes let out an evangelistic "Praise God!"

The feeling of success was overwhelming.

"Yell louder!" Karnes called out. "We're going to zero in on you!"

The buried men were shouting their heads off, and Karnes and Thomas ran to where they thought the voices were coming from. They yelled at the ground and the muffled cries led them to a hole.

"This is Staff Sergeant Karnes of the United States Marine Corp," Karnes announced down the hole. "Who do we have down there?"

"William Jimeno and Sergeant John McLoughlin!" the voice, which belonged to Jimeno, yelled back up. "From the Port Authority Police. PAPD!"

Now that Karnes had found survivors, he needed to get help. He made sure he got their names right, because in Karne's regimental way of thinking, it made sense if he gave the telephone operator the names of the two police officers, they'd believe he had really found two trapped men. He pulled out his pocket-size tablet of paper and a pen and bent

The First Responders

down on one knee and asked Jimeno to say his rank and full name. But the officer had a thick Spanish accent and Karnes couldn't understand him. "Hey, buddy," said Karnes. "Could you spell your name?"

Over and over again Karnes asked Jimeno to spell his name. Ten, twelve times. Then, with every 'i' dotted and every 't' crossed, he said a quiet prayer *Please God let this work* and turned on his cellphone.

Karnes didn't dial 911. He called his wife, Rosemary, in Connecticut. He gave her instructions that were exact, detailed, clear, and methodical. He said to her, "I'm in the center of the World Trade Center collapse. Nobody knows I'm down here. Me and another Marine found two trapped Port Authority police officers, and I need you to get rescue teams in here. When I hang up with you, I want you to call the operator and ask for an emergency patch through to the NYPD Command Center. I want you tell them to enter in from Church Street and go through the courtyard to where the gold sphere used to be, because it's still there and it's sitting on top of the rubble. Have them pass that about twenty meters and then bank south twenty meters and they'll see us."

He then gave her the names of the two police officers and said, "Make sure you tell them their names, Will Jimeno and Sergeant John McLoughlin, so they'll believe you."

Calling his wife, however, wasn't good enough. He had to make a second call to his sister, Joy, in Pittsburgh, Pennsylvania, and he gave her the same instructions.

Karnes told Thomas to stand in a conspicuous spot and use his flashlight to signal in the responding rescue teams. Then Karnes stood at attention, and with his eyes glued in a thousand-yard stare, he watched and waited for an army of rescuers to come across the twisted landscape. But when help did arrive, it was only one man hopping across the rubble—a lone paramedic who wasn't even a paramedic anymore, who had woken up that morning and seen what was happening on the news. He put on his expired uniform and his expired shield and grabbed his medical kit and came down to help.

Sereika had spent the whole day tagging behind a group of cops, but eventually he lost track of them and then hooked up with a volunteer fireman from Long Island. Then he lost him, and somewhere in the shuffle of rescue workers, Sereika found another fireman from the FDNY. The two men paired up and made their way on the pile and started a search. It was getting late and the sun was starting to set and they were losing light.

They heard Karnes shouting and headed in his direction, but halfway there the fireman stopped in his tracks, pointed straight ahead, and said, "It don't look too good that way." Then he pointed in the direction they had just come from and said, "Goin' back ain't a good idea, either."

The pile was dangerously unstable, with steel beams on top of steel beams that shifted and creaked under each step. The fireman was tittering on limbs of steel and razor sharp edges that cut his boots and pant legs.

"I gotta wife and two kids. I can't do this to 'em," said the fireman, nervously. He looked in all directions as though he was evaluating the best route out. Then he pointed in a direction that was neither toward Karnes nor the way back and added, "I'm goin' that way."

Sereika said he understood and it was okay if he left. So the fireman turned and walked out and left the paramedic deep inside the pile.

Sereika kept heading towards where Karnes was shouting. He was frightened walking over the rubble. He knew every step he took he was taking his life in his hands. One movement here or one movement there, and his foot could go plunging through a loose cinder block or high beam. But he had already made peace with himself he wasn't getting out alive.

The second Sereika's flashlight lit up Jimeno's hand at the bottom of the hole, he got down on his stomach and squeezed through the small opening and wiggled his way down the tunnel. It was dark and smoky. As he moved deeper, he had a nagging feeling again he wasn't coming out alive. Then he felt his cellphone pop out of his pocket and disappear in the dark. Sereika stopped to look for it. He reached around in the dust but he couldn't find it. *Goddamnit, now I can't even call for help when I know I'm gonna die!*

Suddenly, he heard somebody scrambling behind him. Sereika looked back and saw the circle of light from a flashlight and an Emergency cop crawling down the tunnel. It was Police Officer Scotty Strauss.

The First Responders

23 BURIED ALIVE

Scotty Strauss was part of the second wave of Emergency Service Units that had arrived at the Trade Center after the collapse of the Twin Towers. As many of the second responders, Strauss was off-duty and at home in Long Island when the attacks began. He packed some extra clothing and kissed his wife goodbye, because he knew he wasn't coming home for a long, long time. By 9:30 in the morning, all tunnels and bridges were closed to the public, but they still had not been cleared of rush-hour traffic. Strauss jumped in his car and joined a caravan of off-duty firemen and cops barreling behind the lights and sirens of a New York State trooper and made their way back into Manhattan.

By the time Strauss got to his ESU command at One-Truck between 2nd and 3rd Avenue on 21st Street, rescue equipment, police vehicles, and radios were scarce. It was a first come, first served basis, and he was out of luck. He grabbed the only vehicle available, and that was the Light-Truck, a flat bed truck mounted with high-powered searchlights. Other guys showing up at the same time had to go next door to beg, borrow, or steal an RMP from the precinct.

Strauss and the other off-duty cops from his unit—Jim Derby, Greg Welch, Kevin Keuchler, John McCarthy, Jim Monran, Paddy McGee, and Sergeant Gene O'Connor—were geared up with whatever equipment they could find and were ready to go. Suddenly, the pistol range instructors from the Academy started banging on the side door of One-Truck

Excitedly, they said, "We need big guns! We need to protect the building!"

The range cops distinguish themselves by wearing a light tan uniform. Although they carry side arms, the guys were asking for rifles, shotguns, and MP-5 semi-automated submachine guns.

Strauss had the impression that police headquarters had been moved uptown to the Academy. Major buildings were being evacuated: Gracie Mansion at 9:14 AM and, two minutes later, the United Nations, all municipal buildings, and the Empire State Building. At 9:30 AM, One Police Plaza lost its phone lines. Out of desperation, the police department threw wires from the windows and draped them across the street as tenement clotheslines and hooked them up to neighboring federal buildings.

One-Truck didn't have any "big guns" to give to the range cops. Everything they had was in their Big Truck, down at the Trade Center. The range cops returned to the Academy, empty-handed. One-Truck headed downtown, driving cross-town to the FDR Drive.

For Strauss, the ride down the FDR Drive was as a dream. Everything moved by in slow motion. Things would come up gradually, then suddenly zoom by. He looked down the highway and saw hundreds of dust-covered people running towards them. They drove slowly down the Pearl Street exit ramp, and the people swept around them as water swirling around a boulder in the middle of a stream. They abandoned their vehicles at the bottom of the ramp and made their way over to a mobilization point at City Hall Park. Other Emergency cops were arriving at the same time and, as they walked in the park, an ESU boss would point to a man and say, "You're tactical," and then point to another and say, "You're rescue." Sergeant O'Connor and his men—Strauss, Derby, and Welch—were assigned to rescue.

O'Connor turned to his team and said, "Everybody stick together. Go to Tac-g. We have no equipment. Let's go find some."

They grabbed Scott-packs off the BAT (Breathing Apparatus Truck) that Five-Truck brought in from Staten Island and walked across Broadway to the Trade Center.

They passed Saint Paul's Church and its old graveyard. (St Paul's is the little 18th century church opposite the Trade Center on Church Street and that everybody made a big deal of because they thought it had been saved by a miracle). When O'Connor and his men reached Church Street, they saw police vehicle after police vehicle on fire. The Big Truck from Nine-Truck was burning. REPs and RMPs were burning, and what wasn't on fire had been flattened as tin cans. Most of the cabinets on the trucks were blown open, their contents in flames. Strauss, Derby, and Welch were frantically trying to get to the equipment in spite of the fire and damage. They pulled out some of the rope bags, but they were blazing as candlewicks, and whatever bins they could get to had been picked clean.

The First Responders

They felt naked with no tools, but there was nothing to be done. They abandoned the search for equipment and made their way into the shopping mall promenade under the Trade Center. The entire area was roaring in flames. There were structures that had survived the initial collapse but were now coming down. A group of firemen were trying to drag a body out of the fire. It was a big, heavy man lying half in and half out of a plastic bag. The cops ran over and helped rig the body and, in one big heave-hoe, they pulled the body clear.

There was another level below the promenade connected to it by escalators. On this level was the station to the PATH trains (PATH trains are a special subway system connecting Manhattan with New Jersey under the Hudson River). O'Connor and his team tried to get to the train station, but the escalators were so badly twisted that there was no room to put their feet. They had to crawl down the steps until they could go no further. The bottom of the escalators and the train station were obliterated under a cave in of rubble. O'Connor took one look at this and ordered everyone out. The men spun around and crawled back up.

The rest of the day was nothing more than a frustrating picking through the fringe of the pile, looking inside voids and coming up with nothing. Officer Derby was trying to climb over some high beams when he slipped and snapped his ankle. He hobbled off and spent the rest of the day sitting it out in the ER.

Somewhere along the way Strauss went from Sergeant O'Connor's team over to Sergeant Timothy Adrat's team, and there were other guys with him: Sergeant Andy Oberfeldt, Officers Greg Matthius, Greg Welch and Paddy McGee. By 5:30 PM, Building Seven had come down and Buildings Four and Five were roaring as Roman candles. There was no water to put out the fires and everything was left to burn.

Adrat took his men south of Liberty Street. They did searches in some of the buildings that had been gauged out by the blast of the collapse. They went in and out of rooms, elevators, and basements marking doors with chalk to indicate they had already been checked. They climbed over debris, moving as steel balls in an arcade game, making their way around the pile and below the scaffolds. At sunset, they were exhausted and dirty, and all they wanted to do was catch their breath, but suddenly a fireman charged over to them, and they could see from his expression he was livid.

He ripped in with an incredible attitude, and yelled, "Yo! Two of your fookin' buddies got 'emselves stuck in the rubble. You fookin' guys are always fookin' 'round doin' whatever you fookin' like. I'm tired of this bullshit. They told everyone to get out but you fookin' guys never listen!"

"Whoa! Who's stuck?" Spoke up one of the officers. They had no clue what he was talking about. Radios were scarce and nothing was coming over.

"Two of *your* fookin' ESU buddies," said the fireman, incensed. "Up there in the fookin' pile." He made sure he put a little extra conviction on the word 'your'. That way it would be no mistaking who was screwing up. Apparently, the fireman had heard about the two police officers trapped under the rubble and assumed they were ESU.

It had been a long, miserable, depressing day, and they weren't in the mood for some barking fireman with a bug up his butt. One of the sergeants gave it back to him, and while differences of opinions were being exchanged, Strauss, McGee, and Welch did a one-eighty and headed to the forbidden zone. They raced into the pile, climbing over the debris with no idea where they were going.

The pile was as a mountain. The Trade Center itself was elevated from the street. In addition to that, there was all the debris from the collapsed Towers. The greatest amount of it was around the edges. To get to the top of the pile you had to climb over a large amount of rubble. If you were standing at the top, facing the center of what had been the plaza, it was as if you were looking down into a crater. When you were walking over the pile, you were at a constantly changing elevation off the street, some areas quite steep, others almost level.

Welch was leading the run; suddenly, he tripped and took a tumble.

"Greg, you okay?"

"Yeah, keep going!" said Welch. One of his pants legs was ripped up to his knee, and there was a long red gash on his pale skin. He clapped his hand to his wound and rocked forward. Welch was out of commission.

Strauss and McGee kept running. When they climbed to the top, they found themselves standing between two burning buildings. To the left was Building Four and to the right was Building Five, and in the distance they could see the globe sitting as a dented golf ball in the rubble. Suddenly, just below the globe, they saw a light moving back and forth as a SOS, and they took off in that direction.

A fire captain was standing in the rubble between them and the globe. He had his hands up, palms out, and he shouted, "Whoa, guys! Where're you goin'?"

"There's two guys stuck over there!" Strauss yelled to the fireman without breaking his run. "We gotta get to them!"

"You can't come in here," said the fireman, indignantly. "It's a collapse zone. Those buildings are comin' down."

But Strauss and McGee weren't about to listen to him. They had people to save. They kept running towards the dot of light swinging in the dark. It was a man holding a flashlight and waving his arms as Robinson Crusoe trying to get the attention of a passing ship.

It wasn't possible to know who the man with the flashlight was. He wasn't wearing a uniform; he was in civilian clothes. Although according to Karnes he was with Sergeant Thomas, the police officers don't remember seeing anybody else dressed in military fatigues. When Strauss and McGee ran up to the man, he pointed his flashlight to the ground and shouted, "In the hole! In the hole!"

Strauss dropped down the hole. Inside, he saw Karnes squatting and aiming a flashlight down a second hole. The Marine looked up and said, "I can hear him but I can't see him."

Two seconds later, Chuck Sereika jumped in the hole, too. Strauss was surprised to see the medic. Maybe he hadn't been paying attention to who was standing around, but he seemed to come out of thin air. Sereika didn't waste any time. He got down on his stomach, pushed his medical bag out in front and then hurried down the hole as the March Hare.

Strauss was wearing his bulky Scott-pack, his Department-issued-personally-assigned rope harness, and his gun belt. He knew he'd have to take it all off if he was going to fit through the opening. It's a bad feeling giving up your gun, because when the shit hits the fan that's just about the only thing you've got. He dumped everything where he stood and, armed with only a flashlight, took a deep breath and mentally said goodbye to his wife, Pat, for he didn't think he was going to come out of this alive. He went in headfirst and squeezed through the narrow hole and down the tunnel.

Strauss was six-foot-four-inches tall and as slender as an eel, but he could hardly fit inside the tunnel. In order to move forward, he had to lay flat on his stomach, his chin practically scraping the ground, arms outstretched in front of him, dig his fingers in the dirt, and drag his body. He crawled at an angle for twenty-five feet and caught up with the medic. The path they followed swung around as a horseshoe. In the center was a burning heap that separated them from the buried cop. They could hear Jimeno talking from the other side of the fire. They followed his voice until they came to a lattice obstruction of standpipes and sprinkler piping. The two men threaded their bodies through the spaces between the pipes until they reached a wall and an open elevator shaft. There the ceiling rose a couple of feet above their heads and they were able to sit up. To their right was the wall of the elevator shaft going up into darkness and down into an abyss. The pressure of the collapse had peeled back the metal doors as a sardine can. Looking at this, it was hard to tell what floor the elevator came from.

Then they saw lying in front of the elevator shaft the lifeless body of a police officer. He was buried up to his waist in dirt and was slumped forward. A heavy slab of concrete laid across his back. It was obvious he was dead. Carefully, they climbed over his body and continued to search for the second officer.

It was a hard thing to ignore a dead cop. You wanted to do something but you couldn't. The situation required you forget him—he was dead, and it was necessary to move on to help the guy that was still alive.

They made a left turn pass the elevator shaft, and the ceiling lowered again to a tiny space with no room to lift their heads more than a few inches. They crawled on their bellies through the concrete crawl space

The First Responders

and used their flashlights to sweep across the dark as a spray of radar.

They couldn't see Jimeno, but they could hear his voice. He sounded close, but everything was made invisible under a foot of gray, powdery dust. They told Jimeno to stick his hand up and, if he could, to move his fingers back and forth. He said he was doing it, but they still couldn't see him.

"Guide the light to your hand," said Sereika.

Jimeno told Sereika to move the light to the right and, when he did, Sereika saw his dust-drenched uniform. He lifted the light and it fell on Jimeno's hand poking up through the cement dust. The dust was so tightly compacted around his body he looked as though he was on the beach, buried up to his chest in sand. Sereika reached out and grabbed his hand and Jimeno laughed and cried with relief.

Sereika began his vital-sign check. He didn't have a blood pressure cuff; he used his fingertips to feel Jimeno's pulse. His radial pulse was good and his blood pressure seemed okay. Sereika figured the weight of the debris pinning Jimeno's chest and legs was keeping his pressure up.

Strauss and Sereika plowed and scratched at the compacted dirt around Jimeno's body. They had no tools; only their hands and a pair of handcuffs that Jimeno had been using to dig himself out, but before long he dropped them and they fell out of reach. Strauss was thinking he'd give his eyetooth, remortgage his house, anything, for a garden trough.

Paddy McGee had followed Strauss down the hole but could only get as far as the small space by the elevator shaft. There wasn't enough room for him to squeeze in with Strauss and Sereika. But he wanted to help, he said, "What do you want me to do?"

"See if you can clear that stuff outta there," said Strauss. He was referring to the fallen pipes. He was thinking ahead, because he knew when the time came to move Jimeno, there would be no way to get a stoke basket through that mess.

McGee was about six feet away. Strauss and Sereika tried to clear the area around Jimeno. They'd push broken chunks of cement block in McGee's direction, and he'd carefully lean over the dead police officer's body, grab the debris, and drop it down the elevator shaft.

The whole time they were digging, Jimeno kept pleading, "Get to my partner. You gotta help my partner."

They didn't want to tell him the other officer was dead. They hemmed and hawed and made up excuses. They told him not to worry and they'd have to get him out first before they could work on his partner, but Jimeno seemed to know what was up and he didn't want to believe it. Then suddenly they heard a voice.

"Hey, guys," said the groggy voice. They didn't know where it was coming from, and it caught them by surprise.

"Who are *you*?" said Strauss, amazed. He pointed his flashlight in the dark to see who was speaking.

"It's McLoughlin," said the disembodied voice.

"*He's* my partner," said Jimeno in an I-told-you-so tone.

Strauss was confused. If McLoughlin was his partner, then who was the dead guy? It would turn out the deceased police officer was Dominick Pezzulo. He was one of three other police officers who had been with Jimeno and McLoughlin before the collapse of the first Tower.

"Where are you?"

"I'm buried about another ten, fifteen feet in," said McLoughlin. "The pain is excruciating. You gotta get me outta here."

It was just as Sergeant McLoughlin said—he was trapped fifteen feet directly behind Jimeno. Their flashlights could barely find him; they could only see a blurry outline of his head and shoulders.

"Listen, we'll get you out," said Strauss. "We're workin' on Jimeno and then we're gonna dig right to you."

They could only work on one trapped cop at a time. And they couldn't have been more cramped if they had squeezed inside a gofer's hole. The "ceiling" was right on top of their heads. There was no way to get to McLoughlin until Jimeno was out of there.

Unbeknownst to them, the world outside was turning into a three-ring circus. The news that somebody had been found alive was spreading as wild fire. In the hole were five men, but outside, hundreds of spectators had began to gather. Whether just curious or truly concerned, everyone

The First Responders

wanted to be part of the rescue. It was giving the nurses and doctors something to do. All the emergency rooms throughout the city had been on stand-by all day, anticipating the arrival of hundreds of injured people, and the only survivors so far were these two men. So they needed something to do. It made them feel part of it.

By this time, McGee had company. A fireman named Tommy Ascher and Sergeant John Scrivani from One-Truck had climbed in the hole and positioned themselves in the long part of the tunnel. They were helping to clear out the pipes. In a corner just above their heads they started to dig a second exit. This was going to be important when the time came to get these men out.

Karnes was still sitting in the six-foot drop outside the second hole. He'd been digging as a squirrel trying to make an opening so he could look in and watch what was going on. But his digging caused dirt to fall on top of the guys in the hole.

Strauss didn't appreciate the dirt coming down on his head. Plus, it was getting in Jimeno's eyes. He knew the Marine wanted to help, but he was starting to become annoying. Somewhere in the hole, a blue fireman's helmet was found in the dirt and Sereika passed it to Strauss. He had no clue how a helmet ended up in the hole, but he placed it over Jimeno's face to block the dirt (actually, it belonged to Jimeno, knocked off during the collapse).

He yelled up at Karnes, "Hey, Marine. Cut it out!"

Strauss didn't know the Marine's name. He said, "You got something I can call you other than Marine?"

Strauss was really exhausted. He had been up since Sunday morning, with maybe three hours sleep in that whole time. He had worked two late tours and had been at the Trade Center since ten-thirty that morning. Now it was way passed 8:00 PM and he was in this hole struggling to breathe through the dust and the smoke. He was coughing and he was cramped and he was sweating because the hole was on fire and everything he touched was hot. It was an effort to say the two syllables of "marine" and, all he wanted was one simple name he could grunt out but this Marine was not going to oblige him, "You can call me staff sergeant," said Karnes.

If Strauss had had the strength, he'd have rolled his eyes and shook his head. He turned to Sereika and asked for his name. The medic was more sympathetic. He said, "Call me Chuck."

Sergeant Adrat arrived at the hole shortly after Strauss and McGee. The first thing he did was to take out his radio and confirm two men had been found buried alive under the South Tower. The next thing he wanted to do was to coordinate a staging area in order to get equipment and tools across the rubble to the rescue workers down in the hole.

Winkler and Lambkin heard Adrat's transmission. They grabbed a few extra guys and went around to the Ten-Ten Firehouse on Liberty Street, opposite the devastated South Tower. They took a ladder off one of the fire trucks and leaned it against the pile and climbed to the top. This would be the designated portal to get equipment over the rolling hills of rubble and to Adrat and the buried men.

A chain of hundreds of volunteer and FDNY firemen had lined up to pass this equipment from Liberty Street all the way over to where they were digging out the buried cops. There was only one problem. There was no equipment. The specialized, heavy duty torches and surface-air supply systems that were needed were not coming in. And even if they had had this equipment, it was too big and heavy to drag up and over the pile. It took forty-five minutes just for a man to get to the globe. The walk was a dangerous up and down sweep with secondary collapses, spontaneous fires, and zero visibility.

The only equipment that could be passed along was bottled water, air packs, and hoses. Adrat would ask for this stuff, Winkler and Lambkin would send it up, and then Adrat would ask for it again. They kept on sending it, and Adrat kept on asking. After about the sixth pass, Winkler and Lambkin couldn't understand why Adrat kept asking for the same equipment over and over again. They decided they needed to know where everything was going. They climbed up the ladder and followed the long line of men and found the chain suddenly came to a halt. The firemen at the end of the line were gone and all the equipment had been dumped in the rubble.

What Winkler and Lambkin didn't know was the vanishing firemen had to divert their attention to the fires popping up through the rubble. The hoses were gone, and everything else had been discarded for someone else to worry about. Winkler and Lambkin picked up what they could carry—bottled water and air packs—and headed over to where the buried men were being dug out.

As Winkler was walking, he could feel the heat radiating from the steel. He had never gotten around to changing into his uniform. He was still wearing his summer shorts! He could hear the creaking sound of the still-standing façade all around him. It rocked and moaned as an old wooden boat berthed in the harbor. All he had to guide him in was a flashlight and the distant, portable-generator lights of the rescue site. The firemen had encircled the hole and were scrambling to put out the fires, and this enveloped the area in bellowing white smoke.

When Lambkin arrived at the hole, he turned to a young firefighter. He could see from the red mark on his helmet that he was a "probie," and Lambkin said to him, "We gotta get water here." But the probie looked back at him as if he had three heads. The kid was overwhelmed. The fire department had tragically lost their command structure when many of their top brass had been killed in the collapses, and they didn't really have anybody they could turn to that would get things done. This was the probie's first job, and now he was in the middle of a large-scale operation.

Fortunately, some of the ESU guys had volunteer fire-fighting experience and they knew what kind of hoses and nozzles were needed. They told Lambkin what to ask for, but it didn't make any difference. The probie left to get the equipment, but he was never seen again.

It was so smoky in the hole there were moments when Sereika and Strauss, wedged stomach to stomach as conjoined twins, couldn't see each other's faces. When a fire popped up inside the hole, Ascher, the fireman, would try to put it out with an extinguisher, but all he'd succeed in doing was create a lot of smoke that blinded everybody in the hole.

Strauss, McGee, and Sereika could hear McLoughlin moaning down in the smoky hell and calling out, "Medic! Medic!" And all they could do was yell back, "Hang in there!"

It was disheartening. The sergeant would fade in and out of consciousness and McGee would call out to him trying to keep him alert and his spirits up. They did a great deal of talking and joking to help them keep their mind off the pain. Sereika didn't want to administer morphine to Jimeno. It might sound cruel, but he felt Jimeno was better off in pain and alert than with a drop in his blood pressure and powers of concentration. They kept him talking. He talked about his family, his wife and kids. "I hope your wife is a good cook for when you invite me over to dinner for gettin' you outta here," said Strauss. But they never told Jimeno the two Towers had collapsed.

The last thing Jimeno remembered from before the collapse was he and Sergeant McLoughlin and three other officers he worked with—Dominick Pezzulo, Antonio Rodrigues, and Chris Amoroso—were standing on the promenade of the South Tower waiting for a freight elevator. In an instant the building fell, and Rodrigues and Amoroso were killed. The other three officers lay buried and incapacitated.

Pezzulo was a strong man—a weight lifter with beefed-up biceps and washboard abs to prove it. He had pushed the chunks of debris off his chest and twisted and pulled and pried his body out as a cork being squeezed from a bottle.

Finally, he was free. He crawled over to Jimeno and tried to dig him out with his bare hands. "I'm gonna get you out, Will," said Pezzulo. But his digging was making little progress so he decided to climb to the surface and look for help.

McLoughlin called out for him not to leave. He wanted him to stay and dig out Jimeno and then the two of them could come over and dig him out. Pezzulo said he'd be back and then he climbed out of the hole. Outside he saw the collapsed South Tower, and the fire and the smoke. He shouted for help but there was nobody around to hear him. He didn't want to venture through the rubble and far away from the trapped men, so he crawled back in the hole and went back to digging out Jimeno.

The First Responders

As Pezzulo clawed with his fingers and scraped away with his handcuffs, they had heard a voice. A man on the surface was shouting. What was he saying? It was somebody's name, but they couldn't tell what name it was. The three cops began to yell, "Down here! Down here!"

The man came over to their hole and shouted, "Is [so-and-so] down there?"

"No!" the cops called back up. "It's the Port Authority Police. We're trapped!"

"I'm looking for [so-and-so]."

"He's not here! Please help us!"

The man walked away. As he left them, they could still hear him calling for his friend. Soon his voice disappeared, drowned out by the sound of a deafening roar.

The ground began to shake violently and a cement slab broke loose and it crashed down on top of Pezzulo. It hit him hard, and he knew his injuries were fatal. He could feel his life breath leaving his body. He moved his arm slowly down to his side and unholstered his gun and, with the little strength he had left, he emptied the magazine of his 9mm into the dirt. Eighteen shots. Eighteen calls for help.

When Strauss and Sereika finally got Jimeno's upper body uncovered, they saw the straps of a Scott-pack fitted across his shoulders. The instant they cut the straps and pulled out the air bottle from behind his back, he flopped down. This opened up some space. The distance from his stomach to the concrete slab crushing him was now eight inches apart. Hope, at last. Strauss took his extenders, a part of his rope equipment used when climbing bridges, and he wrapped them around Jimeno's chest and under his arms. Strauss and Sereika grabbed hold of the extenders and together they tried to pull Jimeno free.

"My leg! My leg!" Jimeno cried out in pain. Immediately, Sereika and Strauss stopped pulling. This was unbelievable. They had been down here digging for hours, and just when something looked hopeful, they hit a snag.

On the surface the firemen were yelling, "Hurry up! Hurry up!"

Strauss was thinking to himself, *Do you really think I'm taking my time down here?*

"We can't control the fire! Get outta there!" the firemen kept shouting. Building Five was right over their heads. It was a roaring inferno and it was about to collapse.

"You hear them?" said McGee, in disbelief. *How could these firemen think that he, Strauss, and Sereika would abandon the buried men?*

"Fuck 'em."

Yeah, right. Fuck 'em.

Strauss reached his hand down into the little space between Jimeno's stomach and the slab of concrete to see why his legs were stuck. He felt a big piece of cinder block pinning Jimeno's left leg.

Strauss yelled over to McGee, "I need a para-tech airgun!"

The airgun was also known as a "rescue air chisel." McGee shouted this request to Sergeant Scrivani and he shouted this over the radio. Two minutes later, Scrivani yelled back to McGee and he yelled over to Strauss, "We can't get one! How about an air bag?"

"I'll try," said Strauss. These were the air bags used for jacking up crashed trains to remove people out from under them. They are thin in depth, but with a big surface, area-wise. As Strauss feared, he couldn't fit the bag inside the cramped space.

"How about a battery operated Hurst tool?" suggested McGee.

That was probably the best suggestion all day. This tool was a smaller version of the "Jaws of Life," used on "pinned" jobs to cut off car doors. The only problem was even though it was the size of a fax machine, it weighs about forty pounds.

"If it fits, I'll try it," said Strauss.

The Hurst tool was dragged down the hole and passed to McGee. Then Strauss and Sereika humped on their stomachs over to him, grabbed the clumsy, heavy box and humped it back to Jimeno.

Strauss knew this was going to be a big production, and he knew it was going to cause more pain and discomfort for this poor man, who was already in a miserable and uncomfortable situation.

"Listen, Will. I'm sorry," said Strauss, in his typically soft-spoken and polite manner. "I gotta get this tool on the other side of you."

In order to do that, Strauss had to roll on top of Jimeno. He slid over his chest and leaned on his left shoulder. He never had to use this tool while flat on his stomach before, and he was finding out the hard way he couldn't lift his elbows to get any leverage. He was rolling the Hurst tool, pushing against Jimeno, trying to fight it through the small opening, and he was pulling on his left arm, and Jimeno was calling out in pain, and Strauss was apologizing again and again. Strauss struggled to get the tool in the right spot. He had a flashlight resting on Jimeno's chest, and Sereika was holding a second light. Jimeno moaned from the pressure. Strauss stopped, but Jimeno said, "I can take it. Do wha' you gotta do. Get me and the sergeant out."

Finally, Strauss had the spreaders right where he wanted them. He was ready to turn the switch, but he paused for a second and, as a doctor about to perform a delicate surgery, he told McGee and Sereika to be quiet. He wanted them to watch and listen for anything that might go wrong. This was a powerful machine, and if the vibration starts something moving that shouldn't be moving, he wanted to know before they were all buried alive.

The silence spread out. It passed through the tunnel and out through the hole and all the shouting and craziness on top of them suddenly stopped. It wasn't that it had gone away. Strauss wasn't listening to it anymore. He was completely focused on what he was doing, and all he could hear was this moment.

"Will, I'm goin' to operate the tool and I don't know if it's goin' to pull you out or not. But there's a thousand people out there that know exactly where we are," said Strauss, earnestly. "And if it goes bad, they'll be diggin' for us right away."

"Do what you gotta do," said Jimeno. The moment of truth had finally arrived.

"Okay, Will. We're in this together."

The tool was turned on. It was humming as a chain saw and it was creaking and it was cracking. He felt the cinder block move and rubble start to drop. He slowed it down but kept on going. Moving it, moving it, moving it, and then suddenly—the tool just quit.

Shit. I got nothing. It was a small battery operated tool, and its "throat" didn't have the power and the strength as the big Hurst tools used to pry open car doors. It had only opened up six inches. It wasn't enough.

Sereika suggested using some rocks as leverage and Strauss agreed. McGee tossed over a few good size rocks, six and ten inches thick. The men squeezed over and under each other, exchanged places, fitting the rocks between the jaws of the Hurst tool and the block of cement. One more time Strauss operated the tool by over-riding the automatic shut-off and restarted the battery and the motor was ripping and, boom! He could see the pressure come off Jimeno's leg.

Excitedly, Strauss said, "He's free! He's free!"

They grabbed the extenders and pulled and pulled. Again, Jimeno wasn't moving. He was lying there as a sack of potatoes, and every attempt to pry him loose was twisting his foot around as a screw. He cursed the pain and they stopped pulling.

Strauss couldn't believe this. There must be something under the cinder block he couldn't see. He'd need to take a closer look. He crawled on top of Jimeno, and the ceiling pressed down on his back as a vice. Strauss slid down his body until his head was by Jimeno's knees and his knees were around Jimeno's head. He felt embarrassed to be in this Kama Sutra position, and he quipped, "It figures it can't be a female."

It hurt Jimeno to laugh. It jiggled his insides and made the pain worse.

Strauss struggled to crawl down to Jimeno's foot still under the cement slab that was crushing him. Strauss stretched out his hand, but his fingertips could barely reach. Then he saw a piece of rebar was lying across the top of Jimeno's left boot. Maybe if they cut off the boot, they could slip his foot out. Sereika passed Strauss a pair of paramedic shears, but he didn't have enough room to lift his elbows to get the leverage to cut the leather.

Jimeno was frustrated with exhaustion and pain and he was begging them to cut off his leg. "Please get to my partner," he begged, over and over again. "If this is gonna take too long, take my leg. I wanna get out with my life."

Right above their heads, Karnes was watching and listening. He peeked through his little hole, and said, "Okay, Will."

He reached back and removed an eight-inch blade, Marine Corp K-Mar knife from its sheath and passed it down through the portal and handed it to Sereika.

"That's razor sharp," said Karnes, with dry humor. "It'll do a nice, clean cut."

Jimeno's eyes widened in horror and he became silent. At first he didn't get the joke, and later he was relieved nobody was serious. In the moment, he had been serious. But Sereika had no intention of taking that leg. First of all, he wasn't qualified for amputation, and second of all, it was never an option.

Sereika dragged over a three-foot rebar he found somewhere in the dust. It was bent, but they could use it as a tool. Strauss jammed it down into the small space and beneath the metal bar pinning Jimeno's foot. They pushed down on it and at the same time pulled on the foot. Suddenly, the foot shot free.

"He's ready to go! We got him out!" Strauss shouted.

That was the signal to lower the stoke basket into the hole and next to the elevator shaft. Strauss and Sereika grabbed the extenders and dragged Jimeno through the crawl space. McGee reached out and grabbed Jimeno, and the three men heaved him into the basket, strapped him in, and carried him over to the wider hole everybody had been digging for the past three hours.

Jimeno wasn't a lightweight, so it took one good heave-ho to lift him out of the hole. It felt as another rebirth of life, the air outside hit his face and the people waiting on the pile exploded into applause.

Jimeno raised his head and looked around and, in the fire lit landscape, he finally saw for the first time the collapse of the Twin Towers.

He was mortified.

"Look what these muthuhfuckers did to my buildings," said Jimeno with anger and astonishment.

A gauntlet of firemen, cops, and construction workers were standing at the hole and over the pile of rubble to Church Street. Using planks of wood and ladders, they laid down a path. Jimeno's basket was passed from man to man until he met the doctors in the street.

Sereika crawled out of the hole. He was exhausted and his eyes and lungs were on fire.

There was a deputy fire chief, a big man, standing at the mouth of the hole, and he said something to Sereika about how a second crew was coming in for Sergeant McLoughlin. But Sereika couldn't do this anymore. His arms were weak and weightless. He walked blurry eyed down the wooden path. At the bottom, several cops were waiting for him.

"Go right, if you're injured," a cop said, pointing to an ambulance. "Go left, if you're not."

Sereika went left.

Strauss went back in the hole. He wanted to speak to McLoughlin and he crawled over to him. He couldn't see. Every time he blinked, he could feel the grit scratching on his eyes. He couldn't breathe. All he wanted to do in the world was to stand up and take a breath.

He called out to McLoughlin, "Sarge, Will's outta here. You're next. A fresh team is comin' in"

"Okay"

"Sarge, is your first name John?"

"Yeah. Who's this?"

"It's Scott Strauss from Emergency."

It turned out he knew the sergeant, but he'd never put it together until now.

McLoughlin ran the Emergency Service Unit in the Port Authority Police Department at the Trade Center. McLoughlin had cross-trained with many of the NYPD ESU cops in rappelling and rescue exercises in the Towers.

"John, they're comin' for you," reassured Strauss. "They know you're here. I'm outta here. I'm shot. I'll see you in a few days."

Strauss backed out of the hole and, at the same time, he saw Officer Steve Clifford from Nine-Truck, crawling in. Strauss said to him, "He's a personal friend. Take care of him."

Strauss didn't know why he said that—he certainly knew the other officer would take care of the sergeant—it was just, because he had to leave, it felt as though he was abandoning him. It made him feel better to say those words.

Strauss climbed out. He tried to breathe and even though he was out, he still couldn't do it. The air outside was just as crappy as it was down in the hole. The fires were still roaring and the smoke was suffocating. Through his half-closed eyes, he saw Winkler, and he wanted to speak to him, but the mechanism in his throat couldn't get the words out. He was trying to say, "Kenny, they need hand tools—small tools—garden tools," but, his words were short gasps. "We took a beating in there—rotate them in—you can't stay long in there."

"We got it from here," said Winkler. He could see Strauss was struggling to stand on his feet and was ready to collapse. "Get outta here! Go! Go!"

Greg Welch, who had recovered from his fall, and another ESU cop, Tommy Rowe, grabbed Strauss and steadied him. They helped him down the long trail of cops and firemen. His eyes were swollen shut, and he was so exhausted he could barely hold up his head. He was hanging on to Rowe on one side and Welch was picking him up on the other side and they were walking over piles of rebar, high beams, rubble, and what was left of desks, computers, and chairs. All the way down, there were cops and firemen on either side reaching out a helping hand. Suddenly, he heard somebody on the line say, "I see you didn't make the meeting either."

Strauss immediately recognized the voice. It was his best friend, Zeus, a City fireman he knew from the neighborhood. Strauss was a volunteer fire chief in his hometown of Mineola, Long Island, and tonight there was a meeting at the firehouse.

He slowly lifted his head in the direction of the voice and said, "Hey, Zeus. How ya doin'?

"A whole lot better than you look."

Strauss looked as a long, skinny, Pillsbury doughboy. He had white stuff caked on his head and his dark blue uniform was completely white, as though he'd just been rolling around in flour.

When he got to the street, Welch and Rowe put Strauss on a stretcher, and the medics got busy and pulled out their shears and pinched up his pants leg, and were ready to cut him a new pair of Bermuda shorts.

"I'm not hurt!" said Strauss, protesting. He knew how medics love to cut off clothes, and he didn't want to loose his uniform, dirty or not. "I just can't breathe."

During the trip to the hospital and then in the emergency room, Strauss was wailing, "I can't open my eyes! I can't open my eyes!" The medics poured water non-stop over Strauss's face, but there wasn't enough water in the world to put out the fire in his eyes.

Then Strauss heard somebody say, "Hey, what're you doin'?"

He recognized that voice, too. It was his ex-partner, Gerard Sullivan. Strauss tried to look at his face, but there was too much water and grit swishing around on his eyeballs.

"What're you doin' here?" said Strauss, surprised.

"You think I'm gonna stay home with all of this goin' on?" said Sullivan. "Somebody's gotta look out for yer."

Strauss and Sullivan had been partners for thirteen years in Emergency Service. They received the Medal for Valor together and Sullivan had literally saved Strauss's life many times, and Strauss, in return, had saved Sullivan's life many times.

Sullivan had retired from the job back in March, and he was home when he saw the Towers collapse on TV. He ran down in the basement and rummaged through the bags he'd thrown his uniforms in when he cleaned out his locker. Meanwhile, his wife was standing there watching him and saying, "What'd'ya think you're doin'?"

"I'm goin' to work."

"Oh, no, you're not."

"Oh, yes, I am"

Everybody walked off the hill. All the noise and excitement was gone, and it grew strangely quiet. Winkler looked around and saw he and Lambkin were the only two people standing by the hole. It was eleven o'clock at night and there was still a man trapped below. But all those rescue workers, and the hundreds of spectators that had been standing around all evening, had just simply disappeared.

Suddenly, Winkler saw coming from the direction of Church Street dozens of small circles of light jiggling around as fireflies, marching towards the hill.

"What the hell's this?" said Winkler. It looked as the scene in *ET* where there was a parade of lights coming through the mist in the forest. Lambkin and Winkler watched the lights get closer and closer. Then they were able to make out what it was: a new batch of ESU cops coming in for the second rescue. They saw Sergeant Kennedy, Sergeant O'Rouke, and Sergeant John English, with their team of guys.

"Okay. We're takin' over," said English, stepping up to the plate.

Winkler gave him a quick run down: the first man was out and at Bellevue Hospital; the second man was buried in deep. The conditions were bad: smoky, and hot. There was no room for a Scott-pack or for big tools. Work in pairs; don't let anyone stay down there longer than fifteen minutes.

"All right," said English.

Now Winkler and Lambkin were being relieved and they walked out towards Church Street along the same path they saw English and the others came inbound. The trip away from the hole and down was an near-effortless straight path that only took ten minutes. Initially they had taken the long way from Liberty Street, and that was an exhausting forty-five minute climb.

Winkler turned to Lambkin, shook his head in exasperation, and said, "Holy Christ, we just broke our asses walkin' from Liberty Street and the whole time we could've come this way."

THE RESCUE OF JOHN MCLOUGHLIN

John Busching was an ESU cop and a paramedic. He was tall and lanky with boyish good looks that made him appear a decade younger than his thirty-five years. He had been a cop for fifteen years and, ten of those years he was in ESU. His father was a retired City fireman, and that put rescue work in his blood. Busching was always in some kind of a uniform. He had his cop job, and a part time paramedic job and, in his free time, he was a volunteer fireman in Rockville Centre, Long Island.

His four-man team had been split in half by Inspector Wasson when Busching arrived by helicopter to Lower Manhattan. Two men had been sent to the middle of the debris pile as part of the team to dig out the second buried cop. Busching stayed behind on Church and Vey, in front of Century 21, the discount department store. He saw a large crowd of rescue workers—firemen, police, and paramedics— standing in the middle of Church Street. He walked over to them to see what was going on. It was the tail end of the rescue of the Port Authority cop, Will Jimeno. The ambulance transporting him to the hospital had just pulled away.

Busching could hear talk around him a second man was still trapped under the rubble. He looked up over the debris pile and saw it was pitch black except for a tiny glow burning as a campfire on top of a mountain. Specs of light juggling from hand-held porta-lights flashed around the glow, and men moved up and down the hill as worker ants.

ESU Captain Jim Yee was overseeing the rescue effort from Church Street. He noticed the medical backpack slung over Busching's shoulder and asked him what he had in there. Busching gave him a brief inventory, and Yee then radioed up to the hole and asked Sergeant English, who was in charge of the second rescue operation, if a paramedic with IV solutions was needed.

Nobody was treating McLoughlin medically, and a medic was more than welcome. "I'm sending John Busching up," said Yee.

English, who knew Busching from when they worked together at Seven-Truck in Brooklyn, said, "Oh, good."

Busching walked the by-now, well-beaten path between Buildings Four and Five. About twenty minutes later he reached the spot where the rescue was being attempted. The hole didn't look anything as he imagined. The whole area was dark, and the huge crowd that had been there all day either watching or assisting the rescue of Jimeno, had dwindled to a few men. There were still some lights here and there that came from a few small Onan generators and from the porta-lights some of the guys were holding. And there was an eerie glow of fire creeping in from the nearby burning buildings. Busching was looking around with his flashlight expecting to find someone on the ground pinned under a high beam, but he couldn't have been more wrong

English was waiting for Busching. When he arrived, English said to him, "You have to go down a hole," and pointed to a three-foot drop. This was not the hole Strauss and McGee had initially entered, but a new one that had been dug out by the rescue workers while Jimeno was being dug out. It was an easier way of getting down to where McLoughlin was still trapped. Busching would have to walk on a beam down twenty feet and pass underneath two sections of boarding that had collapsed together as a teepee

Standing near the hole was a young doctor named John Chovanes. He was a former paramedic, a second year resident, and an emergency room trauma doctor at the University of Medicine and Dentistry of New Jersey School of Osteopathic Medicine. He approached Busching, conferred with him, and gave him a vial of morphine. Chovanes had found the vials discarded in the rubble. He plucked them as poppies out of the dust and, thinking they might come in handy, put them in his pocket.

Chovanes was younger than Busching. He had a clean cut, preppy way about him—the kind of thing one acquires being from a family of doctors and lawyers, and brought up with a wardrobe of J. Crew polo shirts and Docker pants. Chovanes had driven all the way to New York City from Philly, stopping at checkpoint after checkpoint until he had talked his way into Ground Zero. He ran into Police Chief Garry McCarthy, the Deputy Commissioner of Operations, somewhere around the perimeter of the pile, and told him he was a doctor and wanted to help. McCarthy motioned towards the pile and said, "Emergency is doing something in a hole over there." Then he pointed to an ESU sergeant named Kenny Bowen, who was standing in the pitch black on Church Street in front of Century 21. Bowen was monitoring the staging area from where rescue and medical equipment was being sent up to the hole. Bowen sent Chovanes up the pile; and in the heart of New York City, with its thousands of medical experts of every skill in excellent supply, it was this lone doctor from Pennsylvania that arrived at the hole to assist in the rescue of McLoughlin.

Busching hopped in the hole. Standing on the next landing was a battalion fire chief. The chief was in charge of everything going on inside the hole and he was monitoring the time each man spent with McLoughlin. He looked at Busching and thought he was the relief for the guy who was just crawling out, but the fire chief wanted a medic, so he cupped his hands around his mouth and shouted up the hole, "Where's my paramedic?"

"I'm the medic," said Busching.

The fire chief swung around and gave him a surprised look. Busching didn't have to be a mind reader to know what the fire chief was thinking. Emergency Service cops were usually trained as EMTs, and the odds of coming across a cop who was a paramedic were pretty slim. But Busching had been trained and certified as a paramedic in 1999. He was also part of a new project the Department had recently approved called the "Tactical Medic Program." The idea of the project was to provide a paramedic to accompany ESU teams when they execute a warrant and just in case things got rough and someone got hurt. Tonight was going to be the first field test of the new program, so to speak.

The fire chief said, "Let me have your bag and I'll pass it to you."

Busching wasn't too eager to give up his equipment. He hesitated for a moment and said, "Why?"

"Because you're not gonna fit where you have to go."

The fire chief bent down and shined his flashlight in the hole and showed Busching how narrow and cramped everything was. It looked dangerous and unstable as a collapsed mineshaft.

As they were talking, an ESU cop, Eddie Reyes, was crawling out and climbing up around their feet. When Reyes saw Busching, he said, "You're gonna be takin' care of McLoughlin? Who're you with?"

Busching said he was with no one, and Reyes volunteered to go back in there with him. The fire chief didn't like that idea and snapped back, "No. It's fifteen minutes in the hole and you're done. Stop playin' games."

Busching took exception to the fire chief's attitude. ESU cops have a policy of working in pairs; plus, Reyes was a registered nurse and would be useful if Busching needed assistance. They had to convince the chief a second guy was needed, and when they succeeded in doing so, Busching and Reyes climbed in the hole, got down on their stomachs, and crawled pass pipes, the elevator shaft, and Pezzulo's body. As Busching crawled over the corpse, he tried not to look at him. This was a shorter route than what Strauss and McGee had experienced. To make working down there easier, a fire hose was funneled down the hole to suck out the smoke. Busching made a right turn and then had to worm eighteen feet through an area so tight he had to put his arms outstretched in front of him and keep digging his fingers in the dirt to pull his body forward.

When his flashlight found McLoughlin he was shocked to see him sticking halfway out of the ground and lying faced down in the dirt. He was buried up to his waist in what looked as compressed concrete. To Busching, it reminded him of those scenes in *Star Trek* when someone is "beamed up" and something goes wrong with the transporter and the atoms are scrambled around in space and time and the guy materializes with his upper body sticking out of the floor.

Another thing that surprised Busching was the sergeant was wearing a tan fireman's turnout coat and a blue fireman's helmet. He had never seen a police officer wear something as this. What he didn't know was the Emergency Service Unit of the Port Authority Police Department also operated a fire brigade.

The sergeant was boxed in an area that wasn't more than two feet high by two feet wide. The space was so confining only one man at a time could be with McLoughlin. Reyes had to position himself behind Busching, somewhere around his heel.

Busching pushed himself as close as the tiny space would allow. In this deep dark womb he saw part of McLoughlin's face where the light from his flashlight moved from left to right. He was alert and talking. He was aware something collapsed, but he didn't know what it was and to what extent. He was in pain, and Busching discussed whether to give him the morphine. The sergeant resisted that idea. He had had advanced EMT training and was afraid the drug would lower his blood pressure. But Busching felt since McLoughlin was a big man and his pulse was strong, and he wasn't sweating profusely and he wasn't cold, the morphine could be safely administered.

Busching set up the IV solution bag. It had a long, thin tube with a needle at the end, and he inserted the needle into a fat, blue vein on the back of McLoughlin's hand. He took out the vial of morphine and after looking closely he tried to make sense of what he saw. The vial had no needle. Instead, it had a screw that needed to be pushed into the intravenous line. Busching knew how to work with a vial that had a needle. All he had to do was stick the needle in a pinhole opening in the tube. But he didn't know how to administer the morphine with a screw. And even if he had known how to do that, it was almost impossible to do it inside that filthy, tiny space, using just a flashlight to see what he was doing, all the while lying on his stomach with everything right in his face. Busching was also feeling quite unsure of himself. He had only been a medic for two years and he didn't want to make any mistakes.

Reyes exchanged places with Busching. He tried to work the screw on the vial but he had the same difficulty.

McLoughlin wasn't disappointed he wasn't getting the morphine. He had already spent twelve hours prostrated in cement and in excruciating pain. What difference would a few more hours make?

Their fifteen minutes was up. Busching put an oxygen mask over the sergeant's face and scooted backwards out of the narrow space until there was room enough to turn around. Then he and Reyes crawled out of the hole.

Chovanes was waiting for Busching. When Busching told him he didn't give the sergeant the morphine, the doctor nearly went ballistic and yelled, "What'd'ya mean you didn't give him the morphine!"

Busching told him he didn't know how the screw-in vial worked. Chovanes took back the vial and said, "I'll have to go in and evaluate and give him the morphine myself."

So, the doctor climbed down. He wormed his body through the tunnel and over to McLoughlin. He was scared and claustrophobic and he worked as fast as he could. He unwrapped a straight-needle syringe from a sterilized package, pushed the needle into the vial, drew out the morphine, and injected the drug into the pinhole of the IV solution bag. Fifteen minutes later, he crawled out of the hole with a look of horror on his face, as though he were escaping a nuclear meltdown on a Russian submarine. Busching saw the expression on the doctor's face and wondered if he had had that same look when he crawled out. The conditions in the hole were as close to a suicide mission as you could get.

Chovanes came over and sat down next to Busching on a high beam he had made his personal bench. While still catching his breath, he said, "You have to promise me that if I get killed, my son will be taken care of."

Busching thought, *my, aren't we being a little melodramatic.* But then on second thought, when you sat there for a moment and took in what was really going on around you, death was a real possibility. From where they sat, he could see the remnants of the South Tower with its broken tiers precariously looming over their heads. Sitting directly in front of him was what was left of the Customs House, and a little to the left of that was the globe. To the right was Building Four and Five, and straight ahead was the smoldering heap of the remains of Building Seven. They were all on fire

Chovanes spoke to Busching about formulating a plan for treating the sergeant. It was important to pay attention to the time and to regulate the treatment. When a person is compressed for a long period of time there is a danger of a condition known as "crush syndrome." Acids begin to build up in the body. The good, oxygenated blood can't get in and the deoxygenated blood with all the toxic by-products can't get out. Relieving the pressure can be as dangerous as the pressure itself, because doing so releases the built-up toxins into the system as opening up a floodgate. If this happens, first, a sudden and large release of potassium into the system might send the person into cardiac arrest and kill him on the spot. If this doesn't happen, the toxins still might clog up the kidneys. This would start a chain reaction of organ failures over the course of several weeks.

Busching knew about crush syndrome from his medical studies, and he was trying to put himself back into the classroom where he'd heard about it and remember what the instructor had said in the fifteen minute lesson two years ago. He knew it wasn't good news. He was trying to recall the treatment, but he couldn't remember everything, and so the doctor gave him a little push. Oh, yes, now he remembered. It was important to keep the person hydrated with administration of IVs and to give sodium bicarbonate, an alkaline, to buffer the acids.

"Now, we have to come up with another plan," said Chovanes. This was for the worst case scenario: if the sergeant's medical condition worsened or if the rescuers couldn't free his legs, they'd have to perform a double amputation.

"What's in your bag is all we have, and I want you to think of a way to stop him from bleeding to death," said the doctor, grimly. "And I'll think of a way to take his legs off."

Chovanes described how he would amputate McLoughlin's legs. He told Busching he'd cut high on the thighs with a cordless Sawzall reciprocating saw, because the blade would leave a smooth, and even, edge around the flesh and bone.

Busching's expression dropped. He could feel his nerves rumbling in his guts. He wasn't trained for amputations of limbs, and he didn't want to take anybody's legs off. But, he and the doctor were the only medical team present at this time and place. There were other doctors and EMTs standing out on Church Street, but they might as well have been a thousand miles away.

All through the night Busching had been asking for medical supplies, but for the longest time nothing was coming up the hill. Eventually, some supplies, like needles and syringes started to arrive. It was a twenty-minute climb from Church Street to the top of the hole and it seemed nobody wanted to hike it. At one point, an EMS medic did

The First Responders

show up, but he brought no medical equipment with him and was told to go back. The medic said, "Okay, I'll go back, and you call up and I'll get you what you need." He went back, and that was the last they ever heard from him.

Busching found all this disappointing. He had worked part time as a paramedic on an ambulance in Brooklyn and he knew what a New York City EMS was supposed to have in their bags and boxes, and they were the very things he needed. The one thing that stuck out in his mind: when the first trickle of medical supplies finally arrived at the hole, it came from a small ambulance corps from upstate New York. He was sure it was a lot more of a loss to them, being dependent on community donations and charities, than it would have been to NYC EMS.

To answer Chovanes' request, all kinds of medical procedures went through Busching's head as he tried to piece together how he'd stop the bleeding. He imagined: What would happen to the heartbeat in the vein, or the eight pints of blood? How would they control the pain? And, how would he and the doctor fit together inside that tiny space? He thought about every piece of equipment he had in his bag. Finally he said, "I'll make tourniquets out of triangular bandages and use pen lights as a torque."

"Okay, that sounds pretty good," said Chovanes. "But I don't think it's going to stop the bleeding from the femoral artery. Don't you have any clamps?" *Clamps?* Paramedics don't carry around clamps. Then Busching suddenly thought of a tool kit he carried on his belt. It was called a "Leather-man" and, as a Swiss army knife, he could flip out screwdrivers, knives, and pliers. He told the doctor he would use the pliers as a clamp, bind it closed with electrical tape, and then tape the artery to his stomach.

"See! Now, you're thinking," said Chovanes, one beat short of slapping him on the back.

Sometime around midnight, one of the bosses at the ESU command center at Stuyvesant High School walked over to Sergeant John Politoski and said, "English is somewhere out on the pile. Grab a bunch of guys and go find him.".

Politoski was wearing an ESU uniform but he wasn't ESU—not anymore. He had worked as a police officer at Two-Truck from 1992 to 1996, but halfway through 1996, when he was promoted to sergeant, he had to leave the unit. For the past five years he had been working as a supervisor in Manhattan North Street Crime. But on September 11th the Department wanted anyone who had any experience in Emergency Service to report back to the Unit.

He couldn't have been happier. He had been trying for years to return to the unit, but politics and "hooks" always got in the way. He pulled out his old ESU uniform he still had hanging in his locker at the 2-6 precinct in Harlem and, even though his shirts didn't have any chevrons sewn on the sleeves, it was a great feeling to put that uniform back on. It was too bad it took a virtual declaration of war to get back in.

Politoski put together a rescue team and headed down to Ground Zero to look for Sergeant English. He didn't know why he had to find English. The scope of search and rescue at Ground Zero was so enormous one hand didn't know what the other hand was doing. He didn't know there had been two Port Authority cops buried under the rubble and one of the cops was already out, and he didn't know English was in charge of the operation that was rescuing the second buried cop.

Politoski had a team of eight cops from Two-Truck. There was Steve Elter, Bob Joyce, Mike Sweeney, Vinny Aprea, plus four other officers, and he led them east on Chambers Street and then south on Church. He raised English on Tac-g and asked for his location.

"I'm right in the middle of Ground Zero."

"What's the best way in?"

"Go in by 10-10 on Liberty," said English, in spite of the best way in was from Church and Vey.

Politoski and his team walked down to Engine Ten Ladder Ten firehouse on Liberty Street. He saw two police lieutenants standing on the corner and asked, "What we got? Where's the mobilization point we're workin' from?"

The two lieutenants didn't know anything about a mobilization point. Politoski said he was told to enter the pile from this end. They looked at him as though he was crazy and said, "You're not gonna make it in there," but the lieutenants, who weren't ESU but regular NYPD, had no way of knowing anything about the short cut at Church and Vey.

Politoski and his team went in anyway. They fought their way up the pile of mangled steel and walked over the debris as though they were stepping on hot coals and sharp knives. Building Four was on fire and leaning in their direction. Politoski was worried the building was going to fall on their heads, and he yelled to his men to hurry up; but they could only go so fast because they had a ton of equipment on their backs: oxygen canisters, ropes, Hurst tools, airbags, saws, and cutting torches.

Suddenly Eddie Reyes' voice came over the radio. He was at the hole and said, "I gotta better way in. Come on out and go around to Century 21."

Politoski and his team climbed back out and walked to Century 21 on Church Street and Vey and entered the pile from that direction. It was a less treacherous hike and, twenty minutes later, Politoski found English. The two men had known each from the time when Politoski was in ESU, but they hadn't seen each other in years. English was surprised and said, "What're you doin' here?"

"I don't know what I'm doin' here," said Politoski, in a disbelieving voice. "But here I am."

English gave Politoski a rundown on the situation. He told him there was a trapped Port Authority cop buried in a hole. He told him the conditions were bad and nobody could stay down there longer than fifteen minutes trying to dig the cop out. They exchanged radios so Politoski could be on the right frequency, and then English said his goodnight and left.

Politoski looked around and saw he was the only boss on the hill. Standing behind him were fifty guys—the eight he had brought with him plus the ESU cops who had been brought in over the last hour—all itching to get down the hole and dig. He couldn't believe he was here. His entire emergency training returned to him as easily as riding a bike. He set up a line of guys equipped with Scott-packs, shovels, saws, airbags, and had them go down the hole on a twenty to thirty minute rotation to dig out McLoughlin—he decided to expand the limit from fifteen to twenty or thirty minutes depending on what was actually happening down in the hole. They couldn't fit the Scott-packs on their backs, and a lot of the guys didn't want to drag them down with them, but Politoski made them take one with them just in case there was a collapse.

He put his fifty guys on stand-by, lined up in pairs, and ready to relieve the men in front of them. He had two men in the hole digging, two men sitting on the three-foot drop inside the hole, and two men crouched at the top of the hole. As soon as the two men that were digging came out, the next two men on the three-foot drop would go down to dig. Then the two men at the top of the hole would shift down to the three-foot drop, and two more men from the line would move to the top of the hole. That way, there would never be more than a brief interruption in the digging.

No man went down the hole more than once except for Busching and Chovanes. They sat and waited on their bench of rubble and kept their eye on the clock. Every forty minutes or so there was an interval of no digging, and either Chovanes or Busching, would climb down in the hole to evaluate McLoughlin's condition. Miraculously, it stayed unaltered. His pulse was strong—as strong as his will to live. They gave him morphine each time the pain came back. The smoke made McLoughlin sick, and they gave him ondansetron to prevent vomiting. Sometimes the movement of the digging made the IV needle pop out of his vein, and they'd put another needle in. McLoughlin was going in and out of delirium, and the rescuers talked to him to try to keep him alert. He told this fantastic story about how he was standing on the 86th floor of the South Tower when it fell. Everybody thought, this was amazing. They didn't believe it but, on second thought, it made sense. He was relatively high up in the debris field, poking through the top as if he had been carried down as a skier in an avalanche. McLoughlin's team had actually been on the promenade, although it's possible he received an order that had something to do with the 86th floor, but it was never clear.

Busching and Politoski watched Chovanes with amused curiosity. They joshed he was like the guy in the television commercial where people are taking a tour of a nuclear power plant. There's suddenly a big emergency and a guy runs into the control room and takes charge yelling to everyone what to do. Everybody on the tour is impressed and one of them says, "Wow. Thank God you're here. Are you a top nuclear scientist?" The guy answers coolly, "No. I'm staying at the Holiday Inn."

Busching and Politoski were thinking, *wouldn't it be funny if he really wasn't a doctor but he was just some guy that walked in here and faked it?*

At one point, when things were looking dire for McLoughlin, Chovanes requested the field amputation kit. They radioed this message down to the staging area on Church Street, and Bowen, who was monitoring the radio all night, turned to the doctors standing in the street waiting for something to happen so they'd be needed, and asked them to go get the kit. But the doctors seemed as though they wanted to argue with him about every little thing Chovanes requested. They'd ask: "Why are you asking for this narcotic?" "Under what authority are you asking for an amputation kit?" After a long night of second-guessing, Chovanes flipped his cool.

"Because I say so!" said Chovanes with such force he astonished himself and put the fear of God into anybody standing nearby. "You tell them that under my authority to shut up and give me what I need!"

Everybody was taken aback by Chovanes' sudden outburst. They stopped what they were doing to look at him. There was a pregnant-pause—"what-was-that-all-about?" moment, and then a release of laughter and a congratulatory *You're all right by me, doc.*

At seven o'clock the next morning the sun was coming up, and all the rescue workers who had left for the night started to return. At first it was one man at a time, then two men, then three. Before you knew it, hundreds of people had formed a long congo-line that stretched from the top of the hole, across and over the rubble, down to Church and Vey Street, and then curled around as a giant conch in front of the entrance of Century 21.

In the hole, McLoughlin was getting close to freedom. He could taste it. The level of the dirt had fallen from his waist to his thighs to his knees. As sand pouring down an hourglass, more and more of his body was uncovered. When the rescuers dug down to his feet they saw he was caught up in a complicated web of steel rebars. A Nassau County cop named Richie Doerler was with McLoughlin now, and he was requesting a Hurst tool. He had been down there far longer than his allotted twenty minutes. The guys on top were getting restless; they wanted their turn. *It's been almost an hour since Doerler went down—what's going on there?* A few seconds later Doerler announced the sergeant was freed and ready to come out.

McLoughlin was lifted to the surface and placed in a stoke basket. Busching went over to insert the bicarb into the IV bag. This was the first time he was able to see him as a whole man. Now he could see his face looking up rather than down to the dirt. There was daylight instead of the beam of a flashlight. The turnout coat he had been wearing was removed and he saw McLoughlin's police uniform with its sergeant's stripes.

Busching joked, "If only I had known you were a sergeant."

McLoughlin smiled weakly.

Busching had never met the sergeant before this night. Since midnight, Busching had watched the men climb in and out of the hole, and every time somebody came out, he'd pass by the guy now going in and say, "Guess who's down in the hole? McLoughlin!" And the other guy would answer, "Oh, my God, we gotta get him outta there!" Busching must have heard that comment twenty times tonight. He felt funny every cop in ESU but him knew McLoughlin. Busching thought, *this was a helluva way to meet.*

McLoughlin was shuttled down the human chain to Church Street. At this point the rescue was over, and Politoski wanted the equipment picked up and out of there. As McLoughlin passed by, Politoski yelled orders behind him. He said, "Lets go! All the equipment—lets start passing the equipment, right now. The equipment, the equipment, the equipment—just keep shuttling the equipment down!"

Politoski radioed down to Bowen and said, "Here comes the

equipment. Make sure you grab it so it doesn't grow legs and walk away."

The equipment and tools went down the pile and to the street as smoothly as a conveyor belt in a candy factory. When the last piece was gone, Politoski and his men turned around and walked off the hill and down to Church Street.

As they were putting McLoughlin in the ambulance, Politoski looked up and saw Chief Hale standing off to the side. The chief was a sight for sore eyes in his pressed blues and clean, white shirt. He looked untouchable and glowing in the middle of this dirt and disaster. Politoski turned to the cop next to him and said out of the side of his mouth, "I thought he was dead."

All day Politoski had been seeing ghosts. There was a rumor flying around the entire higher echelon of the police department had been killed in the collapse. Earlier in the day, when Politoski and his men were first heading down to Ground Zero, he saw Chief Michael Scagnelli popping out of a shop on Park Place and West Broadway. Caught by surprise, he blurted out, "Chief, I thought you were dead!"

"No. I was in Canada," said Scagnelli, matter-of-factly. "I was hunting. The Canadian Mounted Police just flew me down."

Scagnelli was the Chief of Transportation at Headquarters, and here he was, in full uniform, gold stars and white shirt, his eight-pointed uniform hat, and looking as spiffy as polished brass, bopping down the street in a laid-back, cop-on-the-beat shuffle. He was the kind of boss that was still a cop. He didn't pull rank or bust chops. The Chief was a likable guy, and it was good to know nothing bad had happened to him.

A few days after September 11th, Busching went to Bellevue Hospital to see McLoughlin, who was in a medically induced coma to help bring down the swelling to his brain. He had developed complications from the crush syndrome and came very close to dying. McLoughlin had operation after operation. His muscles had not been oxygenated and started to die and the necrotic muscle had to be cut away. Then inflamation set in and more muscle was removed. The doctors did grafts and flap procedures, multiple wound debridements, and numerous blood transfusions.

When Busching entered the hospital room, he found Chovanes and the Head Trauma Surgeon of Bellevue Hospital standing by McLoughlin's bedside. Chovanes and the surgeon were good friends and Chovanes wasn't shy about telling the story of what he and Busching had done that day.

The surgeon raised his eyebrows, shot a look over at Busching, and said, "You did that?"

Busching cringed inside, *Oh, no*. He thought he was going to get in trouble. He knew what he did wasn't protocol in New York City. He had broken all the rules and improvised as a combat field medic.

"Well, you saved his life," said the surgeon.

Busching gave him an incredulous look.

"No, I'm telling you," insisted the surgeon. "Without the treatment he got in the hole he would've died."

Busching heaved a sigh of relief, and an embarrassed but proud-of-himself grin spread out across his face. That put him in a good mood for the rest of the day.

Busching went home, took out his notes, and listened to his old classroom tapes for the lecture on crush syndrome from two years before. The taped voice said, "It has a 100% mortality rate if not treated while it was happening prior to being freed."

Hmmmm, Busching mused. I really did help.

The First Responders

THE FLAG RAISING AT GROUND ZERO

A year after September 11th I started hearing about a photograph of the first flag raising down at Ground Zero, but I hadn't seen it yet. From what I can tell, this photograph was never published for the public to see. It appeared only in police publications, *Police Beat Magazine* and, on page 79 in *Above Hallowed Ground*, a photography coffee table book put out by the New York City Police Department. Other than that, the photograph had never been seen by anyone except the guys who were in it and the photographer.

There is a very famous photograph of a flag-raising at Ground Zero: a shot of three firemen published on the cover of *Time Magazine*, in newspapers, on postcards and postage stamps. It wasn't that one. The photograph I'm talking about was of two Emergency cops, Richard Miller and Richard Hartigan, climbing a ladder propped up against the partial remains of the weather antenna from the North Tower. The antenna had broken lose during the collapse, hurtled down, and speared the ground. It stood fifteen feet in the air and leaned to the right.

When it was finally shown to me, it was framed and mounted on a wooden plaque. It was hanging on the wall in the lounge at Nine-Truck in Queens. I'd find out later every ESU command had a copy displayed in quarters.

The photograph was taken on the morning of September 12th. The day started at 5 AM, in the auditorium of Stuyvesant High School. The first shift had arrived to begin the search and rescue. For the next nine months the school would be the command post of the Emergency Service Unit.

It had been a long night. There was constant activity at the site. Nobody had slept, or if they had, it was just an hour or two. Under those conditions one's body got tired and one's mind went racing. A hundred and something beat-tired cops slouched down in the rows of wooden chairs and waited for instructions. They watched the tide of movement among their supervisors, who were supposed to be telling them what to do and, while they waited, sometimes they nodded off to catch some Z's. Some were lost in thought or speaking privately to the guy next to him, and some couldn't talk at all because of that sick, sinking feeling your friend was buried under a pile of rubble and he might still be alive and they had you sitting on your ass.

Richard Miller sat quietly in the auditorium, his stomach all tied in knots because he was anxious to get down to Ground Zero and do some work. Yesterday had been futile—nothing got done. Now it was time to get serious. Miller saw an American flag on the auditorium stage. It was on a short pole, propped in a metal socket on the wall. He could almost hear the Pledge of Allegiance, recited a million times at assembly in the school auditorium or, right hand over the heart, a hundred young voices singing the national anthem. Miller couldn't take his eyes off the flag. He kept thinking about his country being attacked, and looking at the flag made him feel patriotic.

Miller was a member of FEMA and was assigned to the FEMA New York Task Force Team along with twenty-six other ESU cops including Hartigan, Schwerner, Berarducci, Stefanakos, Winwood, Sergeant Buscemi, Sergeant White, Sergeant Hargrove, K-9 cops, and other officers from Trucks Four and Nine. Lambkin was put in charge of the FEMA team. He hadn't been too happy about it at first, but it turned out to be a blessing in disguise, because he and his team worked independently of the NYPD. For the next few weeks, the FEMA team was an entity unto itself. They did their own morning briefings and, based on that day's information, they'd go down to the pile to look for live or viable bodies.

By midmorning, Miller was out among the debris on a search team, and it was time to break for a meal. He climbed out of the rubble and looked back at the bleak landscape of gray, and more shades of gray, and noticed the colors of "red, white, and blue" were missing.

Miller turned to his teammate, Hartigan, and said, "We're gonna put a flag up for Mike Curtin and the boys."

Hartigan thought, *okay, but where're we goin' to find a flag?* He didn't know what Miller had in mind, but he tagged along to see where all of this would lead. Miller went looking for a flag. Hartigan followed him around the perimeter of the debris pile and then down into one of the lower areas (it could have been the Port Authority garage) and they walked up the mound towards Church and Vey. Miller couldn't find a flag. He thought about the flag in the auditorium of the high school, but he didn't know if he was bold enough to walk right in and take it. He did see flags outside the frozen zone on Broadway, but he didn't want to take a flag off a pole already standing or where there were flags on buildings. But Miller was determined to find a flag. His mind kept going back to the flag on the stage, after all, it triggered this whole thing. He might as well take it. He turned to Hartigan and told him about the flag sitting on the stage at Stuyvesant High School and he said he wanted to go back and get it.

"And, you know what? I'm goin' to put that flag right up there," said Miller, and he pointed to the globe and the tall spear-like structure that stood in the center of the debris pile.

Miller had a military background. In 1979, at the age of nineteen, he joined the Marines for four years. He was stationed at Fort McCullen in Alabama, and Camp Pendleton in California, and Camp Smith in Hawaii. Miller knew there were a lot of guys in ESU who had military time, including some of the cops that were missing. Vinny Danz, who was Miller's friend and sniper-team partner, a former Marine and a reservist in the Coast Guard, and Stephen Driscoll was Navy, Jerome Dominguez was Air Force, and Sergeant John Coughlin, a former Marine. There were also guys whom Miller didn't know personally, such as, Claude Richards, an Army Airborne Ranger and a Presidential Honor Guard, and Brian McDonnell, 82nd Airborne in the Army. Finally there was Mike Curtin. In the bombing of the Alfred P. Murrah Federal Building in Oklahoma City in 1995, Curtin had been sent down as part of the New York FEMA team. In the rubble he recovered the body of a Marine and draped an American flag over his body so he might be carried out with the honor that is bestowed on a soldier.

Miller wanted to put a flag up for all of these men, because that was what it was all about—being an American and showing our colors. It was about protecting our country and the soldier's code no man gets left behind. Coughlin had given Miller the book, *Flags of Our Fathers*. It was about the six marines that raised the flag on Iwo Jima during

World War II. Coughlin thought it was a great book, and he knew how Miller felt about the flag and he knew how patriotic Miller was, and Coughlin had gotten after him to read it. Miller never found time until he broke his hand playing sports and was assigned to a desk. Coughlin put that book in front of him and said, "Now, you have no excuse."

Miller and Hartigan wanted to make sure the flag raising went without a hitch. They ran out and found their boss, Sergeant White, and they told him what they wanted to do. White said if they could find a flag, it was okay with him if they did it. Miller said he was going to borrow the one he saw up on the stage in the auditorium at Stuyvesant High School.

"Don't get caught," said White, cautiously. He looked up in the air like he didn't really want to hear this.

The two cops headed back to the school, and before they could get through the front doors, Chief Purtell walked out and stopped them.

"Where're you guys going?" said Purtell.

"Chief, we need a favor," said Miller, and told him the story of how Curtin had draped a flag over a Marine's body when he brought the soldier out of the rubble at the Oklahoma bombing.

"When Mike comes out of this building," said Miller. "I want him to see that a flag is up."

"That's a good idea," said Purtell. "Where're you goin' to get a flag?"

"Well, if you hadn't stopped me," said Miller, coyly. "I was goin' to steal/borrow the flag off the stage."

"Go get that flag!" said the Chief, in a booming voice.

Miller and Hartigan went into the school's auditorium, it was empty except for a conference of big bosses sitting around a table on the stage. The flag was sticking out from a wall behind them. The bosses paid no attention to the two cops walking by them across the stage to the flag. Miller reached up and took the flag down from the socket and officially rolled it around the pole. He turned to Hartigan and told him to grab a blanket from a pile near the stage. Then Miller wrapped the blanket around the flag, not wanting to draw attention.

They had just snuck passed the bosses at the table and headed to the exit when Purtell entered the school surrounded by his entourage of men. He looked the two cops over and asked where was the flag. Miller pointed to the bundle under his arm.

"Unfurl that flag!" said Purtell, loud and firm. "Show it with pride."

"Yes, sir," both men answered.

They quickly pulled the blanket off from around the flag and kept on going. When they got out of the school, Miller held the flag nonchalantly down by his side and hoped that no one would notice what he was holding. He was very proud of the flag, but he just didn't need anyone asking him a million questions about why he was walking around with it. They would know why when he put it up.

Once outside, they looked for transportation and saw an ESU pickup truck parked a block away from the school. They ran to the driver, Sue Scott, an ESU cop from the HazMat unit, asked for a ride, and hopped in the back.

Suddenly, out of nowhere, a reporter ran over to them. He must have had his radar on. Down there the place was crawling with the press and every single one of them was looking for a story. With his press credentials dangling around his neck, he slapped his hands down on the back of the truck and made his presence known.

"Where you guys goin'?" asked the reporter.

"We'll tell you later," said Miller.

"Can I have your names?"

"We'll tell you later".

They drove off leaving the reporter without a story.

Miller and Hartigan rode around the perimeter of the debris pile and stopped at the pile entrance at Vey and Church Street. They jumped off the back of the truck and, wading through a crowd of firemen, cops, and construction workers, they walked towards the site. Miller kept the flag down low but, as he entered the pile, he raised it to his shoulder. He approached a fire chief and said to him, "Chief, can you give me a fireman to give me and my partner a hand?"

"Where you goin' with that?" asked the fire chief, looking at the flag propped up on the cop's shoulder.

"I'm goin' to put it on that pole," said Miller. Then he pointed to the antenna sticking out from the ground near the globe. "Right there."

The fire chief became excited. His eyes widened as a little kid on Christmas morning. He said, "Wha'd'ya need?"

"A ladder."

The fire chief looked around for the closest firemen and called two of his guys over and told them to get a ladder. When the firemen came back with a ladder, the four of them, two cops and two firemen, walked out towards the middle of the pile.

Then something unexpected happened. Everybody working on the pile stopped what they were doing and looked up. Hundreds of faces turned to watch the flag being carried across the rubble. They watched the four men stop at the foot of the pole and they saw the flag being unfurled. The men on the pile knew something important was about to happen, and they put down their tools and started to flood in that direction.

Now, where the pole stood, there was a deep drop of fifty feet on one side and another drop of seventy feet on the other. The area quickly became congested as everybody gathered around, squeezing closer, tittering on the edge. The fire chief yelled for the crowd to get back so one of the fireman could get around and place the ladder against the pole.

Miller was about to pass the flag to the fireman. Hartigan saw this and gave Miller a quick poke to the rib, and said, "Richie, get up there."

"Oh, yeah," said Miller. He had been distracted by the attention. The spotlight was on him and he was nervous. Actually, Miller didn't care who put the flag up. He only knew he wanted it up. But it had been his idea, so it made sense for a cop to be the one to finally put it in place.

Miller climbed as high as he could and balanced himself on the next to the top rung. He wanted to climb higher, but the ladder was a little shaky. Construction workers passed wire and rope to the two firemen, and they passed it to Hartigan and he passed it up the ladder to Miller.

It took some work to tie the flag to the pole, but once it was sturdy and strong, a light wind lifted the flag. Then, the stirring crowd stood still and it became quiet. The fire chief stepped forward and yelled, "Order! Arms!"

The First Responders

Hundreds of rescue workers in their hard hats and dirty faces stood to attention and did a hand salute. Miller looked out over this sea of men, and seeing that moment gave him a chill of pride. He never thought there would have been such a reaction. These were weary men. They had seen their country under attack and their City in ruins. Their hearts were broken, and patriotism was their comfort.

The ceremony lasted a few moments. Then they lowered their hands from their brows and silently the crowd broke up and returned to the work on the pile.

The next day Miller and Hartigan felt nostalgic for those few moments and hoped somebody had taken a photograph. They hadn't realized the effect it would have on them, and they wished that moment had been captured on film.

Over the next few days they started hearing about a photograph of a flag raising at Ground Zero. Somebody said there was a copy of it in the papers. Nobody was reading newspapers; nobody was watching TV; but they were dying to see this photograph. Then somebody managed to tear a page from the Daily News and tape it to a lamppost. It was a photograph of three firemen raising an American flag. The photo was taken in the late afternoon of September 12th. The three firemen—Don McWilliams, George Johnson and Billy Eisengrein—had borrowed a flag from a yacht docked on the Hudson River and then raised it on a flag pole anchored in the rubble about twenty feet off the ground at West Street. When Miller saw the photograph, his immediate reaction was it was a great picture and it reminded him of the Marine flag raising of Iwo Jima. But deep down inside he was a little disappointed that nobody had a camera when he put his flag up.

A few weeks later Miller and Hartigan were called to Police Headquarters. They were invited to take the elevator ride to the "penthouse" and speak to the powers that be. Everybody was waiting for them. There were enough gold stars in the room to light up the night sky. On the chief's desk was a fourteen-by-sixteen-inch black and white photograph of the flag Miller and Hartigan had raised on the morning of September 12th.

It was a beautiful photograph. Its composition was reminiscent of W. Eugene Smith's 1955 Pittsburgh photograph of a young boy climbing over a street sign. But in this photograph there were three police officers. Two were holding a ladder as the third man climbed up and untangled the flag that had wrapped itself around the pole. It was taken with a long lens that pulled the skeletal tier of the South Tower in from the background. The photo was taken by Detective John Botte, the police commissioner's personal photographer. Botte was standing there presiding over his pride and joy.

The chief sitting at his desk lightly tapped his finger on the photograph and asked Miller and Hartigan if they were the two cops who raised the flag.

Yes, we are.

Everyone looked the photograph over and admired its powerful and painful message.

"And you see this?" Miller said, pointing to the structure the flag was attached to. "That's the antenna from the North Tower."

It is? The bosses fell back in their leather chairs with mouths agape.

Then Botte held up a pen and asked Miller and Hartigan to sign the photograph. But the request seemed out of place and confusing. They looked at this black and white picture and they knew it wasn't of them. Although the faces of the men were not visible behind their respirator masks, it was clear to Miller and Hartigan there were two other people standing in their place. They watched the pen in Botte's hand as he brought it over to them, but they wouldn't take it.

"It's a beautiful photograph," said Miller. "I'll find the guys that are in that picture for you."

"But, you're Rich Miller. You put that flag up," said Botte, earnestly. "And, I took that picture."

"That's not us in the photograph," said Miller. "And yes, Hartigan and I did put the flag up. But that's not us. We'll find the guys that are in the photograph and they can sign it."

Miller and Hartigan left the office, and they looked at each other, and they knew they were thinking the same thing. What was that all about? *There were stranger things in heaven and earth, Horatio.*

But, the explanation was simple. Botte had been looking for the three cops in his black and white photograph. He had taken it three days after the initial flag raising. Actually, there are four cops in that picture: Seth Gahr from Two-Truck who climbed the ladder and adjusted the flag, and at the bottom of the ladder were Sergeant Mike McGinnis and John Busching. Busching is the tallest and his medical bag is lying on the ground. The fourth man was Kevin Reynolds, in between McGinnis and Busching, but all that's visible is a gloved hand grabbing a rung of the ladder as an extra arm at chest level. Those hands belong to Reynolds. Unfortunately, the composition and the compressing effect of the telephoto lens pretty much deleted him from the photograph.

Then one day—it had to have been two months later, Miller was not sure, because it was hard to tell time in those days—he and Hartigan were invited to a Lieutenant's Benevolent Association dinner. Before the evening ended, Lieutenant Anthony Garvey, who was president of the LBA, presented the two officers with a colored photograph of the flag raising. Garvey had taken this photograph with a cheap instamatic camera as he stood at the back of the pile on the morning of September 12th.

When Miller and Hartigan saw this photograph they were speechless. They saw themselves on the ladder shot from a distance. The flag was luminous, as though a light was shining on it. The background was devoid of any detail—a dense gray fog of suspended dust and smoke. In the foreground are the blue hard hats and the backs of the heads and shoulders of construction workers, steelworkers, medics, firemen, and police officers. And way back in the background in the bottom right hand corner, a woman was being carried out on a stretcher with an IV bottle held in the air—the last survivor of the North Tower removed from a broken staircase.

The photograph was perfect. It showed everybody working together, not just one particular group.

The photograph may have gone unnoticed by the media, and the public may never see it. But that's okay with ESU, because this was a personal photograph; it was private, as a family snapshot that stays in the photo album.

When people talked about this photograph, it was as a game of Chinese telephone. Nobody could get the story straight. It was something everyone heard about, but never seen. Anyone that wasn't ESU thought Botte's black and white photograph was of the original flag raising at Ground Zero. It was popping up all over the place, on book covers, on T-shirts, and on posters. The irony was they'd show it to Miller and say, "Hey, look. I have the picture of the first flag raising."

Miller would lift an eyebrow and just say, "I beg to differ" and leave it at that.

He knew why he put the flag up. It wasn't for publicity, or for all the hoop-la that followed. It was an expression of a part of him that was patriotic, and it was a personal gesture to his friends. And on that day, and in the days that followed, Miller and Hartigan would work the pile and watch flags unfolding in front of them. They'd jab each other and point at every new flag raised, and say, "Eh, look at that!"

Raising the flag was as therapy, every time one went up. It meant things were coming back together. Rebuilding. It meant the City was regrouping at Ground Zero, and the country was regrouping, too. Flag sales rose, and flags were being attached to cars antennas and stuck on bumper stickers as peel-on tattoos; and flags were being draped across shop windows and planted in front lawns as patriotic sunflowers. And each flag raised was a personal gesture..

"One flag inspired another flag to go up," said Miller. "And another flag inspired a nation."

The biggest satisfaction Miller had from raising the flag that morning came a few days before the first anniversary of 9/11. He was walking through quarters and the phone rang and he answered it. It was a Mount Vernon police officer, named Ted Louy, who said, "I'm lookin' for Lieutenant McArdle."

At the time, McArdle was in charge of Four-Truck and was Miller's immediate supervisor. "Well, you just missed him," said Miller.

"Ah, ya know, I've been tryin' to track McArdle down," said Louy, disappointed. "Because I'm tryin' to find this guy, Rich Miller."

Miller did a double take and held the phone a little from his ear. He let Louy go on with his story about the Green Berets that went to fight in Afghanistan and how he was hoping to ask Miller to come to Fort Campbell to personally thank the guys.

"Well, I'm Rich Miller."

"Oh, my God!" said Louy. "Hey, listen, would you be interested in going down to Fort Campbell, Kentucky to thank the troops that went to Afghanistan? They lost guys in the stray bombing incident."

He was referring to the 5th Group Special Forces A-Team that was hit by an errant air strike on December 5th, 2001. Three of the 2nd and 3rd Battalion of 5th Group Special Forces soldiers were killed and twenty were injured.

Miller was about to accept the invitation when Louy said, "But, there's only one catch."

"Well, what is it?"

"You'd have to go down on your own expense."

"Count me in!" said Miller, excitedly. "'Cause that's the way I want it! I just wanna be able to thank these guys." There was something about going out of his way for these soldiers that struck the right chord. Since 9/11, there had been controversy as to who put the flag up first: the police or fire department. Miller wanted no part of the dispute. He had turned down all requests for interviews and avoided the limelight. Then about a year after 9/11, and when he thought the controversy over the flag had calmed down, he decided it would be okay to do an interview. A reporter was writing a story about Flag Day and wanted to include the flag raising at Ground Zero. Miller thought it would be a harmless story, so he met with the reporter. Everything was going smoothly until the reporter wanted to know if Miller was bitter the firemen had gotten the credit. This really irked Miller. He couldn't believe the subject was brought up. He said, "If this is going to become a negative story over who put the flag up first, FD or PD, and am I disgruntle about that? Then this interview is over."

But Miller was sure the Green Berets *would* get it. They understood he put the flag up for *them*—and for every soldier that came before them, and for every soldier that would come after them.

Miller and Hartigan bought their plane tickets and flew down to Kentucky and stayed at Fort Campbell for four days. It was great meeting the men that actually went "over there" and hand something back to "them." These were the men that went to Afghanistan one month after September 11th and with the anti-Taliban rebel tribes of ragtag freedom fighters, they fought Al Qaeda and sent them packing out of the country and into the mountains. Miller couldn't believe he was standing in their Team Room, surrounded by these living legends of the military.

He said to them, "You guys are dynamite." And the soldiers would cheer and say back to him, "No. You're dynamite."

"No. *You're* dynamite," insisted Miller. "We have a saying in our unit that when a civilian is in trouble, they call a cop. When a cop is in trouble, they call ESU. We were in trouble and we called upon you guys and you really handed it back for us. And I'm here to thank you guys."

Everybody started hooting and hollering and grabbing each other in hugs and handshakes—it reminded Miller of Sergeant Coughlin, who, after every big job well-done, would say to his guys, "Okay, lets do our ESU hugs and handshakes."

In January of 2003, war with Iraq looked imminent. The Secretary of State, Colin Powell was presenting the case against Saddam Hussein at the UN on how much of a threat he was to America, and the UN's International Atomic Energy Agency inspectors combed the Iraq's countryside, desert caves, and baby food factories, to find Hussein's elusive Weapons of Mass Destruction. But it didn't matter what the outcome was, President George W. Bush had already made up his mind to invade Iraq. Military bases went to lock down mode. Deployment was inevitable.

On March 19th 2003, when America went to war with Iraq, Hartigan and Miller folded an American flag for the men of 5th Group to carry into Baghdad.

The First Responders

SEARCH AND RESCUE

On Wednesday, September 12th, Mark DeMarco of Team Three, returned to the Customs House. He had been unable to sleep the night before. He tossed and turned and every time he closed his eyes, reliving the collapse, asking himself the same questions over and over again: *What if I'd made a left turn instead of a right? What if I'd been picked to go on another team? What if I had waited two more minutes in the building? What if I hadn't walked faster than the other guys?*

By Wednesday, the Customs House was nothing more than three standing walls and a big hole, but when DeMarco walked inside, he could reconstruct everything clearly. Most of the dust had settled, and the only obstruction was the dull haze of smoke from the fires still burning in the adjacent buildings. He spotted his medical bag lying on the floor covered with gray dust and knew he'd found the place where he stood when the North Tower crashed through the roof. The bag was on an untouched patch of floor about fifteen feet square where he, Beaury, McNally, Beatty, and Sergeant Francis had fallen and taken cover. The rest of the floor was obliterated. Then he saw hand prints smeared along the marble wall to the edge of a hole that dropped plumb down seventy to hundred feet. The prints were his and those of his teammates.

Seeing those prints made him go all "philosophical" inside. How had they managed not to fall? They'd been grabbing on to each other as they advanced along the wall, and if one of them had slipped, they'd all have been killed. A miracle.

There were a lot of guys that felt they experienced miracles. Things played over and over in their heads as a broken record. For instance, in the days that followed 9/11, while driving back and forth from work, DeMasi would think of a million things that saved his life. He thought about Sergeant Gillis, who had died in the South Tower, standing in the garage at Eight-Truck, and yelling "Come with me!" But DeMasi hadn't gone because he wanted to put equipment in his truck. And he thought Sergeant Sullivan definitely saved his life when he made that last minute decision to switch from rescue to tactical mode. Hell! That three minutes delay kept DeMasi and his teammates from walking into the South Tower before it collapsed.

On September 11th, before the Towers collapsed, Hargrove ran into Chief Purtell. He looked worried and preoccupied. Hargrove asked, "Are you all right?" Purtell said, "My sister might be in the Tower." Hargrove tried to ease his mind by saying, "If it's any comfort, I saw thousands of people leaving the Towers." That night Hargrove saw him again, and again he asked him, "Chief, is everything all right?" The Chief said, "The baby was sick and she didn't go to work."

Joseph McCormack had been in the South Tower with Sergeant Coughlin. In the lobby, Coughlin sent him back to the truck to get a safety harness. When he was walking back to the Tower, Winkler stopped him. Five minutes later (and before McCormack had time to return), the South Tower fell.

That was how luck worked. It takes almost nothing to change fate. In 1983, when McCormack was thirteen years old, his father, Joseph, Sr., was an Emergency cop in Two-Truck. He was killed in the line of duty when a deranged man fired a shotgun and the bullet ricocheted off a tree, striking him in the side, passing beneath a fold on his bulletproof vest, and piercing his heart.

On September 11th, McCormack felt unbelievably lucky. He was sure his father had looked down from Heaven and placed his hand on his shoulder that day.

On Wednesday, New York City was gray. The sky was gray, the buildings were gray, and the military helicopter hovering over Lower Manhattan was gray. It was hard to tell if the gray was a real color or just the mood of so many people.

There was an unnatural silence. Only the whirling sound of the chopper's rotors broke the collective reverie and confirmed the emptiness. The clock on the steeple of St. Paul's Church had stopped at 8:43. It is an old church, as old as New York City. The front of the church faces Broadway, and its graveyard is in the back and extends down behind a black iron fence to Church Street and faces where the Trade Center had been. The church had seen a lot of history. George

Washington was inaugurated there. Now its old graveyard was blanketed in a gray snow that covered the head stones of revolutionary soldiers and New York society millionaires.

For the first few days, the ESU teams didn't have any transportation from the high school to the site. They'd throw the equipment on their backs and walk south down West Street, then cut east on Chambers, and south again to Church and Vesey.

The view on the walk from the school looked as an open market place. A makeshift city had sprung up overnight. Tents and tables lined West Street. Good American folks had driven down from every part of the country and set them up. The guys could grab a cup of coffee, a buttered roll wrapped in cellophane, a 12-pack bag of Hanes socks or a paperback bible. The coffee was for the most part terrible, but the hearts that brewed it were all in the right place.

Stefanakos remembered the first day he set out to work on the pile. He was part of an eight-man team and they made their entry at Greenwich Street near the remains of the South Tower. The men hooked unto each other with their rappel lines, connected together as a Texas chain gang, and descended into the site. They climbed down and up and over the twisted metal that brought them ten stories up to the top of the pile. Stefanakos looked down and saw a huge smoldering crater. The sight was so overwhelming, he froze. He thought about the 12,000 people buried down there (in the first few days everyone thought the number of the missing was that high), and he couldn't imagine how they were going to sift through this complicated and enormous mess to find them all.

All day and all night the rescue workers silently picked through the rubble. They climbed mounds of steel and looked down into voids, and every monotonous step would set off a replay of the previous twenty-four hours, over and over again, until it ground down time and consciousness. Stefanakos remembered walking by body parts—an arm or a finger or a piece of flesh. At this time, the orders were only to look for live recoveries. He came across plane parts. These were to be picked up and placed in a large blue box the FBI had situated outside the perimeter. Stefanakos wholeheartedly believed there were people alive in there—that he'd lift a slab of concrete and Tommy Langone would jump to his feet and in his fast talking banter he'd tell him off for taking so long. Then he'd look at this twisted pile of steel and think, "How could there be anyone alive in there?" Those Towers had pancaked down with one-percent of the energy of an atomic bomb and pulverized everything with their power.

Time was measured by the shrinking of the pile. On the first and second day after 9/11, the big machinery—cranes and bulldozers—came in to clear the streets of debris that surrounded the Trade Center. Liberty, Church, Vesey, and West Streets—the streets that comprise the perimeter just outside the pile where the Towers fell—were covered with a carpet of dust two feet thick, variously shaped chucks of fallen buildings from tiny fragments to pieces of concrete and steel the size of a refrigerator; dozens and dozens of burned and crushed cars. Everyday, Stefanakos would take a conscious look at how the debris was disappearing from the perimeter. It was scooped up and driven away in dumpsters; destination: the Fresh Kills dump in Staten Island. The debris along the perimeter was gone. But the debris inside the site never seemed to go away. As the dust and large chunks of cement were taken away, other things came into view: blue prints, papers, memos, and photographs were everywhere, as junk washing up on the beach. But no bodies washed ashore. They only found *things*. It wasn't until six weeks into the dig they actually began to find people.

Stefanakos found a photo of a woman with her family—a part of someone's life displayed on a desk. There was a game he often played inside his head when cruising on patrol trying to guess what people's lives were like. He'd drive by a house and see a family there and wonder about the personal politics of their everyday lives. Looking at the photograph he wondered where the woman was. Was she okay? Had she made it out alive?

Sometimes Stefanakos felt angry there were so many rescue workers. Hundreds of volunteers had come from every town from every state in the country. The frozen zone around Ground Zero hadn't been closed off yet, so it was wide open for volunteers to come and go as they pleased. There was no command post for the volunteers to report to and place their names on a roster so they could be accounted for. The problem was the volunteers would wander around on the pile looking over the shoulders of the rescue workers. Stefanakos would be trying to get some work done and here would come somebody with no rescue training stepping on his heels and getting in his way. He'd bite his tongue, but he wanted to shout, "Thank you for being here but, get outta my way!"

Machines became the rescue workers' eyes and ears. Some of the ESU cops were search specialist operating gadgets known as "pole cameras." These are low-light cameras mounted on extenders. They can be threaded through crevices and used as underground periscopes to tilt, pan, and swivel around. They also had a "Track Person Locator"—a listening device placed against the ground to pick up vibrations and noises.

Randy Miller, an ESU search specialist, was assigned to a team that included FEMA Task Force One from Florida, two firemen, and a K-9 officer with a search dog trained to pick up the scent of human blood. The team was sent into the ruins of the Marriot Hotel to check for confined spaces where there might be oxygen depreciation, indicating people either were or had been breathing in there.

Half the hotel had collapsed, but a restaurant inside had uncannily been spared. It looked undisturbed, as if it were an ordinary empty restaurant waiting for customers. The tables and chairs were neatly arranged with their linen, crystals, forks and knives. In the bar there were little menus clipped in holders sitting on the tables. The cash registers were untouched, and the money was still there. Everything was covered in a layer of dust, and that gave it an old, haunted look. Looking in there was as peeking in through the windows of the Titanic as it rests undisturbed in its watery grave.

Inside the hotel, apart from the restaurant, they found a Fire Department's search line—a long rope, one end would be attached to the fireman himself so that, as Handsel and Grettel's bread crumbs, there would be a way to find the firemen if he got lost or separated or to help find his way back. There were also hoses and controls for the inflatable bags, and other hoses that dead-ended into the rubble. Their presence showed the firemen had been actively working a rescue situation before something abruptly stopped them.

When the team entered the hotel, the search dog immediately became excited and started to dig. When a dog digs in a circumstance as this, it's usually a good indication bodies were nearby, but the area was too unstable to recover anything. They pulled out the dog and the machines, and left the graves undisturbed.

During one of the descents, rappelling into the crater at the center of the pile, Stefanakos and Winwood dropped fifty feet down a void and found themselves in the underground shopping mall. They saw a GAP store pretty much intact. The clothes rack and the ceiling were only partially collapsed; thirty feet away, the ceiling was on the floor. There was a bookstore with shelves of books and an ATM machine. It looked eerie and dusty, as though time stood still. Winwood wanted to get a better look. He switched on his flashlight and inadvertently shined the light into the face of a mannequin. He wasn't expecting to see eyes staring back at him, painted on or otherwise! The sight of the mannequin made him jump ten feet in the air and bounce on his line as a plastic spider at the end of an elastic string.

A few days after the attack, everybody thought Liberty One was collapsing. Liberty One was the freestanding, twenty-six-story building that sat next to Century 21 on Vey Street, and it looked slightly twisted. The rescue workers were in the process of making contact with somebody whom was alive in a cavity beneath the building. Men were screaming questions down to the trapped person and using a bullhorn pressed against the ground to amplify their voices. They had lowered microphones through crevices and were listening to someone deep underground tapping answers back to them. There was no voice—just one tap for yes and two taps for no. They worked and worked trying to remove the debris to get to him. The steelworkers cut through the tangle masses of steel and pulled it out of the way. Big cranes were reaching down into the pile and peeling back the debris. Suddenly a horn screamed a warning, and voices over the portable radios ordered everyone out of the area. Engineers had been keeping a laser scope on Liberty One. There had been a shift in the building's foundation and they thought the building was coming down.

One of the steelworkers stood his ground as the rescue crew began to move to a safer place. He promised them the building wasn't coming down. He said, "If you see us runnin'; run! But, if we're not runnin' then nuttin's happenin'."

Winwood was part of the rescue crew. He heard what the steelworker said, but he wasn't convinced. He asked, "How can you say that? Where's your degree?"

"I don't need a degree. I built these buildings. I know these buildings," said the steelworker, firmly. "These buildings aren't goin' anywhere. My grandfather built it with my father and my father built it with me."

Winwood felt that was fair enough, but he'd still decide to heed the engineers' warning; but as everyone else pulled away from the site, the steelworker didn't budge. He was defiant and proud of his father's work. He stood there under Liberty One, and the other steelworkers stood with him, while the engineers on the radio fiddlied with their instruments.

An hour later when, as it turned out, there hadn't been any further movement from the structure, and the building had not collapsed, the rescue workers returned, but the person they had been trying to save was no longer tapping. Winwood was sorry he didn't believe the steelworker, and he was determined to never doubt their word again.

Sometimes there would be shouting matches between the firemen and the steelworkers. Although the fire department lost a lot of men—nobody denies them their pain—but they had no control over themselves. They'd yell at the steelworkers, "You cut here and get this out of the way! We have work to do! We have to go find our brothers!" The steelworkers would try to explain, "If we cut *that* we'll loose *this* and *this*." It was a very emotional scene. The firemen would want something impossible or dangerous done, and the steelworkers would run to the police and say, "You're the cops—do something!" But the cops could only promise to watch their backs if things got hairy. They'd say, "Don't do anything that'll get anyone hurt or killed. Follow your rules and we'll back you up." And, that was the way things were run.

Every day there were meetings between the fire department, the police department, DDC (Department of Design and Construction), Port Authority, and FEMA. The Army made aerial photographs of the site dividing it into sectors and, if the manpower was available, a team would be assigned to each sector: A, B, C, D, or, Liberty Street Sector, Church Street Sector, Dey Street Sector, Liberty, and West Sector, etc. There were also Logistic and Relief Teams, and teams assigned to engineers to escort them where they had to go to do their surveys.

It's hard to explain the attitude of the firemen. Maybe it was the arrogance stemming from the power suddenly thrust upon the fire department combined with the devastating loss of 343 men; but, whatever it was, if the police crossed over into their zone, it usually led to a confrontation. On one occasion, the ESU teams were walking in to start their shift and a National Guardsman stopped them and said they didn't have permission to enter the area. The cops looked at him in disbelief. They said, "Who told you that?" It turned out the Battalion Fire Chief in charge of that particular sector had told the Guardsman to keep the police out of the area. Meanwhile, volunteer firemen, showing no more insignia than a T-shirt with some out-of-town department logo printed on its back, were freely walking by the Guardsman. No ID check; just the trust in a T-shirt.

This led to a shouting match. The Guardsman backed off, but the next day it happened again. This time a fire chief found another reason to keep the cops off the pile. He said, "You don't have the proper equipment on," even though the cops were wearing the same gear as he was.

The Fire Department felt it was their job. They didn't want anyone that wasn't a member of the "brotherhood" on the site. On one occasion, a police officer was administering an IV to a construction worker who had a crushed foot. A fire captain came up from behind, pulled the IV needle out of the vein, dragged the cop away, took a swing at him, and screamed, "This is my job!"

Whatever FD's problem was, their lack of cooperation with the police and other agencies interfered with coordination. For example: One day a group of six engineers wanted to check the slurry wall—a three feet thick and eighty-foot-deep slab of concrete that supported the ground that surrounded the basement underneath the World Trade Center. The engineers were concerned the collapse of the Towers might have destabilized the slabs. If the slabs went, the Hudson River would flood the area. Because of this instability, an escort of three ESU cops was assigned to lead the engineers to the slurry wall. Outside, a rescue team was set up near the point of entry just in case something went wrong. Winkler was on the escort team, and he led the six engineers through the basement. They passed two-foot-thick steel columns that had spilt and shifted off their pedestals. There were other columns melted from the intense heat. The men walked through the subterranean parking lots. One side of the lot had collapsed. The cars were smashed with tires melted as wax crayons. The other side of the parking lot was intact, the cars unscathed and covered in dust. Then they turned a corner and were surprised to see five firemen walking around the parking lot as if they were strolling through a park.

There was an awkward moment. Finally, Winkler asked, "What're you guys doin' here?" Nobody knew the firemen were down there. The entire area had been off limits to everyone but the engineers. How they got through and why they were there was a perfect example of lack of coordination.

Below the Trade Center, in the belly of the wreckage, fires were still burning even ninety-nine days after the collapse. There also was flooding and voids as large as locker rooms and hallways where a man could actually stand up and walk, so you never knew whom you would meet.

Richard Miller and a couple of other ESU cops were sent in on the third day to search the sub-levels of the Customs House. When they reached Sub-Level 4, they saw an underground parking lot with State Department vehicles. Some of the cars were intact and some were crushed. As they stood there taking in the cavernous remains, they saw a middle-aged man in civilian clothes, walking towards them in the dark. The man was alone and he was shining a small, one-cell porta light to guide his way. Miller was stunned to see him, and he said, "What're you doin' here?"

The man's name was Lee Ielpi, a retired fireman. He said he was looking for his son, Jonathan, a missing firefighter.

Miller was moved by the father's search for his son, but he was concerned for his safety in this dangerous place. He said, "Come with us."

"No, I'm all right," said Ielpi. Then he turned and walked into the darkness, his flashlight bouncing a small ball of light at his feet.

A few days later, Miller saw him again. Ielpi had teamed up with another retired fireman, another father looking for his son, and they were tagging behind a group of firemen and searching the pile together.

There was always an anonymous voice coming over the radio screaming some building or another was falling. For example, there was a tremendous piece of steel sticking out of a building over by Financial One at Liberty and West and every day somebody on the radio would cry out, "The piece is shifting! The piece is shifting!" But it was never shifting. Sometimes it was One Liberty Plaza that was about to come down: "Imminent collapse! Imminent collapse!" But it never collapsed, and it's still standing to this very day. The workers down in the pile on the bucket brigade were instructed if they heard the whistle blow three times it meant something was about to come down. They added, "Don't bother to run—you'll never make it out in time. Just take cover under a steel beam and we'll dig you out later!"

Just to show how crazy things were, a couple of days into the search and rescue, the fire chief assigned to the Church Street sector wanted a secondary search of One Liberty Plaza from the basement to the roof. Winkler and his team were sent over to meet the FEMA representatives from California to conduct it. They all were thinking, *you got to be kidding!* It was five o'clock, at the end of the shift, and this building was twenty-six floors high.

A group of OCCB cops (Organized Crime Control Bureau, including the Public Morals and Narcotics Divisions) were sent over to do the

The First Responders

same thing. Winkler and his team were looking at them, and OCCB boys were looking back. Half of these guys were so out of shape with one-too-many-Big Mac-bellies and smoker's coughs they shouldn't be climbing one flight of stairs much less than ten. But there they were.

Winkler said, "Okay, you guys take one to eight and we'll take nine to seventeen and the FEMA team can take the remaining floors."

The three teams went in. Winkler passed a group of construction workers on one of the floors. It seemed the cops weren't the only ones in the building. When Winkler got up to the 9th floor, a radio transmission came bursting over the air: *Everybody out of One Liberty Plaza! Evacuate One Liberty Plaza! Imminent collapse! Imminent collapse!*

"Shit, we just climbed these stairs," said Winkler, annoyed. He and his team began the walk down. All over the staircase, out the door and down the street, was a trail of tools. Winkler followed the sledgehammers, the shovels, and pry bars until he caught up with the group of out of breath OCCB cops. Winkler asked them what had happened and the sergeant said, "We heard a loud boom, and a couple of guys felt the building shaking, so we evacuated. Then we saw the construction workers running, so we ran."

Then Winkler approached the construction workers and asked them what had happened. They told him they'd been loading a pile of plywood and it slipped and fell.

"Did you guys run?" asked Winkler.

"Geez, we went runnin' after—those guys!" pointing to the OCCB cops. "They were runnin' outta the building, so we figured sumthin' was up. So, we ran too!"

Winkler rolled his eyes. Now it was back into the building, back up the stairs, and back to searching the building all over again.

The problem was the old fear of being afraid. It made you uncomfortable. People were there because they thought they *had* to be there and they didn't want anyone to think they *were* afraid. But then, when they got there they were so afraid they became a liability.

One Liberty Plaza was never in any danger of collapse. It was true if you looked at it a certain way, with the clouds moving in the background, it looked as though the building was swaying. But it wasn't swaying.

Again, if you looked at it straight on, it appeared to have a bow, but it didn't have a bow. It was all an optical illusion.

For the first six weeks the workers on the pile felt useless. The men couldn't reach the bodies because they were buried deep under the pile. The recovery teams would drop into the voids and follow the strong, decaying smell of the dead, but they could never get to them. Sometimes they were stopped by hot steam sizzling up from bubbling pools of rainwater boiled by the fire burning under the site. Sometimes a metal girder blocked their path. They'd call in the steelworkers to bring in their torches, but even after the steel was cut, it was often still in the way. Then the operating engineers would bring in their backhoes, cranes, and excavators—machines on tracks with a single hydraulic arm, and they'd lasso the steel columns with chains and lift them out with heavy cranes.

When they began to find bodies, what appeared were pieces of people. They'd open up part of a collapsed stairwell and find parts of many firemen: almost empty helmets, turnout coats, turnout boots with nothing more than a trace of human remains inside them. On one occasion, a crushed elevator was peeled opened onto a mangled pile of legs, but each foot wore a different shoe.

Most cops are used to seeing dead bodies in various stages of decomposition. However, the sight of death hit some of the steelworkers and engineers pretty hard. For instance, one day a grappler, who was an engineer that worked the three-ton grappler machine, was digging on the pile when he made a gruesome discovery. This machine used a claw-like bucket that opened and closed as the mouth of a Tyrannosaurus Rex and was attached to the end of a hydraulic arm to bite into the debris and scoop it up. Then he'd shake the bucket and let some of the dirt fall out, little by little, between the "teeth," as sifting flour through a sieve. The engineer using the grappler picked up a big mound of debris and he started shaking out the dirt. Suddenly two arms and two legs flopped out of the bucket. They were from the body of a partly decomposed woman. He took one look and lost his composure. He let go of the controls and the bucket opened and emptied its contents to the ground. Then he fell out of the cab of the grappler-machine, and vomited.

The Fire Department was in charge of the GPS (Global Positioning System). This is a worldwide radio-navigation system formed from a constellation of twenty-four satellites and their ground stations. GPS uses these "man-made stars" as reference-points to calculate positions that are accurate to within a few meters. When biological remains were found at the site, a yellow crime-scene tape was stretched out to partition the area. Then the GPS team would be called in. They'd stand next to the remains and fiddle with the GPS receiver until they got the longitude and latitude of their position. They'd write the coordinates down on a 95-tag (95-tags are also called "toe-tags"; these are three-by-five-inch, glossy piece of paper with a string attached, used to identify human remains for the coroner). Then the information would be transferred to a large map to pinpoint visually the areas where bodies or body parts had been recovered. The only problem was sometimes the Fire Department was getting erroneous readings from the GPS. The errors could have been caused by the satellite signal bouncing off the surrounding high-rise buildings or atmospheric interferences. But whatever the causes, they weren't corrected, so even though the body was actually found in one place, it was documented the body was found in another.

Everything in the rubble was the same putrid color. It was hard to distinguish one thing from another. Curtains, sofas, and bodies conglomerated into gray lumpy slop. Sometimes there would be shapes that looked almost human, as a barely begun sculpture in wet clay. But the only way to know if it was a body was to put your face right up to it and smell it.

For example, one day on the pile one of the guys walked over to ESU officer Bob Brady and said, "Did you see that face laying on the ground over there?"

Brady shot a look over to where he was being directed: a mangled mess of gray muck and twisted steel. He didn't see anything and said,

"Where?"

"There."

Brady walked closer and stared at the ground. He squinted as looking at the sun. He tried to find the shape of eyes, a nose, a mouth, but all he saw were clumps of mud. Maybe the other cop only *thought* he saw a face.

"I don't see it," said Brady.

"It's there."

"Where?"

"There! There!" said the cop, jabbing his finger in the air as a flustered school marm. But Brady couldn't see it, and as far as he knew, there was no one there.

That was the way it was down at Ground Zero—a Rorschach inkblot test. The shadows would play tricks. It was as though the landscape would shift and change shape as colorless rocks tumbling inside a kaleidoscope.

Then there was the time a grappler pulled back a big piece of steel beam and the stench released knocked everybody back. There certainly was a body there, but they couldn't see it. Officer Ronnie Racioppi and another cop, Matt Veahy, put their noses to the ground and followed the smell as bloodhounds on a scent. They were sniffing at everything and anything that looked remotely human. Then Veahy tapped Racioppi on his shoulder and pointed up in the air. Racioppi looked up and saw a steel beam suspended over their heads shaped as a cross. The body they were looking for was impaled in the bolts. They stared in amazement. It looked as Jesus on the Cross.

To remove the body from the beam they had to cut the bolts and gently peel it off, but when they did that, the skin fell apart as wet tissue paper.

On Wednesday, September 12th, Winkler and a few ESU and Port Authority police officers returned to the hole where the two Port Authority cops, McLoughlin and Jimeno were rescued, to retrieve the bodies of Dominick Pezzulo, Chris Amoroso, and Antonio Rodrigues. They had been with McLoughlin and Jimeno when the Towers collapsed, and were killed. In the dust, they found Pezzulo's 9mm handgun. The clip was empty of bullets.

Scotty Strauss, the ESU cop who dug out Jimeno, had lost his watch in the hole. A reporter who was writing a story about the rescue asked Strauss if his children had given him the watch. He laughed and said, "Sorry, no human interest story here. It's just a cheap, twenty-dollar watch."

On Thursday, the hole caved in.

Any time the cops found the remains of a fireman, they backed off and let the Fire Department come in and do the removal. The removal of the body was as a ritual. A bell would ring, an American flag would be draped over the remains and, in a slow, ceremonious procession, the men would carry the dead fireman up the ramp and to a waiting ambulance.

This respect the cops showed the firemen was not returned. In the early days of the recovery, when the police found one of their own guys, they'd notify the particular officer's Command, and his friends would come down to get him; but when they got down there, the firemen on the scene would often say, "No, you can't carry him out."

The cops would look back at them in disbelief and say, "This is a friend that I worked with for fifteen years. I just spent eight hours digging him out."

It was very disheartening. The police were told they couldn't carry a friend out because the fire chiefs and everyone else had to have their chance to pose for the publicity cameras. The guys were angry and they asked: Why did FD have to carry him out? Why couldn't they walk in front or behind the stoke basket? *Let the guys he worked with carry him out. Let them bring him home.*

That was what triggered the tensions between FD and PD at Ground Zero. The big bosses from both departments had to sit down and come to an agreement to quell the bad blood. Eventually the firemen backed off and the police were allowed to carry their own guys out.

Everyday, when their work was done at the site, Hargrove, Stefanakos and Winwood would stop on the second floor of One Police Plaza to see the families that were waiting to hear news about their missing loved ones. The cops would walk in filthy and tired, and every face in the room would turn around and look at them, their eyes wide with questions. Even though Deputy Commissioner Dunne would brief the families twice a day, once in the morning and once in the evening, they still wanted to hear more—especially from the guys who were down there digging and who were their husbands' or sons' friends and colleagues for many years in the unit. But Stefanakos and the others didn't have an answer.

They could only say, "We're workin', we're lookin'."

"We know you are," the families would answer. "Be safe yourself. But bring our guys back home."

The families awed Stefanakos. He fed off their energy and hope, and even though he and the others were dog-tired they all wanted to turn right around and go back to the site and dig some more.

During their painful wait, a police officer from the missing cop's command would be assigned to the family. Starting in November, Randy Miller stayed with Joann Langone throughout the holidays. Every day he'd drive her to the Help Center at Pier 92, and sit with her on the second floor at One Police Plaza to wait for any news. When Christmas came and Tommy's body was never found, Joann decided to have him declared dead. Miller helped her finalize the paper work with the medical examiner, and he helped her finalize his pension. He cleaned out Tommy's locker and he took Joann to the Property Clerk to sign off on all his personal things.

The First Responders

THE BLACK BOXES
27

At Ground Zero, the order was to dig for the "black boxes"—the flight recorder boxes every airplane carries with information about operations right through the plane crash and beyond. The original information from the FAA was they thought the signal from the black box was coming from the corner of Liberty and Church.

A black box sends out a signal at the frequency of 37.5 kilohertz. It doesn't matter if the plane crashes into the ocean and sinks or if it explodes on impact on land: the casing of the box is strong enough to survive it and the signal keeps on coming for thirty days. Though the FAA had been picking up the signal, they were having a hard time pinpointing the exact location of the box. They could hear it humming over the earphones, but they couldn't tell exactly where it was coming from.

When they thought the "ping" was coming from the corner of Liberty and Church, the men were sent to dig. As they were digging, Dave Burkart from Eight-Truck saw something amazing. Pointing towards the sky was the roof of the South Tower, it was a big triangular chunk, as a piece of pie, still intact. He stopped digging and stared at it for a long time trying to imagine if someone had stood right on it before it fell and hung on would they have survived the ride down? Eventually he realized it wouldn't have been possible. It was a nice thought though. He shook that fantasy from his mind and went back to his digging.

Meanwhile, after a few days of digging for the black box at Church and Liberty, the FAA changed their mind about where the signal was coming from. On Friday, September 21st, the FAA now said the "ping" was coming from inside Building Five, on the opposite end of Church Street, at Vesey.

The fires in Building Five were extinguished by this time, and what was left was a blackened and gutted eight-story building, with smashed windows, and dangerously unstable, or missing staircases. The FAA pinpointed the black box directly underneath, or inside, the roof of the building. ESU Lieutenant Dehlia Mannix, from Ten-Truck, was in charge of the operation to retrieve the black box. She decided the only way to get to the roof was to send a small team of three men and have them brought up to the top of Building Five in a "bucket," a contraption similar to a shark cage that divers would use to drop in the ocean to protect themselves from sharks, except the bars on the bucket were wider apart and the railing came up to the men's waist.

Stefanakos, and two other ESU police officers, were picked for the mission. They stood in the bucket and held on to the railing, a crane lifted them in the air and then lowered the bucket on the roof of Building Five. The men unlocked a gate on the bucket and stepped carefully onto the roof. The FAA had shown them a photograph of the black box and they knew they had to look for something orange and about the size of a large shoe box, and they also knew it was suppose to be under, or embedded in the roof. Stefanakos, and the other two cops, were looking for a hole, something where the black box might have punctured the roof of Building Five when it was catapulted out of the plane at the moment of impact into one of the Towers. But when they looked out across the roof they didn't see any holes, or dents. All they saw was a large grey smooth slab of tar.

Without any markings, the three cops didn't know where to look for the black box. Stefanakos tried to contact the FAA personnel on the radio, who was handling the transponder, for coordinates of the black box's location.

"Transponder on the air?" he said. There was no answer, only static. Stefanakos radioed a second time, and then a third, but still there was no response from the FAA.

Finally, after a few minutes of radio silence, a voice came on the air, and said, "The FAA aren't here. They went home for the weekend."

Stefanakos, and the other two cops, looked at their watches and saw it was only about five o'clock in the afternoon, then they looked at each other, and shook their heads in disbelief. The cops got back in the bucket, and on the way down, they laughed and commented to each other, in an incredulous tone: *We've been workin' every day for 16, or 17 hours straight, with no days off. And here we are inches away from the black box, and the FAA just get up and leave in the middle of a recovery just because they don't wanna screw up their weekend?*

THE MISSING

On the morning of September 12th, ESU Sergeant Timothy Farrell came up with an idea for finding the missing police officers. He brought down to Stuyvesant High School a plot map of the sixteen-acres plaza with all the buildings part of the Trade Center. It was an aerial view, drawn as an architect's blueprint. It showed every detail, every corner, every alleyway, and every little blob of shrubs peppered around the perimeter. It peeked inside the buildings as though the roofs had been lifted off so one could see the position of the stair wells, elevator shafts, and the offices. Everything was drawn in, right down to the sun rays radiating from the globe fountain on the plaza.

Farrell went up on the stage in the auditorium of the high school where everybody could see him and spread the map out on a table. Cops in the teams who had been on the plaza or in the Towers were called up on the stage. He asked them if they had seen a missing officer, and if he had, to pinpoint where he last had seen them. Then Farrell would circle the area on the map.

The ESU cops knew where to place the fourteen ESU officers and the one Bomb Squad detective who were missing, and the bodies of these men were soon found near to where they were last seen. But it was harder to find the nine precinct cops who were also missing. On September 11th, they hadn't reported to a command post and there was no way to account for their whereabouts. Patrol officers from their precincts were sent to the high school to speak to Farrell and he was able to draw up a rough idea as to where they might be. The missing precinct cops were: Sergeant Timothy Roy, from the Control Division Bus Unit—he was last seen on the concourse; Police Officers Mark Ellis and his partner, Ramon Suarez, from Transit District 4, had been climbing the stairs from Church Street to the plaza; Glen Pettit, from the Police Academy Video Production Unit, was at the base of the South Tower taking pictures with his video camera. Also missing were John Perry, 40th Precinct; James Leahy, 6th Precinct; Moira Smith and her partner, Robert Fazio, from the 13th Precinct. The body of Moira Smith, who was one of two female police officers killed in the disaster, was never recovered and no evidence of her death appeared until the spring. Two days after the attack, Winkler and Sergeant McCarthy hooked up with her supervisor, Sergeant Joe Canney. He had been injured on September 11th and had just been released from the hospital after he had surgery to remove debris from his eyes. The three men went back to look for Smith inside the concourse. Part of it was intact, with stores still in perfect condition except for a layer of dust, and part of it was collapsed, and part of it was still on fire. They tried to retrace her steps, but they could only get so far because the section of the concourse where Canney had last seen her was buried under the collapsed plaza. Smith and her partner, Fazio, had been together. They had gone into the lobby of the South Tower, brought out injured people, and then gone back in again. Daily News photographer Corey Sipkin had snapped a picture of Smith on the street escorting a bloodied-face man out of the building just moments before the South Tower fell: she was in uniform, with the sun in her eyes, and her blonde hair shining. When the Tower collapsed, Smith and her partner ran south, but Smith ran further south than Fazio, and both were caught in the shower of steel and cement.

A memorial service was held for Moira Smith on her birthday, February 14th, at St. Patrick's Cathedral on Fifth Avenue over an empty casket. Five weeks later, on a rainy night of March 20th, 2002, at four o'clock in the morning, a group of Port Authority cops raking in the rubble found a single collar-brass "13" and Smith's bent and dirt-impacted shield, number 10467.

Smith's partner, Fazio, was recovered two months earlier. He was unmarried and lived in Freeport, Long Island. He loved fast machines and wanted to open a motorcycle repair shop when he retired in three years. He was laid to rest on January 9th, 2002.

Police Officer Victor Laguer last saw his partner, James Leahy, in the North Tower. They had been on patrol in the West Village on 7th Avenue and Grove Street when they saw the first plane crash into the Tower. They rushed down to the Trade Center, parked their RMP on the sidewalk at Vesey Street, and ran into the main lobby of the North Tower. Just as they entered, a stampede of hysterical office workers rushed the lobby doors. People were dog-piled in the doorways; hundreds of bodies were trying to squeeze through at the same time. Lauger and Leahy tried to maintain order but the crush was too overwhelming.

Then Leahy saw four or five firemen enter the lobby. One of the fireman was laden down with canisters of oxygen, and Leahy could see he was having difficulties carrying them. He turned to his partner and said he was going to help the fireman carry the canisters up the stairs. Lauger thought this was crazy. Leahy wasn't wearing protective gear, and the lobby was full of smoke. Lauger tried to talk him out of it, but Leahy insisted he'd be fine and the firemen told him the plane crash in the building was only an accident and the building was safe. So, he went up with the firemen and Lauger stayed in the lobby.

When the second plane struck the South Tower, the North Tower teetered. Leahy screamed over the radio, "Vic, you on the air? What was that noise?"

Lauger told him the South Tower had been hit by a second plane and begged him to return to the lobby, but Leahy stayed with the firemen. In his last transmission, moments before the collapse of the North Tower, he told Lauger he was coming down with the firemen from the 27th floor.

In October, evidence of the death of the first two police officers were found. They were Tommy Langone and Paul Talty: guns, a pair of handcuffs, and some badly burnt bony remains. When remains of this sort were found, records at the command were checked for data relating to the missing men. Randy Miller, Langone's steady partner, did the match on the serial numbers of the guns and handcuffs on the "ten-card"—an index card containing personal and equipment information. When he saw that the handcuffs belonged to Langone, he just had to smile. They were the cuffs he bought during his cadet days in the academy: seventeen years later he was still using the same pair. This was funny, because most cops lose their handcuffs over the years through the movement of prisoners. It's pretty much expected this will happen, especially if you let another cop use your cuffs. (It often happened a cop would borrow a pair of handcuffs to transport a prisoner to Central Booking. He'd take them off that prisoner and then forget to return them to his buddy. Later, perhaps, he'd lend the borrowed handcuffs to another cop for a prisoner transport, say, to the hospital. And then the handcuffs would end up on somebody else's prisoner, and then another prisoner, until one pair of handcuffs had been passed as a hot potato through all five boroughs!)

Miller had been Langone's partner for one year. They had a lot in common and became fast friends. They were both A-type personalities, and they'd race from job to job at mach-5 with their hair on fire. If they were in Corona, Queens and a "pinned" job came over the radio five miles away in Flushing, Langone would insists on getting there before the Fire Department. He knew every short cut. He'd fly through the back streets of residential Queens at 90 mph and be the first truck on the scene before the Fire Department could get the rig half way out the garage.

Miller never forgave himself for not working on September 11th, and for the longest time he had survivor's guilt. He wanted to quit ESU. The senior guys talked him out of it. They told him it was important to carry on Langone's legacy—to be a teacher.

For Langone, being an Emergency cop wasn't a job; it was his life. He was a volunteer Fire Chief in Roslyn, Long Island and an instructor at the Nassau County Fire Service Academy and an instructor at the ESU school. He was the foremost technical expert on everything to do with rescue, and, if you needed to know something, he'd always spend the time showing you rope loops or how to safely hold a buzz-saw.

When Langone went on patrol he'd have four radios going at once. His partner would carry the Division radio they were in— the 110-115 precincts. Then another radio was on for the adjoining precincts (108-114), the Transit radio, and SOD (Special Operation Division). If there was a dark cloud somewhere, Langone was under it. He was omnipresent. When the other guys were anxious to get a day off for Christmas or a Fourth of July barbecue, Langone would work the holidays because, he said, "That's when the best jobs happen."

If you drove with Langone down a street in any part of the City, he'd inevitably point to a corner or a building and say, "We had a good job there! We had a good job here!" And his kids, Catlin, age 12, and Brian, age 10 knew all their father's stories. They'd sit on the edge of their chair and with the same intensity and rapid-fire talk as their father, argue about the details of the story, "Not that jumper. This jumper Dad was talking about!" They were truly their father's children.

A fellow officer once asked Sergeant Hargrove if he had any regrets letting Langone and Talty go with Coughlin to the South Tower. "No, I don't," said Hargrove. "I made that decision to let Paul and Tommy go with the other sergeant because that's what we do. I've made decisions like that before and I know I'm going to make them again. Hopefully, they won't have those kinds of results. The decision wasn't the thing that took their lives. I don't feel that."

The worst thing was the Langone family lost two sons on September 11th. Tommy's older brother, Pete—who was a firefighter in Squad 252 in Brooklyn—was also killed in the South Tower.

The way Miller finally dealt with Tommy's death was to tell himself this was how Langone would have wanted to die. Langone was his best friend and mentor. They worked together eight and a half hours a day and they talked about everything under the sun, including death. "I don't wanna grow old," Langone used to say. "I wanna die the way I'm living." 9/11 was America's biggest rescue job. If he was going to die as an Emergency cop, that was the job to die on. Miller knew Tommy smiled all the way to Heaven.

There are three types of people in the world: The first, *wait to die*, the second are *afraid to die*, and the third, *hurry up to die*. If you were to ask an ESU cop what type he was, he'd probably say the third, because these guys know there is no greater feeling in the world than to skate by death on the skin of your pants. They lived for the thrill. "Come on! Let's go!" they'd shout right in the thick of a firefight. They loved the adrenaline rush of going in on a high-risk warrant and standing outside a door holding a machine gun and knowing the other guy inside the room had a machine gun, too, and any second now, they were going to crash through the door and have a shoot out with the guy.

John D'Allara told the guys at Two-Truck a million times if he ever got killed, he had money in the back of his locker for the guys to throw a party. He wanted an Irish wake where everybody would drink, tell stories, and laugh. And sure enough, after his death, they did find money tucked inside a white envelope in the back of his locker.

D'Allara was wiry and strong. He had a dry sense of humor and, for a guy who had to drive on the job, he was a terrible driver. He'd drive his truck as if he were the lead car in the last lap of the Indy 500, but in his own car, off-duty, he drove as slow as molasses. Politoski used to pass him on the Palisades Parkway driving to work. The first thing he'd see when he zoomed by him was an ugly cockroach doll D'Allara had stuck on the rear window. When Politoski got to work, he say, "I passed D'Allara again. He'll be in in about a half an hour." And thirty minutes later, D'Allara would walk through the door.

D'Allara was into bodybuilding, and at one time he was as big and ripped as Arnold Schwarzenegger. He had pictures of himself in training but kept them in the back of his locker and only showed them to a select few. When he stopped working out, he lost a lot of his weight. His face got very thin, and his angular, high cheekbones and square jaw became very pronounced. Everybody called him, Skeletor—after the comic book muscleman with blue skin and a skull for a head!

Every day he'd go through the same routine, double-checking every nut, bolt, and screw. If they were loose, he'd tighten them. If they were in the wrong place, he'd put them in the right place. He was precise, analytical, and neat. All the guys at Two-Truck knew what D'Allara was like, and any time a guy had a certain way about him—some kind of an idiosyncrasy, or a habit, that struck everyone funny—they'd immediately pick up on it and it would become his signature banter. "We wouldn't tease you if we didn't like you," was the usual excuse. Sergeant John Politoski remembered the first day he was assigned to the unit in 1992. He was a cop then and working in Two-Truck. D'Allara was in charge of the RMI, the Remote Mobile Investigator—the robot with an attached camera used for spying inside hostage situations. D'Allara taught the new guys how to work the robot. He'd drill through plywood to demonstrate how to drill through walls so they could use the robot from a remote position. One time, D'Allara set-up the drill and plugged it in, but somehow he didn't set it up right and the cord twisted and he ended up stripping it. Exasperated, D'Allara said, "That's it—I gotta throw the drill out!" Politoski looked at him incredulously and said, "John, you're in Emergency Service—you can fix anything." Politoski took the cord, stripped it down, fixed it, and gave it back to D'Allara. But D'Allara didn't like that. If something looked off—even by a tiniest fraction of an inch—he'd throw it out and buy a new one.

After that, Politoski declared open season on D'Allara. He must have "got him" at least ten times in one month. For instance, he came back to quarters after a job, and said, "Bad news, John. We had a barricaded EDP (emotionally disturbed person) today, and he took our hostage phones and threw them ten stories off the balcony!" D'Allara flipped out and headed for the garage to check out the phones. Politoski tried to stop him, saying, "I'm just kiddin' with you," but, D'Allara was already pulling out all the phones just to make sure they were okay.

Though D'Allara was anxious about detail, sometimes he couldn't see what was right in front of his nose. When Politoski was promoted to sergeant, he was assigned to the 3-0 Precinct in Harlem on 125th Street. One night there was a homicide in front of a bodega. Politoski had the whole block cordoned off with yellow crime-scene tape, so it was obvious where the shooting had been. Then he called Emergency Service to the scene for an "evidence search," and here came D'Allara pulling up and parking his REP right in front of the yellow tape. He jumped out and got on the division radio and said, "Yes, Central, it's Emergency Service-Two. Can you advise me of the location of the crime scene?"

Politoski laughed and ran over to D'Allara and said, "Are you kiddin' me or what? It's right in front of you, knucklehead!"

Two weeks before 9/11, Stefanakos flew to Two-Truck for the day and worked with D'Allara in the Adam-car. D'Allara talked the entire tour about how much he was looking forward to retiring next year. Stefanakos was disappointed to hear the news. He asked,"John, are you really gonna go?" But D'Allara never had the chance to retire. He died under the collapse of the North Tower.

Joe Vigiano and Vinny Danz were on Sergeant Curtin's team on 9/11, but they had run up ahead and gotten separated from the team when first approaching the North Tower. But the surviving members on that team don't remember ever seeing them. The last person to see them alive was Kenny Winkler, who watched them from across Church and Vesey putting on their gear. Winkler can tell you exactly where they parked their truck, and he can tell you how far up the block they ran ahead before climbing the plaza stairs. After that, nobody knows what happened to them. Their bodies were found against the west wall of the *South* Tower. How did they get there? We can only guess what happened. Perhaps they were with the firemen and had climbed so high up in the North Tower that when the building fell, they were thrown all the way to the other building.

On Tuesday morning Danz left a message for his wife, Angela, on their home answering machine. He said, "It's nine-fifty. I'm in the building. Say a prayer that we get some of these people out. I'm okay, but say a prayer for me. I love you."

After the collapse of the Towers, a paramedic found a ringing cellphone on the street. He picked it up and answered it. It was Kathy Vigiano, who was desperately trying to reach her husband. The medic had Joe's phone. He told her how he found the phone and he didn't know what had happened to her husband. After he hung up the phone with Kathy, the phone rang a few more times—friends and family frantically calling to see if Joe was all right. Each time the paramedic had to give the disappointing news he didn't know where the owner of the cellphone was and he'd drop Joe's phone off at the 2-6 precinct for the family to pick up.

Vigiano was a volunteer fireman in his hometown in Suffolk County. He came from a family of firemen. His older brother, John, was a firefighter, and his father, John Senior, was a retired and highly decorated fire captain. Joe had become a cop, but he knew about fire fighting. He was thirty-four years old, six feet tall and strong looking, with short-cropped hair and a Roman face. He came on the job in 1987 and was assigned to the 7-5 precinct in Brooklyn. Here, he met Mike Curtin and for nearly three years they were partners on the midnight tour. Vigiano's mischievous sense of humor was his trademark. He was charismatic and funny. When he walked into a room everybody would turn around and look at him, and when you looked at him, you wanted to laugh, because you knew he was sneaking up behind somebody getting ready to pull some prank.

Dave Norman tells a story about Joe and a fire at the police academy. One day while he and Vigiano were sitting in quarters at One-Truck, somebody started frantically ringing their bell and banging on the door as though the devil was on their tail. They looked up at the surveillance monitors and saw a Pistol Range Officer standing there. Vigiano and Norman looked at each other, as if to say, "What the hell does *he* want?" When they opened the door, the Range Officer burst in and screamed, "The range is on fire! The range is on fire!"

"Okay, did you call the fire department?" asked Vigiano and Norman.

"Yeah."

The two cops grabbed a pair of Scott-packs, water cans, and fire extinguishers and walked downstairs to the pistol range in the Academy, and there was a stack of cardboard boxes blazing away. This was more than a little fire. Vigiano put down the fire extinguisher and picked up the standpipe and a hose that had a "suicide nozzle" on it—an open nozzle with no shut off valve. He turned to Norman and said, "Count to five and then charge the line" ("charge the line" meant releasing the water through the hose). The five-second count was to give Vigiano time to get a good grip. The release of the water forces the air out through the nozzle with such force it would kick up and hit you in the face, the hose struggling in the hand as a cobra on a hot plate. Norman walked down the hall and turned on the water. Then he ran back to where Vigiano was knocking down the fire.

After they put out the fire, all that was left was a smoky and soggy pistol range. The fire department had not arrived, and Vigiano thought this would be a good time to give them a little surprise.

"Quick. We gotta vent this out," said Vigiano, coyly. "That way, when the firemen get here, they won't have anything to do!"

They turned off the water and rolled the hose back up, nice and neat.

They threw on all the blowers to shoot the smoke out of the vents, and moved the burnt and water-soaked boxes out of sight.

The fire chief and his men walked in and Vigiano went into his fire-lingo spiel saying things as, "All visible fires knocked out at this time," and "Basically, we're over hauling," and so on. But the fireman wasn't amused.

"You guys have done it now!" bellowed the fire chief. "You're in OSHA violation. You're operating a fire brigade without a license!"

The chief pulled out his little note pad and pen and told them he was going to make a complaint and said, "I want your name and your partner's name."

The cops told him what he wanted to know, and the fire chief mulled over the surnames—Vigiano and Norman—two names that were legendary in the fire department and then he stopped writing.

"Are you—?" Asked the chief.

"Yes. My father," said Vigiano. Then he pointed to Norman. "And, his brother."

The fire chief had nothing more to say. He put away his pen and pad and left in a huff.

In 1991, Curtin joined ESU, but Vigiano stayed in the 7-5. Joe met his wife, Kathy, who was also a cop, moved to Medford, Long Island and had three sons. He worked patrol and over the years he was involved in two shootings. Between the two he took a total of seven bullets in the chest, and both times his bulletproof vest saved his life. The Department gave him medals and a detective shield. One of the guys, Winwood, called him "a warrior among cops." He thought a saying he once saw written on a T-shirt applied beautifully to him: "Decent people sleep peacefully at night because rough men stand by to do violence on their path." Vigiano was a man who would sit back and watch and just observe whether things were going right; but if the shit hit the fan, watch out, because he'd charge in as a bull with a bee sting.

When Curtin was assigned to Seven-Truck, in the back of the 7-5, Vigiano made it a daily ritual to drop in and hang out with his old friend. Curtin told him since he was always hanging around quarters

The First Responders

he might as well join the unit. Vigiano took his suggestion and, on July 4th, 1998, he worked his first day in Emergency Service. Everybody just knew he'd come in with a bang. After Curtin was promoted to sergeant he was assigned to Two-Truck in Harlem, Vigiano followed suit. He could have stayed in Brooklyn and be closer to home, but no, he wanted to work in Harlem, because as he said, "it was busier there."

Vigiano owned a set of "Billy Bob" fake teeth and he'd put them on whenever they'd be sure to get a laugh. They were buck-toothed and crooked and made him look as though his IQ had just dropped about 100 points. Joe carried them with him wherever he went, just waiting for the most inappropriate moment to put them in!

One day President Bill Clinton was in town. For the Presidential escort, a CAT-car (counter assault team) was assigned. It was a covert black van with heavily armed ESU cops inside. They'd function as the back up for the Secret Service should somebody try to harm the President. Inside the CAT-car were Sergeant Mike Curtin, Mark DeMarco, Joe Vigiano, and Alex Ciccone.

The CAT-car was pulling into a reception area where Clinton was going to give a speech. The motorcade slowed as the President's limousine passed an area where people were lined up on the sidewalk waving to him. The CAT-car was three cars behind Clinton's limousine. Vigiano rolled down his window and poked his head out. He was sitting there looking very serious with his ballistic helmet and holding a machine gun—and his gorgeous face full of those fake teeth. He looked at everybody on the sidewalk as the car ceremoniously passed by and all you could hear was a roar of laughter from the spectators. One woman screamed, "O, my God! Did you see that policeman?"

The President made a second stop at Brooklyn College. The CAT-car parked across from the school near Junior's Cheesecake, a restaurant at the corner of Flatbush and Dekalb Avenue, and since 1950, had boasted the world's most delicious cheesecake.

As the CAT-car sat there a Secret Service agent walked over, opened the van's sliding door and climbed inside the front seat and sat down next to Curtin. It was standard operational procedure on every Presidential escort to send an agent over to discuss plans with the sergeant, and it was usually an exchange in the form of "If this happens, you do that" and "You stay outside; we'll stay inside."

Curtin listened carefully to the instructions. He'd nod and say, "Oh, yeah, yeah."

Meanwhile, Vigiano, sitting in the second row of seats directly behind the agent, nonchalantly took out his special dentures and put them in his mouth. He didn't have to do or say anything, but just sit there and look ridiculous to send DeMarco and everyone else in the back of the van into a laughing fit. They laughed so hard they were in tears.

Now the Secret Service are serious people. They don't take to humor kindly. The raucous laughter from the second row was making the agent uneasy. He stopped talking and prepared a look on his face that said *You guys making fun of me?* But he made the mistake of turning around to see what was causing the hysteria, and there was Vigiano sitting there looking cock-eyed. The Secret Service agent didn't say a word. He gave everybody a blank look, opened the van's door and left.

By late afternoon it was getting hot inside the van, so DeMarco cracked opened his side of the door to get some air. Now, from where they were sitting they could see Clinton was leaving the school and was walking down the sidewalk and would have to pass the CAT-car to get to his limousine. Vigiano was ready. With you know what in his mouth and in fake-teeth-distorted speech, he muttered, "Open the door. I wanna say hello to the President."

Vigiano was climbing over DeMarco and Ciccone struggling to get to the door, and they were laughing and pretending to be trying to hold him back. Curtin was laughing so hard he could hardly get his words out, but finally he commanded, "I'm ordering you NOT to open that door!"

Somewhere, pinned to a bulletin board, there is a photograph of Joe Vigiano. He has his arm across the shoulder of a smiling homeless man, and their heads are tilted together as two old down-and-out buddies. Joe was smiling and wearing his "Billy Bob" teeth.

It's a sad memory, but it still can make you laugh.

The First Responders

For the most part, Farrell's map of the Trade Center grounds where the missing cops had last been seen was accurate, but there were some surprises.

On March 6th 2002, the bodies of two of the missing police officers were found. It happened during the changing of shifts, just as everybody was coming off the pile and all the machines had been turned off. A few workers were staying on the site picking and searching in the vicinity of the Customs House. The entire section was considered unstable, and no big machinery was allowed in the area. If any digging was going to be done it would be by hand, using shovels and rakes.

A group of firemen found some bony remains on the rubble and called for K-9 to bring in a dog for a cadaver search. Police Officer Steve Smaldon and his dog, a German Shepherd named Hansen, and Cliff Allen, who had been working with Smaldon all day, responded. The dog sniffed around but no more body parts were found.

Allen and Smaldon turned around and left the firemen. Because it was the end of their tour, Allen headed back to where his command, One-Truck, was gathered, and Smaldon walked towards his four-wheel drive gaiter parked at the bottom of the mound. Smaldon let Hansen run ahead so he could stretch his legs and get some exercise before the long drive back to his command at Fort Totem in Queens. As the dog was running around the rubble, he must have caught the whiff of something, because he suddenly stopped and started to dig. Hansen was going nuts, jumping around, wagging his tail, and poking his wet nose deep in the dirt. Smaldon had never seen his dog react like this. It was as if he'd caught whiff of a T-bone steak buried under the rubble. Smaldon had been down at Ground Zero for a 150 days and his dog had found over a hundred bodies. In all that time never once had Hansen gotten this excited. But Smaldon and Allen didn't think the dog had found anything important as human remains. The air around the Customs House was so thick with the stench of decaying flesh they couldn't imagine the dog could zero in on a specific body. Smaldon put the chain back on Hansen's collar and gave the dog a tug to abandon whatever it was he found intriguing. But Hansen pulled away and jumped right back to the same spot to dig.

It was obvious to Smaldon and Allen the dog wasn't going to quit. They decided to take a closer look. Allen crouched down, and with his hands he started to dig. Immediately, he recovered something: a key-shock watch—still ticking! Now the two men were excited, because they knew ESU cops wear this type of watch for their shock resistance and durability. And they also knew three of the missing cops, Mike Curtin, John D'Allara, and Claude Richards, had last been seen near the Customs House and could be buried underneath precisely where they were standing. Smaldon took out his radio and tried to raise somebody over at Barclay Base, ESU's Communication Center, but nobody was answering. He looked back at the firemen he had just left, but he wasn't going to call them over because he knew what they found belonged to a cop. He felt it was only right ESU recovered their men. Then they saw, about two hundred feet away, at the bottom of the debris hill, a group of ESU cops raking in the dirt. One of the cops was Winkler. Smaldon and Allen frantically waved their arms above their heads until they grabbed his attention. Winkler ran up the hill to them and now the three men started digging.

The word a body might have been found spread as wild fire. The other guys— Dave Brink, Danny Coan, and Sergeant O'Connor ran up the mound to join in the dig. Hansen was still excited and he wanted to join in too. He was jumping among the cops, and Smaldon had to keep pushing the dog out of the way.

Suddenly a finger poked out from under the rubble. Then more fingers and a hand, then an elbow. The grappler came over with his machine, and he dug for a long time until the midsection of the body was exposed. It had a business jacket and a white shirt with two Bic pens sticking out from the breast pockets. Everybody assumed they had found a civilian, until somebody moved the jacket and they saw a 9mm handgun holstered to his belt. A cop! Now they thought they had found the Bomb Squad detective, Claude Richards, but couldn't understand why he was in civilian clothes. Winkler removed the gun. It was in pristine condition, clean as a whistle. O'Connor radioed-in the gun's serial number, and a few minutes later it came back the gun belonged to Police Officer John Perry of the 4-0 Precinct. Everybody was surprised.

The First Responders

Nobody expected to find Perry here. Witnesses had placed him either on the concourse level or in the lobby of the North Tower. Plus, the three surviving members of Curtin's team had made no mention of seeing Perry. Winkler wanted to double-check, so he reached into the pockets and pulled out some identification. He cleaned it off and read the name. It was, indeed, Officer Perry.

They draped a flag over his body and, after the ceremonial walk down the mound and to the ambulance, they returned to the spot where Perry was found. They wanted to keep digging and Winkler asked an excavator to bring in a compact four-wheel-drive, tracked Bob Cat (a small construction vehicle with a shovel in the front) and concentrate his digging on the recovery area. The machine bit into the rubble and, in one sweep a body was lifted to the surface. An empty leather machine-gun sling was across the torso and a MP-5 machine-gun was lying at his feet. They had a strong feeling it was Curtin, since he was the only ESU cop who went into the Towers with a machine gun. The teeth of the scoop had hooked into the sling of the MP5 and it pulled him out of the dirt. He was halfway up when Coan yelled out for the engineer to stop.

The body was intact. They saw his short-sleeved uniform shirt with its sergeant's stripes. No doubt it was Curtin. He was wearing his Scott mask, crushed and burnt. They wanted to see his name, stitched on the front of his shirt, but his uniform was caked with gray dirt and the name was illegible. They didn't want to touch the body, so they radioed the coroner and asked him to respond to the dig. When the coroner arrived, he took a rag and some water and cleaned off enough letters to confirm his identity. Curtin's body was dry and stiff, as a mummy. Perry's body had been in the same condition. The coroner couldn't explain it, but they thought the dust might have had something to do with it. It is still a mystery

Sergeant Curtin and John Perry had apparently died side by side. Curtin's body was removed from just underneath where Perry's had appeared. Perry had been at One Police Plaza on 9/11. He was about to put in his papers for retirement to pursue a career in law. When the North Tower was struck everybody in Headquarters ran out into the streets and over to the Trade Center, including Perry. One witness saw him on the stairs to the PATH train. That would have put him on the concourse level, towards the vicinity of the South Tower; but a Brooklyn Housing police captain, Timmy Pearson, was with Perry as they helped an elderly woman who was suffering from chest pains get out of the North Tower through the lobby doors. When the South Tower collapsed, the blast of heat, shattered glass, and dust threw Perry, Pearson, and the woman in three different directions. The lobby filled with blinding smoke and Pearson couldn't see anything or anyone around him. After a minute or so, he saw an opening of light. It was a firefighter with a flashlight. Pearson followed him out of the North Tower, but he never saw Perry again. When Perry's body was found he was wearing a construction helmet, and he must have gotten injured at some point during the evacuation, because his arm was tied up in a triangular sling.

Whenever someone was found, everybody would try to piece together the last few minutes of their life. In Perry's case, they figured when the North Tower began to rumble, Perry must have been running across the plaza and Curtin reached out and grabbed him.

THE TOXIC DUST

During the long months of the retrieval operations, every morning there would be posted on a pole in front of Stuyvesantt High School a hand written message on a piece of paper telling everybody what the asbestos level in the air was that day. And every day somebody would scribble underneath this message, "very high/wear something."

Knowing the level didn't change anything. The men would have gone in there no matter how dangerous they knew things were. If the possibility of falling into a fifty-foot hole of burning embers didn't deter them, knowledge about the toxicity of the air wouldn't have either. As long as the asbestos level didn't go higher than 0.1% f/cc, the air at the Trade Center was supposed to be safe.

The rescue workers would be here in the morning, rain or shine. Some days they'd wear their HEPA masks and some days they didn't care. The press photographers would often ask the workers to remove their masks for pictures. It looked less ominous, more personal, to see their faces.

On the third day after September 11th, God came up with a rainstorm. It was the greatest rainstorm that ever rained: it settled all the dust and it made life easier for the rest of the week. Once the ground dried out, it was there again.

The landscape became a part of the workers. It was in their hair and on their skin and on the soles of their boots. But mostly it was in their lungs. Beside asbestos, they breathed in silica, carbon monoxide, fiberglass, cyanide, plastics, pulverized concrete and glass, mercury, ashes of human bones, lead, polycyclic aromatic hydrocarbon, furans, dioxins, polyvinyl chloride, and polychlorinated biphenyls: a heavenly cocktail to cook your lungs. And if coughing your brains out wasn't fun enough, you could spend the rest of your life worrying about cancer.

The EPA was down there vacuuming up air-bound particles and looking at things through a photo-optic microscope. *They said there was nothing there!* And the Occupational Safety and Health Association (OSHA), and the International Union of Operating Engineers National HazMat Unit (IUOE), were all taking samples too. Con Edison's

Union Lab was conducting an independent study, and no two groups of experts had the same results. They squabbled about the numbers, but it didn't matter because there were too many guys with coughs that won't go away.

Much of the discrepancies in the findings between the different agencies had a lot to do with the equipment they used. The EPA based their findings on Ambient Air Quality Standards, a guide on the safety levels of six pollutants: lead, carbon monoxide, ozone, sulfur dioxide, particulate matter, and sulfur dioxide. The EPA only tested the air. They didn't test the loose dust that settled in and around Ground Zero. Asbestos is a mineral fibre that can only be positively identified with a special type of microscope. The EPA's photo-optic microscope, with a magnification power from 10x to 10,000x, couldn't possibly confirm the presence or the absence of asbestos. Why? Because 13,000x is the minium magnification for detection of asbestos. The IUOE were using the more powerful scanning electron microscopes. It has a magnification power from 25x to 250,000x, and is 250 times the magnification limit of the best photo-optic microscope. They found that 60% of 150 samples collected inside the cabs of heavy equipment operating at Ground Zero showed asbestos concentrations greater than the EPA's clearance criteria of .1%.

Everyday the rescue workers would return to their digging, and when they looked up from their work and saw men in bulky "spacesuits" with Geiger counters walking around the pit as men on the moon, they wondered what the hell they weren't being told. In the rubble of Building Seven all the needles swung off the scales. The area was contaminated with high levels of radiation and nobody would say where it was coming from. The experts explained it was the smoke detectors or the bunker might have had an indigenous medical facility that could have leaked cesium from x-ray machines. But cesium gives off low-level radiation, and the most it can do is cause burns if you hold it in your hand for a long, long time—as the children in Mexico who played with the pretty colored rocks that once littered the grounds of abandoned American medical labs.

The First Responders

The culprit was a hidden cache of anti-tank weapons that had contaminated the area with "depleted" uranium. Depleted uranium is the radio-active substance used to coat shells to increase their lethal nature. It isn't dangerous unless it's burning. Then it can break out of its casing and the first rainfall will turn it into toxic dust (so maybe it wasn't God after all who brought the rain!). The wind blows the dust and it settles here and there. A rescue worker could accidentally touch it with his fingers and put his fingers to his eyes or mouth, or inhale the dust so it ends up in the bloodstream and lodges in the bones. In any case, it seeps a low but steady dose of potentially lethal radiation throughout the body.

There were a lot of weapons, a lot of evidence, and a lot of paper money littered around the area of Building Seven and the Customs House. Building Seven housed the offices of the DEA (Drug Enforcement Agency), the CIA, the DOD (Department of Defense), and the Secret Service. When the two buildings were destroyed, anything safeguarded in their offices and vaults were scattered to the wind as a smashed pinata at a child's birthday party. Officials from these agencies came down to police the area. There was a rumor the President's limousine he used on his New York City visits was kept in the garage below Building Seven. The Secret Service was very anxious to get to that vehicle. They hovered around the debris pile as a nervous bridegroom. They watched the digging and the raking, and they waited as their "secrets" were unearthed.

One day the cops were sent to Building Seven on "Stinger" detail. Stingers are the military's basic fire-and-forget, shoulder-launched, infrared heat seeking anti-aircraft missiles. Their orders were to just sit there and watch the grapplers scoop up the debris, and if something evil looking popped out—such as, a cylindrical infrared Seeker head—they were to alert an official who would recover it, secure it, and take it away.

During the nine-month clean-up the hazardous chemicals and radioactive waste was dumped on a barge sitting in the Hudson River. The police escorted the waste to an undisclosed area in Staten Island. Men in white HazMat suits met the barge, unloaded the waste, and buried it. Then they locked the gate, turned to the cops and said, "There'll be no more dumping here."

Buried deep beneath the mountain of debris in the basement of the World Trade Center was 60,000 tons of Freon gas stored in tanks as large as double-decker buses. Here the largest refrigeration plant in the world sat in the middle of Lower Manhattan, and it took the whole nine months of the recovery period to reach these tanks. A New York newspaper wrote nobody was sure whether the Freon was leaking. I don't know what reports the newspaper was looking at, but the engineers at IUOE confirmed from samples of acetone, hexane, and benzene that large quantities of Feron was found at the site and inside the cabs of the construction cranes and bulldozers.

Every time a rescue worker entered a void, he'd pull out a gas meter and test the air for Freon. This equipment never found any, but given the enormous quantity of Freon present, it's likely their rudimentary equipment simply failed to detect it. Inhaling Freon itself is bad enough: it can cause nausea, headaches, and it can temporarily depress the nervous system with effects like dizziness, confusion, loss of coordination unconsciousness, and temporary alteration of the heart's electrical activity leading to an irregular pulse or palpitations. But there was something worst. If escaping Freon is exposed to fire, it transforms into a dangerous acid gas called phosgene.

Phosgene gas was used as a chemical weapon during World War I. The Germans invented it and exploded it over the French army. It has the dusty sun burnt smell of freshly, cut hay. Symptoms usually take a few hours to a few days to appear, and they can include cardiovascular collapse, dizziness, vomiting, headache, irritation of mucus membranes and lungs, mental disorientation, coughing, a bizarre choking sensation, acute pneumonia, or lungs filling up with liquids, and severe burns to skin or eyes.

The experts neither denied nor confirmed phosgene gas was present at Ground Zero. All they'd say was, "We are sure it has dissipated by now" or "The inferno wasn't hot enough to make phosgene." But Freon will change to phosgene gas at approximately 375 F. Steel melts at 2,190 F.

The First Responders

A fire burned for ninety-nine days deep inside the pit and since it was hot enough down there to melt steel support columns, it was certainly hot enough to create phosgene gas. Furthermore, anybody with a high-school knowledge of chemistry can tell you phosgene gas is heavier than air and lingers close to the ground. It takes months to dissipate. True, rainwater breaks it down into weaker compounds, which then seep into the ground. But in between the rainstorms, the earth was dry and more Freon would always leak out

One month after September 11th all ESU cops who had worked or were working on the pile were sent to Beth Israel Hospital, a block off Stuyvesant Square in Lower Manhattan, for physicals, including chest x-rays and a pulmonary function test to measure lung capacity. Some of the guys had been wheezing and showing signs of asthma. In most cases, the doctors prescribed Advair, an anti-inflammatory asthma medication. For other guys, they were told to do a follow-up exam with their personal physicians.

A few weeks later, ESU was sent over to Kingsboro College in Brooklyn for another day of medical testing. At first glance, the cops thought the Department had rolled out the red carpet. Everybody received a catered breakfast and a catered lunch, and the staff was waiting on them hand and foot. This was something the cops never expected from the Department. Everyone was walking around in disbelief and thinking, "Wow, this is great, the Department really does care about us. Pinch me, am I dreaming this?" The cops' disbelief were correct. Eventually, they found out it wasn't the Department at all sponsoring this royal treatment, but the Police Foundation, a charity group that has nothing to do with the NYPD but comes to help out cops when they are in need. They were paying for both the catered meals and medical examinations

In any case, the doctors drew blood and did another pulmonary function test. They had the cops sit one-on-one with a psychiatrist for fifteen minutes. The Early Intervention Unit came in and did a stress debriefing. Then they selected individuals for long-term physical screenings—for instance, men with asthmatic symptoms—to be reevaluated every six months. Among the men selected was Sergeant Hargrove, not because he was showing such symptoms, but probably because he was fifty-four years old at the time, and older than most of the men in the unit.

The psychiatrist interviewing Bob Brady, a cop from Nine-Truck, was a man in his seventies. He was very sympathetic. He asked, "How are you doing?"

"I'm okay," said Brady. What else was he going to answer?

"Tell me about your career. I know 9/11 was a big thing. Is there anything else you'd like to talk about?" asked the doctor. "Were you on any other big job?"

"Well, this is my ninth plane crash."

"Oh, my God!" exclaimed the psychiatrist as he shot back in his seat.

Brady thought, *Hey, slow down, Johnny. This is about me here—don't you start opening up!* Then the doctor asked Brady if he'd come up to Cornell Hospital to talk to him about his experiences. Brady was puzzled by the doctor's interest in his police career. After all, seeing gory things came with the territory. "You get used to it," he said. But the doctor was intrigued and explained the human brain was not capable of handling traumatic events and the stress level from what he said had happened was overwhelming. He said they still get post-traumatic stress cases from Vietnam and WW2 veterans. Brady didn't know what to tell the doctor. He felt fine.

"How do you handle it?" said the doctor.

"I just bagged two-hundred and forty-seven bodies in the Rockaways," said Brady. He was referring to the American Airline's Flight 587 that crashed into the beach front community of Bell Harbor, Queens. Then he shrugged his shoulders and added. "I was tired at the end of the day."

The crash happened two months after September 11th and New York City was traumatized a second time. Two-hundred-sixty-two people were killed on the plane and six were killed on the ground. Brady remembered a moment where it did get just a *little* too much. He was standing there holding a body bag, picking up another arm and

The First Responders

a leg, and he got angry. He turned to the guy next to him and said, "I'm sick of this shit." He dropped everything and stormed off. He took a walk and got it out of his system, came back, and, just as if nothing had happened, picked up the body bag and resumed stuffing it with human remains.

People take cops for granted. They take what they do for granted. *Mangled bodies, gruesome homicides, man's cruelty to man.* It's what cops see on a daily basis. That's what makes a cop or a fireman different from the average citizen. A fireman runs into the fire, John Q. Citizen runs out. Cops run towards gunfire, the ordinary man runs away. There is a fascination with police work, that's why cop films and TV shows are so popular. It's a way of living the intensity of it all vicariously.

It's only in recent years the Department came up with a Traumatic Stress Debriefing Team. There had always been a policy after a cop had a shooting he'd be treated for trauma. The Department would give the cop a couple of days off to get his head together. If he wanted to speak to a shrink, he could. It wasn't mandatory. This new program was to help cops deal with stress other than shootings. Participation in the program was also not mandatory, but because the shrinks knew they couldn't get a cop to come to them, they'd go to him.

A few years back, before September 11th, a Department mechanic was killed at the garage when a truck fell off a lift and rolled over him. Sergeant Lambkin and Winkler were part of the Emergency Unit that responded. They picked the truck off the man and did their best to save his life, but unfortunately, by the time he reached the emergency room, he was dead. Lambkin remembered on that day some Departmental shrinks came to the hospital to talk to the cops. They explained they had a new program when something traumatic happened, such as, a train accident, plane crash, car accidents with fatalities, etc., they'd go to the scene and debrief the first responders, who were usually a precinct sector-car assigned to the job by the 911 radio dispatcher.

Lambkin politely listened and then he said, "What do you do with the guys that are in the train bed picking up the body parts?"

"Oh, *that's* ESU," said the Department shrink. "We don't do anything."

Then he realized what he was saying and he caught himself in mid-sentence.

"It's not that we're looking for it," said Lambkin.

Lambkin wasn't trying to put the idea in the shrink's head to start psychologically analyzing every cop that saw something gruesome. He was just pointing out the irony of how typical it was for the Department to ignore the obvious.

Cops debrief each other. They'd go back to quarters or at the precinct and talk about what they did, or what somebody else did. They express their feelings to their partners or even their wives, though talking to the wife isn't the same as talking to the guy that stood with you through the same ordeal. The wife will *try* to understand what he went through, but she didn't *really* understand. Some marriages suffer because of this, and some grow stronger.

On September 11th, Hargrove never called his wife, Marilyn. He called his son, Paul Jr. He was concerned the attacks would be an all-day, on-going thing. He said, "Get your mother and your sister and stay out of the malls and away from large crowds of people." If he didn't call his wife, it wasn't because he didn't think about her or because he didn't want her to know. It was just an old habit of never worrying the wife. For twenty-eight years as a cop he did one thing: he came home every night with a laundry bag of dirty uniforms, walked into the house, and his wife took it from him. Then he got in the shower, she threw the laundry in the washing machine. He fell asleep; she woke up in the morning, threw the clothes in the dryer. He left for work, and she handed the clean and pressed uniforms to him going out the door.

If he was stuck on something at work, he'd call home and get one of his two children on the phone. They were younger then and they'd be watching TV, jump up, and answer the phone, and then they called down the stairs to their mother, "Dad's stuck on a hostage in Brooklyn." And his wife would yell up, "Okay."

It was understood if his wife didn't hear from him, everything was okay. In a cop's world, no news is good news. A phone call from work is always a nuisance. It meant ruined plans, because roll call perhaps had nabbed you with overtime you didn't want, or a day-off was denied, or a boss on your back. But a police officer knocking on the front door meant the worst news. Every spouse or mother knew it could mean a husband or a wife, or a son or daughter, was dead.

September 11th hadn't been any different in regard to the way Hargrove handled talking with his wife. Then one day in March of 2002, they were driving in the car and the subject of 9/11 came up. They talked about what they did and where they were. Hargrove didn't know she was at her job at Chaminade High School in Mineola, Long Island, sitting in the teacher's lounge, watching the Towers collapse on TV. He didn't know the only way she knew he was okay was when their son passed his message to her. He sat there silently, taking this information in. Then Hargrove said, "I can't believe it took seven months for us to have this conversation."

On the days following September 11th, the Department tried to do the right thing by sending ministers, priests, rabbis, and imams to the command center at the high school to say prayers and talk to the men. But the men didn't want to talk. The only person who could understand what they were going through was the friend sitting next to them. In the locker room somebody threw a bunch of brochures on the table. It was for some kind of confidential counseling service. It had phone numbers to call just in case you needed someone to talk to about your feelings about 9/11. The brochures got tossed in the garbage or ended up being used as scrap paper. Cops don't talk to strangers about their problems, especially if they think the Department is asking questions.

30. 'CHERNOBYL ON THE HUDSON'

When the Twin Towers and Building Seven fell, a cloud of chemical smoke enveloped Lower Manhattan. Residents in the area, first responders, and the rescue workers on the pile at Ground Zero wondered what they were breathing. For three days after September 11th, many rescue workers wore no protective respiratory masks. They had no choice, because there weren't any respirators available. Neither FEMA, nor the NYPD, nor the FDNY were providing masks. The Scott masks with the air tanks weren't an option. They were too cumbersome to wear for any extended period of time, and only provided a thirty-to-forty-minute supply of oxygen. So the firemen and the cops tied cotton handkerchiefs around their noses and mouths or wore those cheap Home Depot paper masks secured with a rubber band around the back of their heads.

Working on the pile was as standing inside a volcano. It was extremely hot, and a green, noxious cloud hovered over the site. Sometimes exposed skin on the face and arms was stained with a strange dark red color.

Finally, on Friday, September 14th, 2001 the EPA personnel arrived at Ground Zero and stood at the corner of Spruce and Broadway, West Street, and outside Stuyvesant High School, and handed out pink plastic HEPA masks with purple canister air-filters, to the rescue workers. Unfortunately, after wearing the mask for two or three hours, the filters would clog with particulate matter, and it became impossible to breathe and the canisters had to be changed. .

In spite the haze of dust and smoke, hacking coughs, and stinging eyes, on September 16th, the EPA stated in a news release: "Our tests show that it's safe for New Yorkers to go back to work in New York's financial district" and "that the asbestos levels in the area are only slightly above the 1% trigger for defining the presence asbestos." In other words, the air was safe to breathe. But, they couldn't have been more wrong. What the public didn't know was, four days earlier, on September 12th, the EPA's Administrator, Christie Todd Whitman, circulated a memo throughout the agency with the instructions to not release any information to the public in regard to the air quality of Lower Manhattan until it had first been cleared by the National Security Council in the White House. The first draft of the agency's findings was heavily edited: all cautionary information was removed and replaced with reassuring statements.

Ailments that didn't show up immediately after 9/11, began to appear in the months and years following the catastrophe and are continuing to show up to this day. Since 2002, more than 650 NYC firefighters had retired from the job because of respiratory problems. That amounts to more than one-half of the 1200 firefighters that actually responded to the World Trade Center attack on September 11th. During the same period, the Fire Department's medical board had also seen an astounding rise in sarcoidosis, a lung scarring disease. The exact number was twenty-two cases, a five-fold increase over what they'd expect generally in the overall department. While the Fire Department had linked sarcoidosis to working at the Trade Center site, the Police Department—with one case of sarcoidosis amongst their rescue workers—did not.

Unlike the Fire Department, that did an excellent job of monitoring sick fire fighters, the Police Department's medical board didn't monitor the cops at all. Even though 2,000 of the 3,000 cops who worked at Ground Zero reported early on they were sick, the Police Department's doctors said the incidence of 9/11-related illness was merely a blip on the radar. The cops' health complaints were ignored and filed away in their personal medical history folders as if they were as insignificant as a cold. If an officer wanted their health to be monitored, they had to go to Mount Sinai Medical Center in Manhattan

In the spring of 2002, the National Institute for Occupational Safety and Health (NIOSH) gave Mount Sinai a grant of $11.4 million to start the World Trade Center Workers and Volunteer Screening Program. Then in April 2004, they were awarded an additional $90 million by NIOSH to continue the screening program, now renamed the World Trade Center Monitoring Program. The service was free and accommodated any worker or volunteer involved in rescue, recovery, clean up, or the restoration of essential services. The doctors did routine physical exams, took blood and urine samples, administered breathing tests, and made mental health assessments. If these exams showed that a rescue worker was ill, however, they'd get free treatments only if their ailment was limited to sinus or throat irritations. For anything more serious, Mount Sinai had to turn them away. Plus, Mount Sinai didn't have the funds to help Ground Zero workers pay their bills. If they needed extensive treatment and couldn't afford it, the sick rescue workers were thrown to the mercy of private health insurance companies.

On January 5th 2006, Detective James Zadroga died from brain and respiratory complications. He was the first police officer and the first rescue worker to die from exposure to toxic materials at Ground Zero. He had worked in the rescue and recovery efforts there for 470 hours. Within a year after 9/11, he had begun to suffer from a chronic cough and sore throat. He knew he was sick, and he also knew this was the beginning of an uphill battle with the bureaucracy, so he began to keep a journal. He wrote the Department didn't believe he was sick and they continued to send him back to work. A biopsy of his lungs found fiberglass and human bone fragments. Ninety percent of the tissue in his lungs was black. An examination of his brain found the presence of mercury. In 2004, as Zadroga's health continued to deteriorate, he retired from the NYPD on a "3/4" disability pension. He spent the last two years of his life confined to a wheel-chair and a portable oxygen tank. Plus, he received no financial support from the City or the Department to help pay for his medical expenses that, at the time of his death, topped $50,000.

When he died, his father, Joseph Zadroga, fought to have his son's name added to the official list of 9/11 victims. But the City denied his request. The NYC coroner Charles Hirsch wrote in a letter to Mr Zadroga, that the death of his son was caused from injecting crushed prescription pills into the bloodstream, scarring his lungs. Joseph refused to accept this conclusion and asked the New Jersey coroner to do a second autopsy. The NJ coroner found evidence of sarcoidosis in James' lungs and stated, it was "directly related" to his long hours at the World Trade Center site. NYC Mayor Mike Bloomberg wasn't convinced, and said Zadroga was "a drug addict"and died from abusing his medications and was "not a hero." Mr Zadroga was furious, and he marched down to City Hall and demanded an apology from Bloomburg.

Most of the cops who worked at Ground Zero, when questioned about health concerns stemming from 9/11, are generally not very forthcoming. There are few statistics showing the actual situation regarding their health issues. But if you talk to the men in the right way, you find out problems abound among them. Of the officers I interviewed, there is one who reports that since 9/11 he has suffered every night from insomnia; another has sinus problems; and one cop has liver damage and is now confined to a wheelchair. There are also men in the ESU unit who never had respiratory problems before 9/11, but now experience shortness of breath every time they climb stairs. There also is an officer who continues to suffer from classic post-traumatic stress symptoms. He's on a constant regimen of tranquilizers and anti-depressants and experiences frequent black outs and occasional convulsions. He wakes up in the middle of the night from nightmares so vivid he sometimes finds himself clawing at the sheets as though he were digging back at the site. There's yet another officer who, two years after 9/11 found a growth on his back. It looked as a zit, except it was hard. He went to his doctor and said, "Listen, I was at the Trade Center." The doctor took a look at the growth and told him not to worry about it. He scooped it out and sent it to three pathology labs. Two weeks later the doctor called him back into his office and said, "It's not cancerous, but we don't know what the hell it is." That didn't make him feel any better. He glanced at the doctor's desk and saw his medical file tucked inside a Department of Defense folder. Knowing the DOD was examining his skin cells in a lab in Maryland made him feel even worse. He left the doctor's office, and now, three years later, he still has no idea what the "nodule" was. In January 2006, his health took another turn. The nodules have now multiplied and moved to his lungs.

In 2003, Congress ordered FEMA to set aside $1 billion to compensate rescue workers for injuries and illnesses sustained during the 9/11 rescue and recovery efforts. FEMA then turned around and created the World Trade Center Captive Insurance Company to disburse the funds. But, so far, not one penny has been spent in compensation. Instead, the money has been dipped into to pay for liquid lunches at Waldorf-Astoria, $1,252 dinner tabs at fancy Italian restaurants, $122 million on overhead, employees, and lawyers, $8.5 million on claims adjusting, and $304,000 a year salary for CEO's Christine LaSala. Six years, and unpaid out-of-control medical bills, is a long time to wait for help when you're sick from cancer and the funds are spent on pencil-pushing and cocktails.

George Tabb, a punk rock musician, author, and resident of Lower Manhattan, was caught in the dust cloud on 9/11. It aggravated his asthma, and in 2003 he was diagnosed with polycystic kidney disease. Medical bills were stacking up, and he became sicker and sicker. Tabb was refused medical treatment from the 9/11 health clinics. The doctors there told him his illness was hereditary(although he has no family history of the disease), and not related to 9/11. But Tabb knew his illness came from breathing in heavy-metals, from inside his apartment, and his neighborhood. Immediately, he went on a public campaign to expose the health crisis surrounding the toxic dust of Ground Zero. He appeared on MSNBC-TV news, in People Magazine, and the Wall Street Journal. However, his outspokenness was drawing the wrong kind of a attention, and "Men in Suits" knocked on his door. They warned if he continued to talk about the health impact of Ground Zero dust he'd be violating national security and would be arrested and sent to Guantanamo Bay.

In April 2003, George W. Bush circulated a memo throughout the White House to all government agencies, that stated: any environmental fallout resulting from September 11th was now considered national security, and will not be talked about. The memo was a result of Patriot Act II, Section 202, Distribution "Worst Case Scenario" Information, and restricts public access to data collected by the EPA under the Clean Air Act.

During a 2008 podcast interview I had with Tabb, he gave an

interesting analogy. He said, "For several years now, I've been calling the World Trade Center: 'Chernobyl on the Hudson.' Americans are worried about a dirty bomb exploding in the city. Well, guess what, a dirty bomb has gone off already. It's the World Trade Center. People have the right to know they're being genetically altered. I'd like for everybody who hears this (podcast) to refer to the World Trade Center as 'Chernobyl on the Hudson.' I've found, the way to get things changed in this country is to use words that wake people up."

31

REMEMBERING THE GUYS

On October 5th, 2001, the first NYPD memorial service was held for Vincent "Vinny" Danz. His body had not been recovered, and though not much time had passed since the attack, the family needed closure and decided to go ahead with the funeral. It was held at Saint Kilian's Church in Farmingdale, Long Island.

Inside the church the police officers sat on the left side and the civilians sat on the right. Mayor Giuliani was there, and he stood on the podium and talked about how wonderful the cops were and how much he supported them.

All this lip service. All this blah-blah-blah.

"I saw Cardinal O'Connor give a eulogy and I'm going to borrow from him," said the Mayor. "I want everyone to applaud the person whom we are eulogizing and applaud his life."

Everyone applauded—family, friends, and fellow police officers.

Then Giuliani walked off the pulpit to the sound of this applause. Of course, the applause wasn't meant for him—it was for the young officer who was still missing, whose body was lost in the dust and smoke. Then it switched gears. The civilians stood up to applaud the Mayor. It became his moment. But on the other side of the aisle everyone remained in their seats—dozens of white-gloved hands folded in their laps, eyes turned away, the blue dress uniforms never budging, backs straight and facing forward.

The Mayor noticed the slight. You could see it in his face. After that, sometimes he came to the police funerals, and sometimes he didn't. He wasn't missed (though Giuliani had shown great strength and leadership in the weeks that followed 9/11, there were still old hurts and disappointments the police never forgot. It was no secret he did nothing for the cops. In 2000, Giuliani gave himself a 50 % raise. Meanwhile, the police were working without a contract, and he offered them "double-zeroes"—0% raise for the next two years. The ironic thing was ESU received the Breast Bar for that year. This is an award given to a unit, or a precinct, for excellent police work. If you know what the bar looks like it has the last two numbers of the year on it. And the joke going around quarters was they'd been given double-zeroes—twice).

Danz was the youngest of nine children. He was a little guy, down to earth and always in a good mood. He grew up on Long Island and graduated from Southampton High School in 1981. He tried his hand at carpentry, joined the Marines, and later, the Coast Guard Reserves, where he worked in the Marine Response Division. In '87, he became a cop and worked in Housing Police Department, PSA 9, in Queens. He joined Housing's Emergency Rescue Service in '93 and, after the merge with the NYPD in '94, he was then assigned to ESU, at Three-Truck in the Bronx. He was married to an Irish lass named Angela, and they had three little girls, Winnie, Emily, and the youngest, Abigail, who was only a few weeks old when he died. He worked the Second Squad and was supposed to do a "4 to12" on September 11th, but he did a tour change that day because he took operating engineer classes every Tuesday and Thursday evening.

The guys at work called him "Angus" because he was, how shall we say, rather "thrifty". It was a nickname that indicated the deepest affection. They'd tease him and say, "I bet you still have your communion money in your wallet" or, "I bet when you take a dollar bill out, George Washington is wearing a pair of sunglasses." They were entertained by Danz's ingenuity to save a buck. For example, he was too cheap to have the cable sports channel, MSG, hooked up to his home, but every season, when the hockey playoffs came around, he'd order it, watch the games, and then cancel it when the season was finished.

Danz and Richard Miller were sniper partners and during the baseball season they'd have the sniper detail at Yankee Stadium. They'd sit on the huge canopy that hung out over the bleachers. Danz was a Yankee fan and Miller was a Mets fan. They'd have a friendly argument about the teams. Danz would walk out on the edge of the canopy, high above the ball field, remove a cigar from a slim pack of Backward cigars he always carried with him, light up, take a few puffs, and then give Miller his indisputable reasons why the Yankees were a better team. Then they'd sit back and watch the game. They'd hand the binoculars back and forth and sometimes they'd look through the rifle's scope—just a quick peek. They didn't want to alarm the people in the bleachers by pointing a muzzle out over their heads.

Santos Valentin was eulogized with funny stories. Everybody, of course, was very sad he wasn't here anymore. But his life was a comic relief and just talking about him filled the church with laughter.

His funeral was the day after Danz's. His body had not been found and the casket was closed and empty. As a substitute, a huge photo of Valentin was placed next to his casket in the church. The photo, taken from the rear, showed him looking back over his shoulder with a twinkle in his eye and a sly smile. Below the photograph was the caption: "I'm watching you."

Valentin was his own best audience. He laughed at his own jokes, and thought everything he did was funny. He'd put on an exaggerated, high-pitched Puerto Rican accent and say something as, "Do you want to see my hairy buttocks?" or "Hello my little lover, Santos is missing you." Then he'd plant a big, wet kiss on your nose or cheek and, if you were meeting him for the first time, you'd wipe off his sloppy kiss and turn around, red-faced, and say, "What'd hell was that?"

Valentin's long time partner was Ronnie Kloepfer, and the two of them together were an unique comedy team. Valentin would do and say all kinds of crazy things and Ronnie was there as the sidekick and straight man. If the guys missed any of Valentin's antics, Kloepfer would walk into quarters and say, "You're not gonna believe what Santos did today." Then he'd get into his stand-up comic stance and put on a falsetto-Spanish accent and reenact whatever Santos did or say on patrol that cracked him up. Kloepfer was such a good imitator of his partner the guys often were laughing more at the way he told the story than at what he reported about Santos.

Kloepfer had his own little quirks. His sergeant was John English and Kloepfer had a habit of mispronouncing his name, calling him "Ingrish". The guys would bust his chops about it, and he'd get flustered and say, "I only said it once like that." "No," the guys would remind him. "You say it all the time like that."

The First Responders

Valentin and Kloepfer were the original counter-snipers in the unit. Valentin was on the range staff at Camp Smith, an Army base upstate in Peekskill where ESU had their Advance Tactic School.

Sergeant Lambkin was assigned as the "safety sergeant" at the Camp and he'd work with Valentin coordinating live round and long range sniper exercises. One of the things Lambkin liked about Valentin was the second he picked up his sniper rifle he'd go from a wacko personality to a no-bullshit professional. He and Valentin would have the teams practice hostage recovery exercises. One of the techniques they used was called a "sniper-initiated entry." This was where the team would be positioned down range outside a building called "the shooting house." This was a simple structure made out of plywood that had rooms, corridors, doors, and windows. It was supposed to simulate a typical apartment or house they might encounter in the projects or in a middle-class neighborhood. The team would wait outside and, on Valentin's signal they'd rush the door and spread out into the rooms. Half of the team went left and half went right.

Valentin's signal would be a live round shot through the window of the shooting house. He'd position himself about seventy-five or a hundred yards up range, in a crouch and coiled as a slick snake around his M-24 sniper rifle. He'd aim his sites on a piece of paper taped to a wall in a room. The paper had a small white mark in the center indicating the "white of an eye." This meant he had the hostage-taker in his sites. Then he'd wait for someone to yell "close the bolt!" a sniper term for "ready to fire," and a live round dropped in the carrier of the rifle and the bolt-handle pushed it forward in the chamber, and bang! One clean shot through the window.

Lambkin remembered a day when they were going through this exercise, just as they had a hundred times, when something went wrong. The team was in their position outside the shooting house, and Valentin was in his sniper spot. He held the rifle steady and focused on the target with such intensity he'd disappear into his zone. His finger was on the trigger ready to fire a round through the wall. Lambkin stood next to him with a pair of binoculars and watched the team down range. Somebody yelled, "Close the bolt!" and Valentin started to pull back the trigger. Suddenly, Lambkin saw some of the men on the team frantically hand-signaling the "not safe" sign. He shouted to Valentin to stop. Immediately, he pulled his finger off the trigger as fast as if he touched something hot.

The problem was the team had "jumped the gun"—literally—and entered the shooting house before the sniper's signal. Valentin couldn't believe it! He jumped back from his rifle, cussed and threw his cap down on the ground. He was furious the men got sloppy and forgot their training. He couldn't believe how close he just came to blasting somebody's brains through the back of his head.

Lambkin knew from years of watching Valentin at the training camp, that on the street, and in a real-life "barricaded man with a gun" situation, he'd be the sniper with the quickest reflex and sharpest eye. For example, Lambkin remembered one night, at 108th Street on the upper westside of Manhattan, a gunman fired shots at a few anti-crime plainclothes cops. The perp (short for "perpetrator"—is what cops like to call bad guys) ran off and locked himself in a house. ESU was called to the scene, and Valentin positioned himself on a roof across the street. Lambkin was in the Big Truck a block away. The rest of the ESU unit put on their ballistic helmets, vests, and shields, and surrounded the house.

Lambkin hooked up the "hostage phone" in the Big Truck, and through the Reverse Phone Directory (which provides phone numbers when you look up an address), he got the perp on the phone and started a dialogue. After some persuasive talk, Lambkin convinced him to surrender. But the perp was afraid he'd be shot the minute he showed his face. He said he wanted the cops to back off and he'd only surrender to Lambkin (it's not unusual for the perp to only trust the negotiator). Lambkin agreed and gave the perp the following instructions: "I'll tell you when to come out of the house. Then you will exit with your hands on your head. This way, I'll know you don't have a gun. My gun will be holstered and I'll walk up to you. I'm going to ask you to lie faced-down on the sidewalk and I'll handcuff you."

Trust is a fine thing that can easily be broken. The perp could be lying about surrendering, or he could panic at the last second and come out shooting. After all, he did fire some shots at the cops already.

Lambkin radioed Valentin on a roof across the street and told him the plan. Valentin radioed back and said he was ready. Then he pointed his rifle over the edge of the roof and aimed it at the door.

Lambkin was still on the phone with the perp. He told him it was time to come out. A few apprehensive moments later, the door slowly opened and the perp stood in the doorway. He had his hands on top of his head. Meanwhile, Valentin watched him in his scope. The crosshair centered on his body mass. Then he leaned into the radio mike clipped to his shoulder and said, "John, I have him."

That was music to Lambkin's ears. He knew he was as safe as a baby cradled in its mother's arms. He holstered his gun and walked down the sidewalk and right up to the front door. He stood as close to the perp as it took to reach behind his back and handcuff him. And he did this with all the confidence in the world if the perp was still armed and came out shooting, that Valentin, who had a rifle with a bullet that could go through all his body armor if he happened to hit the wrong man, would unfailingly hit his target and bring the gunman down.

After Valentin's funeral service, the cops filed out of the church. They stood in formation and waited for the procession of bagpipes and the hearse to pass with the casket. Then, suddenly, the sky opened as a ziplock bag and buckets of rain poured down. It hit them sideways, backwards, and upside down. They were literally standing ankle-deep in puddles of water. The guys looked at each other and they were all thinking the same thing and burst out laughing. *He's up there pissin' on us and he's laughin' about it.*

Of the fourteen ESU officers killed on 9/11, only seven were found. They never found Sergeant Coughlin, Brian McDonnell, Jerome Dominguez, Walter Weaver, Ronnie Kloepher, Tommy Langone, Paul Talty, or Claude Richards, and Sergeant Rodney Gillis wasn't found until August of 2002. It was just a small piece of bone. The coroner made a match with a sample DNA off his toothbrush. Gillis was a handsome man who had a smile that could light up the room.

There used to be a show on NBC called *Third Watch*. It came on every Monday night. It was a dramatic series about a fictional precinct in a fictional section of New York City, and any time they had a scene that involved ESU cops, they'd use the real guys. Gillis would do walk-ons on the show, and Mike Keaton, from Six-Truck, who was the technical advisor for the show, observed the producers really liked Rodney. He was starting to get more lines and longer airtime.

The night before September 11th, Hargrove was at home flipping through the TV channels and he paused on channel four and saw Gillis on *Third Watch*. It was a five-second close-up and a couple of lines. He said, "Ah, there's Rodney" to whoever was sitting in the room with him, and then he went back to flipping the channels.

On September 11th, 2,883 people were killed in the collapse of the Twin Towers, and of that number only 1,700 have been identified. In the morgue, are 10,000 tiny pieces of biological remains so badly damaged they couldn't scrape out the DNA. They are kept in freeze-dried and vacuum-sealed containers, or maybe, one day to be buried in a wall of the 9/11 Memorial, until science can figure it out.

The First Responders

CHRISTMAS AT GROUND ZERO

Katherine wanted to go down to Ground Zero, but there were big walls, made out of planks of wood, built all around the "frozen zone" to keep out anyone who wasn't a rescue worker. Katherine felt she had the right to be there. She wanted to see for herself, to believe or not believe, her life had really changed. Her husband, Robert, had worked in the North Tower and he was killed there.

The family members of the victims could visit Ground Zero only if they had an escort by a police officer or a fireman. But Katherine didn't know anyone who could take her on the site, and every time she tried to get pass the wooden fence, she was stopped by the National Guard or some other security personnel.

A friend of Katherine's said she knew someone who could get her in. The friend gave her Sergeant Hargrove's number and Katherine wrote it down on a bright pink piece of "post it" paper. She folded it into a little square, stuck it her pocket, and carried it with her for awhile.

Katherine waited until December to call Hargrove. She finally felt strong enough, the pain of her loss somewhat diminished. Ordinarily, she'd have been in the holiday spirit, buying Christmas presents for her two sons, decorating the house with twinkling colored lights and Santa-shaped ornaments. None of this was happening this year.

Katherine read in the newspapers the rescue workers had put up Christmas trees around Ground Zero. There was a tree on West and Vesey, one on the roof of Century 21 building on Church Street, shipped from Maine, overlooking the site, and another tree on Liberty, and there were other little trees the workers placed near the tents. Katherine was moved by the Christmas spirit alive in such a gloomy place. She picked up the phone and called Hargrove. She told him she was ready, and said, "I want to come down and see the Christmas trees."

Hargrove met Katherine and he took her to Barclay Base, the ESU Communication Center on Barclay Street across from Saint John's Hospital. It was a large office, as a loft, with maps and photographs on the wall. In a little corner in the back, Father Bob Romano, the police department's chaplain from Brooklyn-Queens Holy Name Church, had set up a simple altar. It was nothing more than a little table with a plain silver cross sitting on top of it. Next to the altar was a Christmas tree decorated with donated glass bulbs in assorted colors and a shiny, tin Star of Bethlehem. On the other side of the altar was an American flag. It stood upright on a ten-foot pole: a makeshift shrine in the corner for God and country.

Every Sunday, starting on September 17th, Father Romano, would bring the altar to the auditorium of Stuyvesant High School. He would stand on the stage and say Mass for the men who came there every morning to dig. It was good for everybody; it gave them strength.

After visiting Barclay Base, Hargrove took Katherine to the site. They went down the ramp from Liberty Street and stood on the foundation that once supported the World Trade Center. It was now a large empty hole squared by the four corners of the slurry wall Hargrove said, "This is where the North Tower stood."

Katherine had brought some flowers—red roses with baby-breath—with the intention of laying them on the North Tower's footprint. But, instead, she opted to place them on the observation platform attached to the sidewalk on Liberty Street. The platform consisted of planks of wood nailed together. It was surrounded by a tall chain-link fence that overlooked the huge hole. Other bouquets of flowers lay there—some fresh and some withered—leaning against the fence, or inserted in the metal loops as scones on a garden wall. She spent a few moments there, her mood was quiet and contemplative. After a while she walked around the site and Hargrove showed her the "Ground Zero Cross"—two huge steel beams fallen in the shape of a cross and upon which rescue workers had written their names and the names of various people who died in the attack.

"You know, I understand now why you guys are here," she said, as she watched men walk by with their tools. "I could pick up a shovel right now and start digging, knowing that there are people here." There was a lot of camaraderie down there and a feeling for the lost people. It was easy to empathize with the survivors, wondering *what if someone I loved was buried here?* If people want to call it "sacred ground," yeah, it was.

The First Responders

THE CLOSING CEREMONY

On May 30th 2002, eight months and nineteen days after two hijacked airliners destroyed the Twin Towers of the World Trade Center, the clean up and recovery efforts at Ground Zero officially ended with a brief and solemn ceremony.

There were no speeches, no prayers. At 10:29 AM—the precise time the second Tower collapsed on September 11th—the sound of a bell signaled the commencement of the ceremony. The bell rang four sets of five rings—the traditional salute in memory of the fallen firefighters.

An hour before the ceremony began, hundreds of people gathered at the bottom of the seven-story pit that was once the basement of the Towers. Among those in the crowd were politicians, such as, former mayor Rudolph Giuliani, the new mayor Mike Bloomberg, and Senator Hilary Clinton. They waited at the foot of the ramp and stood behind six Honor Guards made up of police officers and firemen. At the end of the last ring of the bell, they lifted a stoke basket carrying an American flag and walked slowly up the ramp.

The flag in the stoke basket, representing the 2,883 victims of September 11th, was brought to the street and placed in a waiting ambulance. Then two bugles played "Taps," followed by a flyover of NYPD helicopters. While everyone's attention was on the helicopters, Giuliani lowered his head with the weight of his tears.

The ambulance slowly pulled away and was followed by a flatbed truck carrying the last fifty-ton steel beam from the southeast corner of the South Tower. It was covered in purple bunting and began a three-mile journey through the streets of Manhattan before being driven to Kennedy Airport. There it would be kept in a hangar, maybe one day to be used in the construction of a monument.

At the top of the ramp were two shacks. One was for the Fire Department and the other was for the NYPD and the Port Authority Police Department. Inside the latter shack, the police stood guard. They wore heavy vests and ballistic helmets and carried heavy weapons. They watched the crowd with binoculars and looked for anyone or anything that might start trouble.

The only thing out of place and caused a brief moment of alarm was an elderly fireman standing on Liberty Street, opposite the ramp that led up from Ground Zero. The fireman was standing next to a horse, holding the reins. He wore a faded and frayed turnout coat and a leather helmet with the number 162. From the looks of him, he and his gear must have retired thirty years before. The horse's saddle was wrapped in an American flag, and from it dangled a cavalry sword in a sheath; he had placed a pair of black shiny leather boots, stuck backward through the stirrups, and strangely, a noose was tied around the horse's neck. The fireman didn't move. He stayed right where he was, in a pose of soldierly discipline. He stared straight ahead, not really looking at anything in particular, and people buzzed around him with their cameras and took his picture.

The organizers of the ceremony didn't appreciate the old fireman's tribute to the dead. To them, he was a distraction, and he was told to take his horse and leave.

Officer Bob Brady was one of the Honor Guards. In an interview in 2002, Brady said, "It was probably one of my proudest days. It was a beautiful day. We didn't expect the turn out that came and we followed the beam that symbolized the end. We followed it for three miles and people were lining the streets and cheering us on. You felt proud to be in America that day."

For some the end of the digging came with a sigh of relief.

"I was the most relieved person in the world when May 30th came around," said Stefanakos, a year after 9/11. He was tired of going down to the pit everyday. He was tired of waiting for the other shoe to drop or for something else to happen in the world or in the City or in America and he was tired of eating tent food and drinking canteen coffee.

Others, such as, David Brink, would miss working at the site. Three years later after 9/11, he wished there was still something he could do to help. Go down there and dig again—anything to be near his friends, Wally and Jerome. He wears a silver bracelet engraved with the names of his two dead buddies and the date they died "September 11th 2001". For something more permanent, he has tattooed their initials on his back. He'd pull up the back of his sweatshirt and point to the fancy colored lettering across his left shoulder and say, "W.W.J.D. What would Jesus do?"

34 REPOSE

Though there were hundreds of photographs and hundreds of feet of video footage taken on September 11th, the one image that perhaps best captures the story of the NYPD on 9/11 was never photographed. It didn't even happen on that day. It was something Sergeant Hargrove saw eight years earlier, during the first attack on the World Trade Center.

"I have alotta love for the police department," said Hargrove, as he sat in his office in quarters at Ten-Truck. It was a warm late-summer evening, and the first year anniversary of 9/11 was a few weeks away. The memories were still fresh. "I'm comin' up on my twenty-eighth year. I wouldn't be here if I didn't like it. My father was a cop. My brother-in-law was a cop. Today, I have nephews on the job."

On his desk he had just finished writing his annual Evaluation Reports for the men in his squad, including two, Langone and Talty, who died on that day. It was crazy—checking off boxes and evaluating job performances for people he'd never see again.

"I talk about the Emergency Service cops because I know them personally," said Hargrove. "But I'll never forget something that I saw in '93. I wish I was an artist or had a camera that could have captured the picture, but I don't think any camera could have captured it. I was inside the building—I don't even know which Tower it was. We were in the lobby and we were trying to set things up to go in and evacuate people. Somebody inside the Tower called the local news station and said they were having trouble with the smoke rising up through the Tower from the basement where the explosion had taken place. Frank Fields, the ABC reporter happened to answer the phone and he told the guy to break the glass so he could breathe. So the man broke the glass and it came falling down on the street where the cops had lined-up people exiting from the Tower. Glass was raining down. These were precinct cops—not ESU—these were your street cops, out there directing traffic, and whatever else, answering radio runs. They had formed a line and were keeping the people against the building so they wouldn't scatter while moving them to a safe area. When the glass started to rain down, those cops pushed the people against the building and covered them with their own bodies. The glass just pelted down on the cops. This is the picture people should see in the City. Because this is the kind of thing that happens and then it's gone. That one action is symbolic of what cops do over and over again. That was in '93, and God knows where these cops are today. Some of them might have been the same cops that were down at the Trade Center on September 11th."

Glossary

10-13: A NYPD radio code that means, "police officer needs immediate assistance."

A-Team: A special unit within the Emergency Service Unit that assist other agencies, such as, the Drug Enforcement Agency (DEA), in executing an arrest and/or search warrant within the boundaries of New York City.

Adam Car: Adam stands for "A" and represents an alphabetical designation for the first-response vehicle to an incident.

BAT: The Breathing Apparatus Truck, located at the Emergency Service Unit command in Staten Island, and contains Scott packs and oxygen-cylinders.

Big Truck: An ESU term that refers to their two-ton utility Mack. It's about the size of a garbage truck and carries every conceivable piece of rescue and tactical equipment, from blowtorches to machine guns to jumping bags; (these are the giant, yellow, inflatable "cushions" that fire departments use to "catch" jumpers escaping from burning buildings)

Boy Car: Boy stands for "B" and represents an alphabetical designation for the second-response vehicle to an incident, and/or back-up to the Adam-car.

CARV-Truck: An acronym for Construction Accident Response Vehicle and refers to a specialized ESU unit that responds to construction accidents in order to stabilize structures and rescue trapped workers.

Central: The NYPD radio dispatcher that is located in Brooklyn and coordinates emergency responses of the police department with the 911-Emergency Telephone System and other New York City emergency agencies, such as, the fire department, ambulance services, and etc.

CO: The Commanding Officer, usually the rank of Inspector.

Eighty-Four: Also, referred to as "10-84" and is a NYPD radio code that means, "present on the scene."

E-Man: An ESU term to describe an Emergency Service officer that is respected by his peers to be a highly experienced and knowledgeable police officer within the unit.

The First Responders

EMT: Emergency Medical Technician. EMTs are health care providers that are trained to provide rapid pre-hospital emergency medical care.

ERS: Emergency Response Service was a specialized component of the Housing Police Department of New York City that consisted of highly trained police officers who performed rescues, Special Weapons and Tactics (SWAT), and other high-risk operations. On August 14th 1994, the Housing Police Department merged with the NYPD and many of the police officers in ERS were transferred to ESU.

ESU: The Emergency Service Unit is a specialized component of the NYPD that consist of highly trained police officers who perform rescues, Special Weapons and Tactics (SWAT), and other high-risk operations.

FDNY: An abbreviated acronym for the Fire Department of the City of New York

FEMA: The Federal Emergency Management Agency is an agency of the Department of Homeland Security. It was established in 1979 with the purpose of coordinating the response to a disaster, or a declared "state of emergency," that has occurred in the United States and overwhelms the resources of the local and state authorities.

Fly Guy: A NYPD term, or slang, to describe a police officer that is sent outside his assigned command to fill-in for man power, or to work a detail, at another command. Recently, the term "fly-guy" or to "fly," has become an out-of-date slang word. However, it is still used widely in ESU.

Four-to-Twelves: Also, known as the "late tour." It's one of three "tours of duty" and refers to the work hours of 3:15 PM to 11:35 PM, and is sandwiched between the Day Tour: 7:05 AM to 3:35 PM, and the Midnight Tour: 11:15 PM to 7:35 AM.

HAZMAT: The Hazardous Material Unit that consists of personnel that are specifically trained and equipped in the handling of biological, chemical, and radioactive materials.

HIDTA: Is an acronym for the High Intensity Drug Trafficking Agency. It's a smaller unit within the Criminal Intelligence Division of the NYPD. It was created to keep tabs on drug dealers, but in recent years, they started to include gang members, career criminals, and now terrorists.

The Untold Story of the New York City Police Department & 9/11

Highway Unit: A specialized unit within the NYPD that patrols the New York City's highway system and responds to vehicle accidents and/or incidents on the highways. The unit also administers DWI test to motorists suspected of drunk, and/or impaired driving, on all NYC roadways, and investigates fatal vehicle accidents.

INTEL: An abbreviated term for the Criminal Intelligence Division. Intel is an information gathering unit that analyzes, records, reports, identifies, and disseminates, specific types of crimes, such as, organized crime, or terrorist groups. Intelligence is developed by using surveillance, informants, research, and information that is 'picked-up' on the street by an individual police officer.

K-9 Cops: A specialized unit of police officers that use trained dogs for tracking suspects, or missing people, and to detect the odor of decomposing bodies. Some K9 dogs are also used to detect illicit or dangerous substances, such as, narcotics or explosives.

Light-Truck: A flat-truck equipped with bolted down high-powered spotlights and tower generators and is used to illuminate an area for night time crime scene investigations, or accidents.

Logistic Area: A designated location that is set up during an emergency and where NYPD personnel can distribute supplies, equipment, and manpower to the places they are needed.

MP: Mobilization Point. This is a designated location where police personnel and equipment assemble in order to prepare themselves to handle an emergency situation.

NYPD: An abbreviated acronym that stands for the New York City Police Department.

One Police Plaza: Also, known as One PP. It's the headquarters of the New York City Police Department. One PP is located in Lower Manhattan on Park Row across the street from City Hall and through the Municipal Building archway, and is approximately five blocks east of the World Trade Center site.

PAPD: The Port Authority Police Department of New York and New Jersey is a law enforcement agency that protect and enforce all laws in the facilities that are owned by the Port Authority of New York and New Jersey.

The First Responders

REP: The acronym stands for Radio Emergency Patrol. It refers to a vehicle that is used by ESU, which is a small Ford truck with an attached utility cabin on a four-wheel ambulance chassis. The REP is loaded with everyday emergency tools such as the "Jaws of Life," saws, bolt-cutters, etc.

RMP: Is an acronym for Radio Mobilized Patrol. This refers to the four-door white sedans that are usually driven by the patrol units within a precinct. They are equipped with a siren and turret lights, and are marked with decals that identify the RMP as a "police car" of the City of New York.

Safety-Net Position: Is an ESU term to describe a police officer that is assigned as a liaison between the police officers and the supervisors, and monitors all emergency and police radio transmissions, in order to pass on any viable information to the police teams that may either impede, or ensure their safety.

Scott Pack: Respiratory protection equipment that consists of a heat-resistant face mask, air regulator, and a metal cylinder containing thirty-minutes of oxygen, attached to a body-harness and worn by emergency workers in order to enter an area with hazardous air quality.

SOD: The Special Operation Division that oversees the Emergency Service Unit, Harbor Unit, Aviation Unit, and the K-9 Unit.

Tac-G: Also, known as Tactical-g, is a NYPD radio bandwidth used by ESU to communicate with each other on a one-to-one basis, similar to a walkie-talkie. This frequency operates without a repeater and radio transmissions are not recorded.

Taxi Squad: The Taxi Squad is a city-wide specialized unit that assists the NYC TLC (Taxi and Limousine Commission) in their law enforcement duties pertaining to medallion yellow cabs. Other duties of the Taxi Squad also include the investigation and the prevention of crimes against taxi drivers.

Third Squad: A squad is a military/police term that refers to a small unit that consists of eight to fourteen men and is supervised by one sergeant. A squad is a component of a platoon, which has a division of three squads, each with a numerical designation, such as, First, Second, and Third. In the NYPD, the squads work overlapping work hours and days off.

U-4: A supervisor, either of the rank of sergeant or lieutenant, that is assigned to patrol Upper Manhattan and the Bronx.

Task Force: The Task Force is a unit that is organized in each of the five boroughs and specializes in rapid mobilization for disorder control anywhere in New York City. The Task Force also assist precinct patrol units as additional manpower, such as, in the incidences of missing person, or perpetrator searches, motor vehicle violation check points, and supplement patrol in high-crime areas.

The First Responders

Afterword

Before the release of the *9/11 Commission Report* in the summer of 2004, the New York Times did a preview of what was going to be revealed in it. On both May 19th and May 20th, the NYT did a big spread on the various highlights of the *Report*. I counted four articles that blamed the police for poor communications and a lack of coordination with the Fire Department. One article said the reason so many firemen died was because they didn't hear the warnings from the police helicopters that the collapse of the North Tower looked "inevitable." The NYT stated these warnings reached the cops, and insinuated the police should have communicated them to the firemen but didn't. One article went on to say the police received guidance from their commanders to get out of the building based on the information from the police helicopters. Again, allegedly this guidance wasn't passed on.

This wasn't true. None of the cops I interviewed for this book ever heard the helicopter pilots' transmissions. Some of the cops had their radios turned off and the rest were on Tac-g frequency and therefore only in contact with their command post at Church and Vesey. The pilots were transmitting over the City-wide channel (a radio bandwidth where transmissions can be received in all five boroughs). But the cops wouldn't have listened to the pilots anyway. They take their orders from their own unit, so the whole matter of direct transmissions to the cops from the pilots are irrelevant.

Furthermore, when the police were ordered to evacuate the North Tower it didn't come from a police chief, or an inspector, or even a sergeant. The order came from a silver-shield police officer: Kenny Winkler, who was at the ESU Command Post on Church and Vesey.

At 9:59 AM, the South Tower collapsed. Eight minutes later, at 10:07, the pilot from the police helicopter, Aviation 6, made this observation of the North Tower: "Advise everybody to evacuate the area in the vicinity of Battery Park City. About fifteen floors down from the top, it looks like its glowing red. It's inevitable."

At 10:20 AM, the pilot in the other police helicopter, Aviation 14, stated the North Tower was leaning. Nine minutes later the building collasped. Winkler, however, didn't need the helicopter pilots to tell him what was going to happen. The instant the South Tower collapsed, he was on Tac-g with his teams. In total darkness, with a dust cloud roaring all around him, Winkler ordered everyone out of the North Tower.

There was ten times the number of firemen in the Towers than there were police. Cops work in small teams: usually one supervisor and eight cops. With a small number as this the cops can easily keep an eye on each other. This also enabled Winkler to effectively stay in radio contact with them during the entire evacuation and then to systematically guide them out. At one point, when Team Three called for assistance, he was able to direct Team One over to them. When moments later, Team Three canceled, he went back to directing Team One out of the building. Again, when Team Five was trapped, he was able to put Team Seven together to go and get them, and when Team Five self-rescued, it was easy to cancel Team Seven.

Communications between the police command post and the small teams of police officers were excellent, and this explains why so few of the ESU officers were lost. On the other hand, the first responders whom I interviewed for this book believe one of the reasons so many firemen were killed may have something to do with the large number of firemen on the scene and they were more spread out through the 250 acres of office space in the North Tower. They'd have needed more time to organize their exit and unfortunately that time didn't exist (also, the Fire Department was still using the outdated Saber-brand Motorola radios. During the 1993 World Trade Center terrorist attack, these radios had been unreliable, and were never replaced with a more efficient radio. On September 11th, many firemen reported their radios weren't working, and they didn't hear the order to evacuate from their own command post. However, every cop I had interviewed had been in the company of firemen and, all of them say they had heard transmissions from the FD radios. But that isn't to imply FD radios weren't malfunctioning elsewhere in the Towers).

The police officers in this book would like to say they believed their communication with the firemen was very good. They spoke to them

The First Responders

and exchanged information with them every time they met in the street or in the stairwells, and they did nothing but cooperate with them. In the uncut version of the Jules and Gedeon Naudet's film, *9/11*, the ESU cops, Team One, are clearly seen at the Fire Department's command post under the North Tower. Not only were the police videotaped talking to the fire chiefs, but they were also taped talking to the Fire Commissioner, Thomas Van Essen. Also, there was another attempt by the NYPD to establish communication with the FDNY. On September 15th 2001, the New York Post reported, in a two-paragraph article, Police Chief Esposito had ordered his Executive Officer, Deputy Chief Tom Dale to go find a place to set up a Command Center close to the Towers. Dale looked for a location on West Street, but wasn't having much luck. Then he tried to set up a police command center in the lobby of the North Tower next to the Fire Department's command center, but the firefighters threw him out, stating the building was being evacuated. So the repeated claims on the part of FDNY personnel and the media to the effect the cops didn't try to establish communication with them are patently false and have been painfully insulting to the officers involved.

In 2002, on the day Kenny Winkler retired from the NYPD, the cops of Team One—Dominick Amendolare, Cliff Allen, Dave Norman, and Roger Mack—who had been the first ESU team into the North Tower, presented him with a small bronze statuette of a police officer holding a flag and standing next to a little boy. It was a fourteen-inch replica of the artist Attilio Piccirilli's 1939 sculpture that stands in the lobby of One Police Plaza. They had it engraved with their appreciation for saving their lives on September 11th.

The police, in general, are the first responders. Whenever a call comes over the emergency 911 phone line, whether it's a fire, a car accident, a missing person, or a robbery, we are expected to be the first on the scene and assess the situation, verify the location, and clear the streets. And when it's all over, we're the last to leave. We stay behind to clean up everybody's mess and to do the paperwork.

In 1999, I went to Tactical Training in Whitestone, Queens. This was something the precinct cops are sent to once a year. What we did here was a kind of role-playing training session based on a set of six scenarios. A group of cops in plain clothes would pretend to be civilians, and they'd act out a scene patrol officers might encounter on a radio run. We'd pretend to respond to it, and the training staff would observe how we handled the "situation" tactically.

For some reason Tactical Training is always done in the winter. It's a two-day course with a class size of twelve. Day One is outside in the freezing weather and Day Two is in a nice, warm classroom with a long lecture guaranteed to put you to sleep. On the first day, the twelve of us stood out on a rutted tar road next to the bay. A wicked wind whipped up from the water and we shivered and tried to get through the scenarios as quickly as possible.

The six scenarios are done in pairs. On this particular day my partner and I were picked for the last one. We were assigned to a "radio run" of "numerous bodies down at such-and-such location." I drove the "RMP" to said location and found about six of the "actors" lying all over the ground.

If there's anything I've learnt about these role-playing scenarios over the years it's that they are all trick questions. The action required is never the obvious. The obvious thing to do in the case above was to jump out and administer first aid to the people on the ground, and that was exactly what my partner wanted to do. The instant he opened the car door to jump out I pulled him back in the RMP. "That's what they want us to do," I said. My partner settled back in his seat and we waited for the training sergeant to get the hint we weren't going anywhere.

The sergeant stopped the scenario when he didn't get the response he wanted. He called us out of the car and gathered the group. "Why didn't you get out?" he asked us.

I said, "It looked like a sniper situation."

"Well, that's not what it was," said the sergeant. "It was a terrorist attack. All those people you saw laying on the ground were exposed to Sarin gas. And when that 911 call comes over, you people will be the first to respond. It'll be a scene like this. Numerous bodies down. What're you gonna do? You're gonna jump out and run over. Guess

The First Responders

what? Now, you're exposed to Sarin gas and, bang, you're dead.

"Just a little reminder: a terrorist attack will happen. We don't know when and we don't know where. But, it will happen. And, when it does happen, it'll be a poison gas attack just like the one that happened in Japan.

"FYI, the Department has written off all first responders. That's right, you guys go in first and we'll see what happens to you and the second responders will take it from there."

What a comforting thought: *a canary in a coal mine*. I felt my stomach turn over. I thought about my retirement in 2002 and I turned to the guy standing next to me and said, "I have three years left. I hope I make it." If the Department was so convinced a terrorist poison gas attack was imminent, why weren't we, precinct personnel, that is, issued gas masks? Task Force has always had them, so has Transit. But, never patrol. Even one year after September 11th, precinct cops were still not getting masks. At least, not in my Queens precinct. Then one day at the quartermaster a light bulb went off inside somebody's head. The supervisor-in-charge realized they had hundreds of boxes of gas masks in storage and they'd better hand them out just in case there was a gas attack and a cop dies and the family sues the City, so they started issuing the masks. We'd line up, put the mask on, the instructor would squirt hair spray in our face and ask, "You smell that? No? Good, it works. Next!"

Then one year after finally issuing these gas masks to the police officers it turned out they were defective and had to be recalled. So for a total of two years after 9/11 they kept us pacified with false security. But to be fair, the Department has since issued working gas masks.

When I interviewed David Karnes—the accountant and former Marine from Connecticut who found the two Port Authority cops—we met in the Yesterday Diner on Jericho Turnpike in Nassau County. He refused all food and drink because he was on a ten-day fast. He was preparing his body and mind with some kind of cleansing ritual so he'd be a new man for his new life. He had quit his accountant job in Connecticut and had re-enlisted in the Marine Corps. He was just a few days away from deployment to Kuwait. Karnes was forty-five years old and over the re-up age limit. When I asked him how he convinced the Corps to take him back, Karnes said, definitively, "I was persuasive."

The NYPD Marine Corps Association—an association of NYPD cops who had served in the Marine Corps—meets every November 11th to celebrate the Marine Corps' birthday. This is a big event, held every year in the large assembly hall at One Police Plaza. The hall is decked out with banners and flags, the Marines wear their dress blues, and a birthday cake with "November 11th 1775" written out in blue icing is brought out. Two awards are presented: the "Anchor Above, Anchor Below" and the "Semper Fidelis." Each is given to a former Marine who had done something extraordinary over the past year.

On November 11th, 2001, Karnes was invited to the celebration and was awarded the "Semper Fidelis" in recognition of him finding the two Port Authority cops buried under the South Tower.

Scotty Strauss didn't see Chuck Sereika any time soon after they rescued Will Jimeno. Sereika was the medic who was first down the hole. He and Strauss had worked face-to-face and stomach-to-stomach for three hours in smoke and fire digging Jimeno out. When it was over, as far as Strauss could tell, the medic had walked off the face of the earth. A year later, Strauss attended the Teddy Atlas Fund Raiser Dinner in Staten Island—a charity event attended by sports celebrities and, low-and-behold, standing across the room, was Sereika. Strauss walked up to him and said, "*You* actually exist?"

Strauss had become good friends with Jimeno. A few days after 9/11, he went to Bellevue Hospital to see him. Jimeno was bloated from the "crush syndrome," and there were dozens of tubes sticking in and out of his body. The minute he saw Strauss walk into his hospital room Jimeno tried to talk, but he couldn't. Strauss held his hand, and Jimeno squeezed back and started to cry. "Will, don't talk," said Strauss. "We'll have plenty of time for that later."

Jimeno's wife, Allison, had been pregnant at the time and their daughter, Olivia, was born on his birthday—the first Monday after

Thanksgiving. Strauss was invited to the christening and he met Jimeno's family. In 2003, when Jimeno was promoted to detective, both Strauss and Paddy McGee attended the promotion ceremony.

Six weeks after September 11th, McLoughlin awoke from his coma. He was in excruciating pain, fatigue, and respiratory distress. The doctors told him he'd never walk again. But, in spite of the dismal outlook, four months later—when McLoughlin was discharged from the hospital—he had recovered well enough to walk out the front door with only the help of a rolling walker. McLoughlin was then transferred to Helen Hayes Hospital in West Haverstraw, New York, for two years of intensive rehabilitation. As of 2003, he now walks with the support of plastic braces on both legs and one straight crane.

On August 9th, 2006, Hollywood released the film *World Trade Center*, directed by Oliver Stone. Stone's film is the story of Will Jimeno's and John McLoughlin's survival and rescue on 9/11. The only comment I'll make, is: The rescue was much more dramatic than shown in the film. Several key rescuers were omitted from the storyline, and the hole that Jimeno and McLoughlin were trapped in, was darker, narrower, and more dangerous than what the set designers created.

Lieutenant Vic Hollifield recovered from his injuries but he couldn't bear to return to Ground Zero. Hollifield felt, because he was the officer who transmitted the initial police call on 9/11, and because he was the highest-ranking police supervisor to lead the first team into the Tower, somehow he was responsible for the deaths of his men. Hollifield retired shortly after the first year anniversary of 9/11.

Lieutenant John Murphy also recovered from his injuries. His finger was reattached, though his hand was badly scarred. He continued to work as a supervisor at ESU's Special Training School in Brooklyn until his retirement in 2004.

If you were wondering about Mr. X—the man with the valise and the bunny rabbit who was handcuffed during the evacuation in the North Tower—I wonder too. The day after 9/11, the arrest was voided and he was released.

To add to the "mystery," a warning was passed to the New York State

Police. One week after September 11th it was declared terrorists might try to get bombs aboard commercial planes by hiding them inside stuffed toys. The toy was left behind in the North Tower and, as far as I know, never recovered. It was presumably lost in the collapse of the Tower and not examined to see whether or not it really did contain explosives; however, Mr. X's cellphone *was* retrieved, but I have no information on what, if anything, it might have revealed.

On December 4th 2001, the twenty-three police officers that lost their lives on September 11th 2001 were posthumously awarded the Medal of Honor. Their names are: Sergeants John Coughlin, Mike Curtin, Rodney Gillis, Timothy Roy, Detectives Claude Richards, and Joseph Vigiano; and police officers John D'Allara, Vincent Danz, Jerome Dominguez, Stephen Driscoll, Mark Ellis, Robert Fazio, Ronald Kloepfer, Thomas Langone, James Leahy, Brian McDonnell, John Perry, Glen Pettit, Moira Smith, Ramon Suarez, Paul Talty, Santos Valentin, and Walter Weaver.

On Medal Day, January 18th 2003, the ESU police officers (now, all promoted to detectives) were awarded their medals. Detectives Scotty Strauss and Paddy McGee were awarded the Medal of Honor.

The men of Team Three: Detectives Mark DeMarco, Stephen Blihar, and William Beaury, and Team Five: Lieutenant John Murphy, Detectives Steve Lanoce, Richard Hartigan, David Brink, Michael Garcia, Evan Schwerner, and Robert Steinman; plus, the men of Team One: Lieutenant Venton "Vic" Hollifield, Sergeant Dominick Amendolare, Detectives Cliff Allen, David Norman, Roger Mack, and Timothy Morley were awarded the Medal for Valor. The Bomb Squad Detective, Danny McNally and the Chief of Special Operations Division, Thomas Purtell, were also awarded the Medal for Valor. The men of Team Six: Sergeant Paul Hargrove, Detectives Stephen Stefanankos, Richard Winwood, Peter Appice, and Franco Berarducci were awarded the Commendation-Integrity Medal. Detective John Busching had a minor delay receiving his medal after a supervisor failed to get his paper work in on time, but finally on June 16th 2004, he received the Medal for Valor.

The First Responders

The firemen mentioned in this book: Firefighter David Weiss and Captain Timothy Hatton of Rescue One, Chief Orio T. Palmer of Battalion Seven, Deputy Chief of Special Operations Ray Downey, and the Chief of the Fire Department Pete Ganci, were killed. I don't know what happened to the firemen injured on the 31st floor of the North Tower, but I'd like to think they made it out safely. Since they had a head start before the guys in Team One, I can only guess the twelve firemen survived. But without knowing their names it hasn't been possible to verify this.

I had thought the ten firemen carrying the heavyset man out of the North Tower were killed. The surviving members of Sergeant Curtin's team who told me the story just assumed this because the firemen and the man were still in close proximity to Curtin when the North Tower fell and that entire area was destroyed; but to my surprise, I recently found out the heavyset man had actually gotten out safely. In the book *102 Minutes*, written by two New York Times reporters, Jim Dwyer and Kevin Flynn, there are a couple of brief paragraphs that mentioned this story. According to Dwyer and Flynn, the man's name was John Rappa and he was carried down from the 7th floor of the North Tower. The book only identifies two of the ten firemen that were helping to carry Rappa out: Lieutenant Greg Hansson, and Firefighter Bill Spade. They also survived.

Port Authority Police Captain Kathy Mazza was also killed. Her body was recovered in February of 2002 along with five other Port Authority police officers. Fire Chief Joseph Pfeifer survived, but sadly, his younger brother, Fire Lieutenant Kevin Pfeifer, from Engine 33, died in the North Tower.

In regard to the civilians mentioned in this book: Beverly Eckert, whose husband, Sean Rooney, died in the South Tower, was killed in a plane crash on February 12th, 2009 in Buffalo, New York.

Aware Talk Radio

Join Us - LIVE - 7 Nights A Week!!!
Or Listen To Past Archvies @:
www.innercirclepublishing.com

http://www.blogtalkradio.com/aware

Call In Number: *(646) 716-8138*

Aware Talk Radio incorporates all fields of science, from the normal to the paranormal, from the physical to the metaphysical. We seek to expand the awareness of humankind. Your Comments, Questions, and Guest Suggestions are welcome.

Printed in the United States
145797LV00005B/9/P